I'M LOST AGAIN

Other works by Robert E. Buckley

The Slave Tag

Ophelia's Brooch

Two Miles An Hour

The Denarius

I'M LOST AGAIN

Seven Bizarre Travel Adventures

ROBERT BUCKLEY

Cover by Taylor Buckley Carlson

Text set in Georgia

Manufactured in the United States of America

3 5 7 9 10 8 6 4

Library of Congress Control Number

978-1537688640

"Twenty years from now you will be more disappointed by the things you didn't do than by the ones you did do."

- Mark Twain

"If you reject the food, ignore the customs, fear the religion and avoid the people, you might better stay at home."

- James Michener

"By the time a man is wise enough to watch his step, he's too old to go anywhere."

- Billy Crystal

"The cool thing about being famous is traveling. I have always wanted to travel across seas, like to Canada and stuff."

- Britney Spears

CONTENTS

THE TALE OF
THE THREE BOMBEROS

MEXICO

It's amazing how quickly you can become accustomed to loud noises. In a surprisingly short time your brain adusts and you hardly notice them any more. Both loud noises and a bumpy ride. Even loud noises, a bumpy ride and cold air freezing your feet. Actually, loud noises, a bumpy ride, cold air freezing your feet, and no room to move around in the cab of a crowded fire engine.

This strange tale started when Sister Magdalen Kilbane of Belmullet, Ireland, made a casual remark to me about the dire need for a fire engine in her small Mexican village of Santa Cruz Xoxocotlán, where she worked as a medical missionary nun with the desperately poor. "It's terrible," she said. "Just a small brush fire and the next thing you know, five houses are gone."

"A fire engine?" I said. "Really? You need a fire engine?"

So there we were — *The Three Bomberos* — or firemen to you gringos, bouncing down I-380 in a vintage fire engine; leaving our cozy homes in Marion, Iowa, and heading to Santa Cruz Xoxocotlán, Oaxaca, Mexico, some 2,500 miles and an entire world away.

We were thrilled to finally be on our way. And although it was one of the coldest days of the year, we knew the frigid weather would be only a faint memory in another few days. Of course, we had to reach I-80 first — then make it to Des Moines — then switch to I-35 and from there head on down to Missouri and points south and west.

Noises, bumps and cold feet were the least of our worries at this point. We weren't even sure if we'd make it out of town, let alone to Mexico!

What if the motor exploded? What if the transmission gave out? What if the radiator froze? What if one of its six monstrous tires blew? What if ... what if ... there were a million 'what ifs' lurking in the recesses of our minds. After all, what did we know about fire engines anyway? The answer, of course, was very little!

Okay, nothing.

Nevertheless, we did know we looked pretty darn snappy sitting up there in the shiny, red cab. With our hands in reach of ear-splitting sirens and flashing lights, we knew we could command some major attention if we wanted to.

After all, how often do three retired old geezers get to drive a fire engine *anywhere,* let alone to some rural Mexican village so obscure I challenge you to find it on a map?

We figured if the feisty old engine would just hold together, we were in for one heck of an adventure.

-o-

In May of 1964, Fire Engine 2362 was purchased brand new by the city of Juneau, Wisconsin. A Peter Pirsch body installed on a

Ford truck frame and powered by a 534 cubic inch Ford V–8 engine which had fewer than 10,000 miles on it. Less than 300 miles a year!

The transmission had five speeds and the tires were like new. The water tank held 500 gallons and the pump worked fine. It had all the ladders, bells, whistles and sirens that you could possibly want. And it was bright, shiny red. This baby was sweet!

One chilly fall day, Bob Whittlesey, a friend and fellow parishioner of mine, joined me on a drive up to Juneau to take a look at it. I had found it for sale on the internet and talked to the Juneau Fire Chief enough times to convince me it was worth the 200-mile drive. Would it be worth the $10,000 they were asking for it?

No matter, we didn't have $10,000 anyway. Actually, we didn't have a dime.

But once we saw and drove Juneau's old No. 2362, it was a slam dunk decision. It was love at first sight. This was the one we wanted!

Of course, as I mentioned a moment ago, we had *no* money. We didn't know how it worked. We didn't have permission from the Mexican Government to bring it into the country. We weren't even licensed to drive it. But these were pesky details.

We left Juneau making vague promises to return soon with cash in hand and went home resolved to plod ahead like we knew what we were doing.

Of course, the Good Lord must have been watching this whole charade, laughing all the while, and He came to our rescue. Money came in — not as much as we wanted, but enough. That December, we offered the City of Juneau $3,750 for the truck and they ended up accepting it.

That was every dollar we had raised at the time and we bought the truck on blind faith that the rest would fall in place. We figured we needed at least $5,000 more to cover the cost of gas, travel expenses, license plates, fees, insurance and a dozen other things we hadn't thought of.

One evening another old friend, Gary Anderson, called me. He had talked to his church elders at First Lutheran Church in Cedar Rapids, Iowa, and they were interested in contributing to the cause if I thought that'd be acceptable. (Of course, he hinted he'd be willing to go along to help drive.)

Hmm ... let me think about that for a second.

"Ok." I said, before he changed his mind. "You're in."

Then things really starting happening. Word in our parish of St. Joseph spread that we'd actually found and bought a fire engine. There were bake sales. The children at our school raised over $400 for gas. Official fund drives were started at both churches. Eventually, all the money came in and we began our final planning.

The first thing we needed were Commercial Driver Licenses; at least one of us did. Bob and Gary, my co-pilots, decided to take the easy way out and just pass the written test and settle for Driver Permits; a tactical error on their part as it turned out, as it put them under my direct command.

I located a Mexican/U.S. insurance company willing to sell us liability insurance, and after months of long distance discussions, I was promised letters of recommendation from the Mexican Embassy in Chicago. I knew this wasn't the same as getting "official permission" ... but I also knew it was the best we'd be able to do.

We bought license plates, drained the water tank and found a place to store the truck until we were ready to leave. We had our local fire department go over the motor and pumps. We loaded it with 30 boxes of children's clothes, medical supplies, gifts and a computer for Sister Magdalen. We also had a large supply of donated pen flashlights and fanny packs which would, I knew, go over big time.

Disappointedly, the letters of recommendation from the Mexican Embassy were the last pieces to fall into place ... and even then, not until the last minute. In fact, they almost didn't fall at all.

January 22nd, 2000 - The Adventure Begins

We originally planned to leave at 7:00 a.m on a frigid morning in January, but the packet of documents that were *"absolutely, positively"* supposed to be delivered to my house the day before ... weren't. I wasn't even sure what would be in the packet. But I knew we'd need everything going for us once we reached the Mexican border. From past experience I knew they could get quite testy down there. I was reluctant to leave.

I called Gary and Bob and told them we'd postpone our departure until 9:00 a.m. and then leave with or without the papers.

At 8:45 a.m. I received a call from the Marion Post Office. A registered package for me had just arrived.

Whew! That was close. Good thing I waited, because it contained an official letter from the Consul General in Chicago to the Head Administrator of Customs, in Mexico City. I only hoped it was enough.

With packet in hand and after posing for farewell photos and saying goodbye to our wives, we were on our way. We were in great spirits — well, perhaps a little nervous.

It was below zero that morning. And even though the motor was warmed up, the fire engine steered like a — well, an old truck. Stiff and unforgiving. And the cold air rushing in under the floor boards was alarming. But we were too excited to worry about that. We were busy concentrating on strange sounds that might indicate something was amiss with the motor or the transmission or the sirens. Anything.

We headed south on Hwy. 13 to Hwy. 30, drove east to I–380 and headed south again to I–80. So far so good, 30 miles without mishap. Time to see what this baby could do. That meant speeding up from 35 to 50 miles per hour!

The problem was we didn't know for sure how fast we were going. The speedometer didn't work. We were advised by our Juneau friends to keep our eyes on the RPM gauge instead.

"Keep it around 2,700," they advised. "That should put you close to 50 or 55 mph. We've never driven it that fast ... but it should work just fine."

"Should?" By the sound of the motor at 2,700 rpm you'd swear we were about to break the sound barrier.

Once we reached I-80 and headed west, we let out a sign of relief. We'd made it out of town, and we began to relax a little. If things broke down now, we could always say we almost made it to Des Moines.

We stuffed newspaper around the floorboards and the cab started to warm up a little. Yankee ingenuity. Things started to look better and better.

Our first stop was for gas on the outskirts of Des Moines. We were apprehensive about the gas consumption, realizing it would not be good. It wasn't. We had hoped on getting between six and seven miles a gallon but found we were getting the low side of five. From this point on, we'd be checking it carefully. We'd budgeted spending $800 just for gas and we needed to come as close to that number as we could.

The truck's manual indicated it had a 50-gallon gas tank. Planning conservatively we figured we'd go no further than 200 miles between fill ups. That should give us a comfortable 50-mile cushion. Wrong! But more about this later.

Around 1:00 p.m. we spied the Osceola, Iowa, exit and decided to stop for lunch. Of course we took the wrong exit — the one marked for the casino guests. A gambling casino in Osceola? Because of a lack of Native Americans in the Osceola area, they'd built an artificial lake and put a boat on it where people could go to lose money. Somehow that didn't seem quite right.

We circled through town and found the Osceola Truck Stop. We swung in and pulled up next to the big boys — the 18 wheelers, and swaggered in to mingle with our fellow truckers, gathering more than a few stares along the way.

I should point out that it was at this early stage of the trip that I, the only truly qualified driver — that is, the only driver with an official CDL, or Commercial Driver's License, felt it necessary to put the "Violations Rules" into effect.

I had been noticing a number of minor infractions committed by both apprentice drivers. I quickly sensed it was necessary to exhibit a firm hand up front so they would fully understand what was expected of them and to put a quick end to the problems their lack of experience could cause.

So it was that while driving through Osceola I caught Bob shifting gears while turning around a corner! A clear violation of Section Three, Line 18. I firmly pointed out this lapse in judgment and penalized him 1 demerit. It was not taken kindly!

Soon after lunch we entered Missouri. Hurrah! We felt pretty good about reaching another state. If something went wrong now, we could say something like ..."Well, we got clear to Missouri before the whatchamacallit blew up and that was that."

We had our first comeuppance when we gassed up again in Bethany, Missouri, and discovered we were now getting only 4.8 miles per gallon. Ugh! Not good. Not good at all.

Unfortunately, it was during this phase of the trip that Bob earned his 2nd demerit. He had the misfortune of driving the truck in such a manner that a severe rattle developed somewhere in the cab area — a rattle, I should point out, which was to stay with us for the duration of the trip. An argument followed that it was not entirely his fault as we were all sharing the cab at the time. Nevertheless, he was driving at the time and the demerit stood. The sign of a firm leader.

We passed through Kansas City at dusk. On the edge of town we pulled off at a prearranged spot and met my son, Michael, wife, Tessa and grandson, Thomas. They were parked cheering for us as we pulled into a side road with siren blaring and lights flashing. Pictures, hugs and kisses, and an exchange of a surplus fireman helmet for a slab of Gates Barbecue Ribs and we were off again looking for a place to stop for the night. Michael suggested that Ottawa, Kansas, several miles down the road, might be a good choice.

We'd gotten into a routine of switching drivers around every 100 miles ... or two hours. Although some might have thought it petty, I felt it necessary to give Gary, who was driving that evening, his 1st demerit for drifting across lanes; an infraction I might have been willing to overlook had our gas mileage not dropped so severely.

He violently objected, claiming the "prairie winds" were not "prevailing" at the time. And couldn't I see the tumbleweeds and other debris blowing toward us? I understood this was mere prattle and promptly awarded him an additional demerit for "insubordination." That put an end to that.

Ottawa was just fine. After a few false starts, we snuggled into a three-bed "suite" at Day's Inn for $60! (Our lodging budget was $25 per night, per person, so we were well within budget.) We stayed in the room and watched a movie on TV, drank beer, ate Gates BBQ ribs, and topped it all off with Little Debbies for dessert. Road food at its best.

All in all, it had been a pretty good day. We had come 404 miles and the fire engine was running just fine. That was further than it was normally driven in an entire year!

We were a little concerned about the gas mileage, and the demerits were of some concern to the 'learners' but, all in all, we were pleased with ourselves and our progress.

It was, of course, early in the adventure.

January 23rd - Brothers of the Road

6:00 a.m. Awake and down to the lobby for our free breakfast. We helped ourselves to juice, donuts and coffee. An older couple was eating there and curious about the fire engine.

"You come from Alaska?" they asked, with their eyes staring at the door of the truck which was emblazoned in gold lettering — *Juneau Fire Department.*

"Why we sure have," I replied before Gary could tell the truth, "and we're on our way to Mexico."

"Why, my land, just imagine that!" exclaimed the wife.

Feeling pretty cocky about things, we finished up and went out to the truck. An awkward situation arose immediately. When I tried to start the engine there was no reaction. Oh no! Had the battery died during the night? Had the starter broken? Who knew anything about fire engines in Ottawa?

Then I noticed the truck was still in gear. That's it. I recalled the Chief telling me the ignition wouldn't work unless the truck was in neutral. I'd forgotten and I was the last driver of the day.

In the spirit of fairness I promptly gave myself 1/4 demerit. Flustered, I accidently killed the engine and received another 1/4 demerit. It was going to be a long day.

We gassed up before leaving town and were encouraged to see our mileage had crept up to 5.1 mpg. Not much of an improvement but still ...

The highway was nice and smooth all the way to the Kansas Turnpike at Emporia. Soon we caught our first glimpses of unsightly oil wells dotting the landscapes, like so many huge grasshoppers bobbing up and down. Flat land, Kansas.

In no time at all we entered Oklahoma. Wait till we told the folks back home. We were cruising!

The bad news came when we filled up at the Oklahoma border. The mileage had plummeted to 4.4 mpg. Drat! I felt it was time to "make another statement" to the apprentice drivers who had not yet fathomed the techniques for efficient driving.

I recalled Gary had not produced the "Oaxaca or Bust" sign we had planned on taping to the side of the truck. In fact, he had never even mentioned it. Did he think I'd forgotten? I felt this was a severe oversight and gave him a demerit. He took it hard, I'm afraid.

Later, to boost his self–esteem I awarded him 1/2 merit for spotting our first longhorn cow. I think that made him feel better. The sign of a good and fair leader.

At 1:30 p.m. we stopped for lunch at Perry, Oklahoma. Oklahoma City was a scant 60 miles away. The truck stop crowd was staring at the fire engine as we entered a well–used diner. *Sausage and Taters* was a featured menu item and I made the mistake of ordering it. A *big* mistake. Out came a platter overflowing with a mixture of American fries dotted with inch-thick chunks of greasy sausage. All three of us couldn't have eaten it even if we'd wanted to. I was still trying to digest it when we entered Mexico days later.

Back in the truck we headed south. Miles zipped by. By 3:00 p.m. we passed through Oklahoma City and again stopped for gas. Our mileage crept back to 5.3 mpg. It looked like my little lesson was paying off.

Around 5:30 p.m., we entered Texas and reached the 820 mile mark — around a third of the way to our destination. It was at that point an over-the road-trucker raised us on the CB radio.

"Hey there Big Red, gotcher ears on?"

Big Red? We were Big Red? I grabbed the mike and answered. "You bet, good buddy, what's up?"

"Y'all from Alaska?"

"That's right, good buddy, Juneau, Alaska."

"Whooooooooeee. Damn! Where y'all heading?"

"Southern Mexico — 1,200 miles south of the border."

"Whoooooooeeee. Damn! Y'all driving that Big Red Engine all that way?

"You bet. We're giving it to a poor town down there. Been on the road two weeks already."

"Whoooooooeeeee. Damn! Now ain't that sump'in. Well, see y'all later. Be careful now. Hear?"

"You bettcha, good buddy. Nice jawing with y'all. Over and out."

Apparenly we had been a topic of conversation among the over-the-road trucker crowd for some time now. As amusing as we found it, it was some form of consolation as well, knowing that if we got into a problem of some kind, we'd have some support. Brothers of the Road.

At this point, our plans were to get to the other side of the Dallas–Ft. Worth area before stopping for the night. Gary was driving during our search for a suitable motel when he accidentally killed the engine in traffic. In fact, we lost all power, lights included. Two swift demerits.

Of course, the reason the engine died was because I accidentally hit the 'kill' switch with my foot. One demerit for me. However, because I so swiftly analyzed and corrected the problem, I immediately awarded myself two merits. The sign of a fair and analytical leader.

Just when you'd think it couldn't get any worse, I caught Gary driving with the high beams on. In addition to earning his third demerit of the day, I took over the driving responsibility for the rest of the evening. Being a leader is hell but someone had to do it.

We eventually settled on a Super 8 in Burleson, Texas. A middle-aged Indian couple were managing the place and offered us a huge, remodeled room ... but at $90, a bit over our budget. We told them about our mission of mercy but they weren't impressed. $90.

Right across the road was the Old Country Steak House. We ambled over for a marginal dinner.

All in all it had been another fine day and the longest of the trip — just over 500 miles! People back home were following our progress. We were right on schedule.

January 24th - Remember the Alamo?

6:00 a.m. The sounds of sneezing, snorting, showers, shavers filled the air. Downstairs the Indians had put out coffee, donuts and assorted cereals for their guests. We ate, loaded up and were on our way by 7:15 a.m.

We performed our routine truck walk around (as required). All the wheels were in place. No sniper holes in the body that we could see. It was cool out but definitely going to be a nice day. It was goo be out of the snow belt so soon. Destination today — Ol' San Anton!

A minor disaster struck immediately.

I started the truck and let it warm up according to correct procedure. It died. I started it up again. It died again and this time wouldn't start.

Oddly it acted like it was out of gas. But we'd driven just 200 miles since the last fill up. How could it possibly be out of gas? We weren't sure what to do but decided to try adding a little gas first.

The good news was we were still in town and, in fact, within 50 yards of a station. I went over to buy some gas but first needed a gas can. The only one they had was a one-gallon can. This could be a problem if we had to go back and forth with enough gas to get it started.

We poured the one gallon into the tank and lo and behold, it started up and stayed running long enough for me to dash to the station and fill up. It *had* run out of gas, but we were mystified how that could have happened after only 200 miles.

The answer became clear soon enough. The tank would only take an additional 39 gallons. Aha! The tank was actually a 40-gallon tank, not 50 as the manual had read. Apparently someone had restructured the tank size in order to make room for the 500-gallon water tank. We'd asked our friends in Juneau how large the tank was but they'd had no idea. They'd never filled it from empty.

As leader of the group it was suggested I get a demerit for this oversight although, in reality, it was not really my fault. I successfully argued that it was a joint error, when Bob noticed the wing window (on the driver's side) had been left unlocked the evening prior and I had been the driver. A serious error. Well, I couldn't prove otherwise so I gracefully accepted one demerit. I do suspect, however that I'd been set up.

Feeling I needed to take control of the situation again before it got out of hand, Gary was given 1 demerit for not preparing coffee in the room that morning, one of his simple, assigned duties. This led to further prolonged grumbling.

The boys needed a mental lift so I took them to the Texas Ranger Museum on the bonny banks of the Brazos River in wonderful downtown Waco. I'd been to the museum a couple of times before and knew it was really great.

We had a good time walking around and thoroughly enjoyed all the marvelous exhibits. The three of us loved guns ... and the Texas Ranger Museum had thousands. Before leaving I called the

Torneys — friends of mine who live in San Antonio — to tell them we were on our way. I've know Don Torney since the 7th grade and we planned to go out to dinner with them that evening.

We reached Georgetown around noon and stopped for gas and lunch at Schlotzsky's Deli. Things were looking a little better — we were up to 5.5 mpg again.

We pulled into San Antonio around 4:00 p.m. It was hot! Don had suggested we stay in a motel along I–37 in an area of town easy to get in and out of, and safe enough that we wouldn't have to worry about anyone messing with the engine.

We found a Motel 8 and took a double room for the night. I planned to stay with Don and Joyce. That would give us a chance to spread out a bit. We were all getting along just fine, but I knew it was a good idea to pamper ourselves now and then. Three adults (Bob and Gary both well over six feet), in a fire engine cab was close quarters.

It had been a short driving day, only 250 miles, but after two long days we were ready for a break and looked forward to relaxing a bit. As you might imagine, driving a fire engine is harder work than driving a wimpy car. A 250-mile trip in a fire engine would be like a 500-mile trip in a car!

Don and Joyce came to pick us up around 5:30 p.m. We headed straight to the River Walk area and visited the Alamo while there was still light. On to Durty Nells for a pint of beer — and then Paesano's, a lovely little Italian restaurant, for dinner. We had a marvelous meal, a great time visiting, and it felt wonderful just getting out and stretching our legs.

After dropping Bob and Gary off at the motel I went home with the Torneys and called Sister Magdalen in Mexico to let her know we were right on schedule.

"That's wonderful," she said in her lovely Irish brogue. "I'll call Señor Aquino (mayor of Xoxocotlán) and tell him you're on the way. He's planning to come up to the border to meet you and facilitate your crossing."

Well, that was a piece of good news!

God speed, Gringo Bomberos!

January 25th - Missing In Action

5:15 a.m. It turns out 6:00 in the morning was tough on all of us. Don drove me over and dropped me off so we could get an early start to the border. We wanted to arrive as close to noon as possible.

Of course, the learners weren't ready. Gary had lost the room key, an offense that promptly cost him a 1/2 demerit.

While they were mumbling and packing and bumping around, I found the key in the parking lot and awarded myself a 1/2 merit bonus. The boys started groaning about this and quickly earned one demerit apiece for insubordination. The sign of a firm, no nonsense leader.

It was early in the day. Things were looking up.

We roared and rumbled out of the motel parking lot, managing to set off several car alarms in the process. Soon we were heading south and, at Don's advice, stopped for gas before we hit a long stretch of emptiness. We were delighted to see our miles per gallon were continuing to creep up and were now at an all time high of five point six. It didn't take much to please us at this point.

By 10:30 a.m. we reached Falfurrias, Texas — a bleak, empty, windblown south Texas town with the dubious distinction of being a major hub for drug entries into the U.S. We were now 1,400 miles into our adventure with around 1,100 miles to go. And the best news was our miles per gallon now crept over six ... six point four to be exact. Incredible!

To celebrate we took an early lunch at McDonalds and stocked up on a few critical, south-of-the-border supplies: mosquito coils, candy bars, and toilet paper.

As we were heading out of town, a car pulled up next to us and waved us over to the side of the road. Was I speeding? Not likely. It turned out they were members of the local volunteer fire department and wanted to know where we were going. Had we driven all the way from Alaska? How old was the fire engine? Then they floored us by offering to buy it for $6,000!

They said the truck they were using was on its last legs. I declined and they immediately upped the bid to $8,000. Hmm.

This was getting tempting but I assured them we couldn't sell it as we were honor bound to deliver it to Mexico.

We left them with the understanding that if we couldn't get it across the border we'd bring it back and sell it to them for $10,000. Deal! Now that made us feel good. It gave us a solid back–up plan in case we really couldn't get it across.

Shortly before noon we actually passed our first vehicle of the trip, a feeble, old Texas farmer in an antique pickup truck. He was so startled he quickly passed us back, but we were feeling pretty jaunty about it anyway.

By noon we arrived at the border town of Pharr, Texas — gassed up with U.S. gas at U.S. prices for the last time. Our mileage had dropped back to around five mpg but at this point we didn't care any longer. We had solid evidence we were good for at least five and that's all we worried about. From that point on we stopped checking.

The night before, Don suggested we cross at Pharr; a fact I had carefully relayed to Sister Magdalen. A brand new bridge had recently been built across the Rio Grande there and it was less confusing and sinister than the old McAllen route several miles further west. With fingers crossed we paid our $4 tariff and entered enemy territory. When we got to the other side we were immediately pulled over and the ordeal began.

"What is this?" shouted a befuddled Mexican guard. "Where do you think you're going with that thing? Where are your papers?"

A small crowd of armed guards drifted over. This was definitely a break in their normal routine.

"This is a fire engine," they yelled. "What are you doing driving it over here? Pull that thing over." Yada yada yada! Gary started to take a picture.

"Hey, cut that out!" yelled one Uzi-waving guard who looked around 12 years old.

To make matters worse, Señor Aquino, the mayor, was nowhere in sight. We talked and showed our 'official' letters and smiled and talked and pleaded — on and on. It quickly became apparent we weren't going to bluff our way across.

15

More and more border guards strolled over and told us we had to go back over the bridge to the United States and talk to the immigration people over there.

My heart sank! I knew for sure that once we did that, we were done. We would *never* get back. We stalled ... and stalled. More people came. Finally one guard who seemed to have more authority than the rest suggested we pull over on the other side of the road heading back, but without crossing the bridge. Then he told us to come back and go talk to someone in Customs.

I liked the sound of that much better, and that's what we did. It was around 1:30 in the afternoon. We'd been at it over an hour by that time.

We turned the fire engine around, parked and walked back to Customs where we met with a couple of lowly, uninterested clerks. Finally a very nice man who spoke excellent English and who seemed to carry an aura of importance came out of an office and spoke to us. He took our papers and told us to wait out front.

Three hours later he motioned us into his office while he phoned the Mexican Embassy in Chicago. Extremely lucky for us, he reached my contact there and that did the trick.

"No problema, Señores," he said, all smiles, "you may go now."

That was it? We could go now? As sudden and unexpected as could be, but we didn't argue. After thanking him profusely, off we hurried away, quickly changed some dollars into pesos, bought our personal entry permits, jumped into the truck, turned it around again and worked our way past a couple of additional check points and drove into Mexico. We were elated and immensely relieved!

It was now after 5:00 p.m. We had to hightail it to get to San Fernando in the State of Tamaulipas, our target town, before dark. Driving a car at night in rural Mexico is a *very bad* idea. Driving a fire engine is a *death wish*.

As fate would have it, in our excitement we got goofed up and couldn't find the right highway. We were lost. This resulted in an additional 45-minute delay. If I hadn't been in such a good mood I would have given both learners at least one demerit each — but what the heck. We were finally in Old Mexico and I overlooked their deficiencies this one time! The sign of an outstanding and flexible leader.

Miles of cactus, fleet-footed roadrunners, dusty side roads, pieces of paper and plastic blowing across the parched landscape. Finally we reached San Fernando by 6:30. We'd come 355 miles from San Antonio and arrived not a minute too soon. It was almost dark!

We stopped at the first lodging we came to — La Laguna Inn — and amazed the desk clerk by asking for three separate rooms. After a tension–filled day, we deserved a little breathing space. Although overpriced at $20 each, I felt we had earned it.

The Laguna Inn was more of a long distance truck stop than a regular motel — but it looked like a safe haven to us. They let us park the fire engine in a semi–enclosed courtyard in front, lighted and safe. Our rooms were in the back, quiet but bleak, two beds each, small b&w TV, lots of cigarette burns in the carpet and holes in the walls — but the beds seemed clean enough and there was plenty of hot water.

I'm sure they thought we were eccentric gringo millionaires driving a fire truck and taking separate rooms.

The clerk sent us to El Granero for dinner. It was just a couple of blocks away so we walked. It certainly was not fancy, resembling what you'd imagine a wild west cantina might look like. They were expecting us. The clerk had called ahead and told them three crazy gringo bomberos were on their way. All heads turned as we entered the dimly-lit, dusty room and followed us as we settled in a corner table and ordered beers and a menu.

Soon bottles of ice cold Carta Blanca appeared on the table. Yes! I ordered grilled chicken; Bob had chicken fajitas; Gary ordered chicken cordon bleu. What? Yes, chicken cordon bleu of all things. It all tasted marvelous!

I asked if there was a long distance phone office in town and was told there wasn't. No problema — I'd call home and report in tomorrow.

Little did we know at the time but we were already reported "missing" as far as the rest of the world was concerned. Sr.

Magdalen had called my house and said we never showed up at the border. She said the last time she had heard from us was from San Antonio. She called the Torneys, who reported we had left early but then disappeared. It seemed everyone but the Boy Scouts within 50 miles of the border were out looking for our bodies.

Ahhh, amigo ... but there we sat sipping cold Carta Blancas in a Mexican cantina — oblivious to the rest of the world. After all, Engine 2362 was safely in Mexico and we were on schedule. Mañana amigo. Mañana would just have to do.

January 26th - Into Old Mexico At Last

7:30 a.m. We checked the fire engine over and headed out of town early; no fancy breakfasts at La Laguna Inn. We were close to our turnoff towards the ocean. When we reached it, we stopped at a remote little country restaurant for breakfast. It was time the learners had their first touch of reality.

The restaurant had no name. I remember lots of dust. No menu. Swinging door. No windows. Dirt floor. Wild west, circa 1920s. But the juice was fresh-squeezed and the coffee was hot and strong. Fried eggs with salsa and fried ham. Excellente!

There were two truckers from Belize eating when we pulled in. Of course, they wanted to know where we were heading. They were driving a flatbed loaded with damaged American cars to get fixed with cheap Latin American labor and then returned to the U.S. Did we want to sell the fire engine? No, we didn't.

Shortly before noon we stopped in a small town where I spied a long distance telephone sign on the door of a shop. We walked in and ordered Cokes and I negotiated a couple of long distance calls ... first to my wife and then to Sister Magdalen.

"Where in the world are you?" my wife screamed. "Everyone's been looking for you! Why didn't you call yesterday? Why didn't you meet Señor Aquino? Are you in trouble? Is anyone hurt?"

Apparently we had created quite a stir.

It turned out Señor Aquino *had* been at the border waiting for us — but at the *wrong* border crossing! We just assumed he didn't come. Later we learned the problem was that the Pharr–Mexico bridge was so new, very few Mexicans even knew it existed and it was not yet drawn on any maps.

I assured her everything was fine. We were all healthy and in good spirits. I told her to call the other wives.

I then called Sister Magdalen, who was equally upset, having feared the worst about us. I explained what happened and she said she would call Mayor Aquino, who was also very upset having flown to the border to meet us and then returned to Oaxaca empty handed. She said she would call him and smooth things over.

"Praise God you're all safe and sound," she said in her lovely Irish brogue. "Call again when you're closer. I'll say the beads for ya. Be careful!"

Roads were a little rough in this northeast part of Mexico but we still made Tampico by 3:00 in the afternoon. This was our first major town and although I wanted to stay in the city center, I sure didn't want to drive a fire engine there.

Instead we parked the truck at the Tampico Airport and took a cab. Before I could stop them, Bob hailed one of the 'tourist' cabs and we ended up paying 80 pesos or about $9 for the ride to town.

There are two kinds of taxis in Mexico. The expensive, newer and larger cabs which feature air conditioning, doors and upholstery — and the smaller, older VWs. To show the comparison, when we returned to the airport in the morning we took a VW and the fare was only 20 pesos. I chose not to penalize the boys for I believe they acted in earnest. But they were warned. The sign of a benevolent leader.

We stayed in an older hotel in the center of town. The three of us shared a room for $57. The price was right, the room was okay and the location was perfect.

The view from our one small window was of the dirty, oily Tampico bay crowded with freighters being loaded and unloaded. The room was air conditioned — or at least it was blowing in

19

damp, cool air at a ferocious velocity. We looked around for a switch so we could shut it off but couldn't find one. Were we doomed to sleep in this wind storm all night?

We cleaned up and walked around town for awhile, visited the *zocalo*, or central plaza, and surrounding downtown area. It was all quite tropical and lovely, a far cry from the freezing weather we'd left behind just a few days ago. Bob and Gary were quite impressed.

We returned to the hotel and stopped in the lobby where they were having a "Feliz Hora" featuring free rum and cokes. I stopped at the front desk. "Is it possible to get the air conditioner turned off ?" I asked.

"But Señor, the air conditioning is *always* on for your pleasure," smiled the clerk, completely puzzled by our bizarre request.

With rum and cokes in hand we sat and chatted with several interesting American workers who were in town drilling a pipeline under the bay. They came from all over the U.S. and each worker seemed to have a different speciality. They were dressed in their work clothes, stood well over six feet each and were old–fashioned, hard–living, rough and tumble characters. It was comical to watch them lumber around the lobby amidst the smaller Mexican hotel workers — like the proverbial bulls in a china shop. They said we'd get used to the air conditioner after a few days. Not likely.

Around 8:30 p.m. we decided to have dinner in the hotel and delighted the dining room staff when we began handing out free flashlights and fanny packs.

Back in the room, Bob and Gary each earned one merit for successfully blocking the air conditioner by removing the vent grate and stuffing bath towels into the opening. Finally, the wind tunnel was temporarily in check and we could sleep.

January 27th - We Reach The Tropics

6:00 a.m. Wanting to beat the morning traffic, we headed to the airport early. The fire engine was still there. Yay! We jumped in and headed south.

We stopped for breakfast along the road at La Estrella, a tiny mom and pop restaurant. It was wonderful. Omelets, beans, fresh squeezed orange juice, coffee and a platter of steaming hot tortillas. The apprentices were beginning to feel more comfortable with the food by now. They'd left home with visions of uneatable meals and daily bouts of dysentery, but I'm pleased to say we all felt great.

The weather was cool and overcast — misting and generally an unpleasant day to drive a fire engine in Mexico. The road was horrible in spots. A very bad winter with lots of rain in the mountains had taken its toll along the coast and we were paying the price.

We had definitely reached a tropical climate at this point. Fields of banana and orange trees and sugar cane spread out in every direction. Every tiny village we drove through had 40-pound sacks of oranges and limes for sale on every corner, $1 a sack.

The weather finally cleared early in the afternoon when we approached the hills north of Vera Cruz. We stopped for lunch at a truck stop near Poza Rica before cutting back toward the coast again. If we thought the road was bad before, we were in for a nasty surprise the closer we got to the coast. Here the roads became even more curvy and crowded with large, smoke-belching diesel trucks loaded down with sugar cane.

We came to one town where the bridge crossing a narrow river had been washed away by the winter floods. We were detoured across fields of packed mud. I wasn't sure we could make it in the heavy fire engine — but we did.

Hundreds of large semis had been stranded in the area since the previous October, caught when the floods hit. They were too heavy to go either way — and just waited there until the roads was to be repaired. That was a little unnerving.

By 4:00 p.m. we were bushed and decided to stop. It had been a difficult driving day and we didn't want to get caught without a place to stay. We were now in the State of Vera Cruz and from my ambulance delivery trips a few years prior, I remembered there were a number of inexpensive resort-type hotels stretched along this section of the coast — an area known as *La Costa Esmeralda* or Emerald Coast.

Near the village of Emilio Carranza we found a hotel that caught our fancy and we stopped. It was perfect. Situated right on the beach, the rooms were huge and completely tiled; the floors, the shower, the counters — all white tile — offering a level of luxury we were unaccustomed to. Each room had two queen-sized beds and looked out over a palm tree-studded beach. Wow!

Again we split up and took seperate rooms as they only cost $22 each. We got them at a bargain price because I agreed to pay *en effectivo* — in cash.

Splitting up every once in awhile was definitely a good strategy; giving us each a little stretching room after being cramped up in the cab of the truck for eight to ten hours every day. And besides, we were still well within budget.

The hotel was very sparsely occupied. In fact, other than the three of us, there were only an elderly German lady and a Swiss man staying there. They had been there for some time and were planning to be there several more weeks.

We took some time to relax and clean up. Later we met in the dining room and had a marvelous dinner. Screwdriver cocktails followed by salads, steaks and fries, pastries and coffee. $8.00!

Back in the room I checked our finances and was happy to see we were very close to our alloted budget in every department. We had come almost 2,000 miles at this point and the goal was within striking distance. Everything was going just great! No demerits earned this day, all drivers were still talking to each other, the fire engine was running fine. And we weren't lost!

Yet.

January 28th - Arriving in Lovely Córdoba

6:30 a.m. I got up early and went out and walked the beach. It was balmy and beautiful. Gary soon joined me and we ran down a couple of fiddler crabs for photo ops.

We left a supply of flashlights and fanny packs for the hotel staff to divide among themselves and were on our way, well-rested and in soaring spirits.

In the nearby village of Santa Ana we stopped at another little mom and pop restaurant on the side of the highway and had our usual great little breakfast. A special touch was tall glasses of fresh squeezed orange juice covered with tin foil through which a hole had been poked and straw inserted. Very chic!

While sitting there we noticed the teenage son was getting ready to leave for school but first took our breakfast orders before he carefully loaded his little sister in the basket of his bike and whisked her off to *her* school, then peddled back and served us breakfast before leaving for *his* school. A typical scene throughout Mexico where siblings take care of each other without being told by the parents to do so.

We didn't stop at the famous archeological ruins of Tajín near Poza Rica because I didn't want to risk driving the fire engine too far off the main road. However, I decided to show the apprentices the ruins of Zempoala, another important archeological site just a short distance away.

We pulled up near the entrance and parked. I was distracted while explaining to the learners the significance of this particular place and managed to walk across a blanket that had been spread across the sidewalk by a small boy. It was covered with "authentic artifacts" for sale.

Unfortunately, I stepped on a couple of these "authentic pieces" and crushed them. That fiasco cost me 50 pesos while the learners got their money's worth in my embarrassment. I fought myself not to give them each a demerit.

Zempoala dates before the time of Christ and is famous as the location of the first major battle Hernan Cortes fought on his way to Mexico City. The Indians living there were the Totonacs who hated the Aztecs. When they found out what Cortes was up to, they offered him a large group of their best warriors to take along on his march to Mexico City. Without them, the history of Mexico may have turned out much differently.

We spent a couple of hours at the ruins before continuing on our way. We were only 25 miles north of Vera Cruz when we spotted a truck wash facility along the highway and pulled in to see if they would wash the fire engine, which looked a mess at this point.

"Oh, sí señor, we would be delighted to wash such a fine vehicle, indeed!"

Five employees stopped what they were doing and started in climbing all over the truck with buckets of water — laughing merrily while wiping and scrubbing and rinsing with great vigor. I think they would have made an entire day's project out of it if we didn't stop them after an hour. The truck looked like a new penny; we paid them 50 pesos and left flashlights and fanny packs for everyone. They waved and smiled as we backed out and headed down the highway once again.

Almost immediately we entered the *Autopisa*, one of several major highways we'd be taking almost all the way to Oaxaca. The drive along the coast was lovely, from the ruins clear down to the turnoff, when we finally turned west and started up the foothills into the dreaded Sierra Madre Oriental mountain range that we had to cross before we descended into the Valley of Oaxaca.

We soon arrived at lovely Córdoba, sitting majestically in the shadow of Mexico's tallest mountain, Pico de Orizaba. It's one of my all-time favorite towns in Mexico and our resting place for the night.

As in Tampico, I wanted to stay in the downtown area but didn't want to negotiate the town's narrow streets and traffic.

We pulled into a Pemex station at the edge of town and asked if we could possibly park the truck there for the night. At first, they thought we were crazy for even asking, but when we explained our mission of mercy, they took a 180-degree turn and welcomed us with open arms. In fact, the entire station crew came out to help us jockey the truck close to the building and security light. Photos were taken. An armed guard assured us he would keep it in sight all night long. They even arranged for a taxi to come and take us downtown and when it came time to pay, the driver wouldn't hear of it. What a wonderful surprise!

The Hotel Mansur is Old World classy! Four floors high, unusual for older hotels in Mexico, with lots of dark tropical woods used throughout. Adjacent to the cathedral and zocalo, I'd stayed there before with my son Michael and his wife, Tessa, and remembered how lovely it was. Each floor featured a wide, tiled balcony looking over the town square. A beautiful setting in this tropical town.

When we walked into the lobby all eyes turned on us.

"Do you have rooms," I inquired.

"Oh sí, señor, and how many will you require?"

Again we each took one as the price was right. Only $23 for a spotless room with queen-size bed, cable TV and phones.

After settling in, we walked around town visiting the cathedral (built in 1688), interesting shop fronts, the palm tree–shaded zocalo, and were treated to an exhibition of Latin American Ballroom dancing by a group of retired citizens.

Córdoba definitely exhibits European influence: seeming much more Spanish than Mexican. Very well–dressed people, light complexions, financially secure.   Founded by Viceroy Diego Fernández de Córdoba in 1618, it's situated smack in the middle of Mexico's sugar and coffee-growing country.

We dined at one of the outdoor cafes on the square, Gary ordering his beloved chicken cordon bleu, Bob going with his grilled chicken, and I, a platter of mixed sea foods and meats, very few of which I could actually identify. Coffee and flan for dessert.

After dinner I called Sister Magdalen again to report on our progress and to tell her we would be arriving the next afternoon. She was delighted to hear from us and assured us that Señor Aquino — the Majordomo — was in great spirits and had gotten over the disappointment of not meeting at the border. She told us the whole town was expecting us.

We made plans to meet around 2:00 p.m. at the Coca Cola bottling plant on the north edge of town.

We were excited. Oaxaca tomorrow. But first, the mountains!

January 29th - The Little Engine that Could

7:30 a.m. There sat the three Gringo Bomberos — breakfasting on the third floor balcony of Hotel Mansur, quietly enjoying their morning fix of fresh juices and delicate *pan dulces*. The hint of bright sun to creep over the mountain top at any second. We were sipping locally grown café con leche while gazing serenely down on the town as it slowly came to life beneath us. We felt like *padrinos*.

A cab dropped us off at the Pemex station where we found the fire engine, secure and ready to go. We quickly slipped out of town and onto the Autopisa, headed toward the towering and perpetually snow-clad Mount Orizaba.

We were out of town before I realized we had neglected to fill up with gas. Whoops! We weren't sure how much we had left but decided to plod ahead rather than do the smart, sane thing, turn around and go back. This could present problems! We were so distracted, the mention of demerits never came up.

On and up the mountain we went — climbing from the 3,000 foot elevation of Córdoba toward the 18,275 foot peak of Pico de Orizaba which we could see looming ahead of us, glistening with snow.

Reaching the pass seemed to take forever; especially when we were trying to watch the road and various gauges as we went. We hoped against hope we would run into a gas station along the way. It was not to happen.

The engine never once overheated and seldom required shifting down to more than third gear. Amazing! Bravo! We passed dozens of other vehicles along the side of the road with hoods up and radiators boiling over.

We eventually crossed over the peak, started down the other side and breathed a sign of relief. Surely, at this height we could coast to the next town if we ran out of gas, the amount of which had to be dangerously low.

Unfortunately, before we reached a station, we arrived at the Oaxaca turnoff where we had to turn south. Should we go straight knowing a gas station had to be somewhere ahead? Or turn south and take our chances? The learners wanted to go straight. I decided to turn. Sign of a gutsy leader.

We turned south and before long arrived at the city of Tehuacan where we coasted into a Pemex station and filled up. The tank took 38.5 gallons. We had a gallon and a half left!

"We could have gone another seven or eight miles," I pointed out to the wimpy apprentices. "What was all the fuss about?"

I considered awarding demerits to both of them for their lack of confidence in my leadership, but I didn't. The sign of a relieved leader.

One more mountain range to go and we had it made. We filled up on water and snacks and headed on. Not as steep as the previous mountain range, but much longer and curvier. We were now threading our way through the famous Sierra Madre de Oaxaca range, slowly but surely.

Trivia experts will be happy to know that we were now within shouting distance of where Alphonso Bedoya uttered his famous line "We don't need no stinking badges" in John Huston's magnificient 1948 movie, *Treasure of the Sierra Madre*.

Stopping often to rest and take pictures of the amazing scenery, we successfully conquered our last obstacle and reached the city limits of Oaxaca, Mexico, by 2:30 in the afternoon.

We came around a final curve and there they were — Sisters Magdalen and Kathleen, Señores Bilvaldo Martinez and Roberto Cruz — standing on the edge of the road waving at us. We had arrived! Bravo Gringo Bomberos!

After a long chat and lots of introductions and *abrazos* (bear hugs) all around, we unloaded the fire engine compartments onto a truck our friends had provided. In the process I managed to cut my head on a protruding ladder and blood started flowing down my scalp and over my face. What a sight that must have been to passing motorists. I laughed it off. Sign of a staunch leader.

The sisters climbed in the cab with me and we followed our friends several miles further into Xoxocotlán and parked it right in front of city hall. Out poured the government officials. *Bienvenido! Bravos amigos!* They were ecstatic!

Mayor Aquino, along with the entire city council, took all of us to lunch at La Capilla, a delightful open air restaurant in the village of nearby Zaachila. By this time we had grown to a crowd of 22!

The lunch lasted from 3:30 to 6:30! Huge platters filled with a wide assortment of grilled Oaxacan meats and other delicacies were washed down with gallons of sweetened rice water and beer, platters of steaming tortillas, and finally toasts with mescal and chapulines (toasted grasshoppers) for everyone. It was a traditional and wonderful banquet! Gary and Bob talked about it for weeks afterward.

By the time we returned to town we were exhausted and half balmy with mescal, but politely spent another hour visiting with Sisters Magdalen and Kathleen before we headed to Las Bugambilias, our bed and breakfast spot for the next few days.

They insisted on treating us to small glasses of Jameson's Irish Whiskey — a bottle of which I had delivered to them on a previous visit. They also gave each one of us a bottle of mescal to take back to the states, and one to enjoy while we were there. Those Irish!

We finally checked into our rooms at 8:00 p.m., being given a very nice two-bedroom suite that included a small sitting room with another bed. Because I had stayed there on numerous occasions, we were charged only $90 per night, a very nice reduction from the regular price, and it included a stunning daily breakfast. It pushed our budget to the max but no one cared anymore. We had arrived in one piece!

I took a shower to rinse all the dried blood from my scalp, and walked down to the zocalo to call home. Lois was relieved to know we had arrived safely and promised to call Bob wife, Mary, and Gary's wife, Alice, with the good news. I then walked the six blocks back to the room and crashed. A long day — and the relief of being in Oaxaca safe and sound. It was finally time to really relax!

January 30th - Oaxaca Doings

Las Bugambilias is a lovely old hacienda close to the center of things — yet on a quiet side street a few blocks from the zocalo. I'd stayed there many times before and found it very accommodating and a good place to take folks who were not that comfortable staying in the busy, noisy downtown area.

It's owned and managed by one family and it's obvious they take great pride in the place and have learned all the intricacies of dealing with the *Nortes*. Although they get top dollar for their rooms, they are still a bargain when compared to the larger hotels that cater to Americans and other foreigners.

It's located less than two blocks from the famous Santo Domingo Church and the adjacent state museum. Numerous restaurants are within walking distance, and the breakfasts are superb and uniquely different each day.

We entered the dining room at 7:00 a.m. The table was covered with spotless white linens and platters of fresh fruit: kiwi, banana, orange, apple, pineapple, papaya, melon, strawberry, and watermelon. Glasses of mixed grapefruit and orange juice were served; sweet rolls, coffee or hot chocolate, and a serving of quesadillas with onion, cheese and Flor de Cabeza; very native and very chic. A delicacy, actually.

Also staying there were an Asian couple, a Canadian couple and a few other guests. Gary and Bob were impressed to read the names of Lute and Bobby Olsen (University of Iowa's famed basketball coach) in the upstairs guest book. Hmm. Was the place becoming too popular? Maybe it was time to look around for some place a little less well-known.

I spent the morning working on our reservations to Puerto Escondido and transportation from there back to Chicago and home. Sister Magdalen called to check up on us and told us the official blessing of the fire engine had been scheduled for Monday morning.

After breakfast we took a cab to the *marcado de abastos* — the central market. It's one of the largest travelling Indian markets in the state, and on Saturday it comes to Oaxaca City and

29

should not be missed. It is several square blocks in size, and we had a great time walking around visiting all the food, spice, animal and vegetable stands — and sneaking photos when we could. Although I'd been there before, I always find it amazing.

Afterwards, we stopped for *nieves* or snows, the delicious Mexican version of ice cream. Closer to snow cones, the ice is finely shaven and saturated in an amazing selection of delicate flavors: vanilla, chocolate, pineapple, tequila, pistachio, papaya, guava, melon, tuna (no, not the fish, but the flower buds of prickly pear) and a hundred other flavors. All natural and all fresh!

When we arrived back at Las Bugambilias we found my old friend, Señor Bilvado Martínez, waiting for us. There had been a mixup. I thought they were coming to pick us up to tour La Estancia at 2:00 p.m. No. It was noon. Oops. But no harm done. We quickly got cleaned up, jumped in his car and headed off.

La Estancia Fraternidad is a large, two-story shelter I had gotten my church, St. Joseph, in Marion, interested in ten years earlier, before it was even built. We have been helping them financially ever since, and over the years I have taken numerous groups there on work trips. I like to describe it as a Ronald McDonald-type house, although it does much more.

My friend, Señor Roberto Cruz, is the administrator and took us around explaining how things were going. The place is used hard, but still looks to be in great shape. They have so many people staying there these days (around 100) that they have to feed them outside in shifts.

One of the ambulances I delivered to them years earlier was still running fine, but the other was out having transmission work done.

Our boxes had been stored in a supply room and we sorted them out and divided them into piles for the sisters and La Estancia. Altogether, we distributed over 20 boxes of shoes, assorted children's clothes, medical supplies, a computer for Sister Magdalen and quilted blankets.. We also gave them several boxes of fanny packs and flashlights, while managing to keep a small supply ourselves to pass out as gifts.

After we visited for awhile, they took us to lunch at a lovely hotel — *Jardines del Lago*, or Lake Gardens, where we enjoyed a marvelous buffet. Like many buildings in Mexico, it did not look very fancy from the street, but as we entered the courtyard it appeared to be one of the nicer hotels in the area. There was a wedding reception going on and we got to enjoy seeing Oaxaca's high society at its best.

Later that afternoon I was able to make our plane reservations to the coast, as well as room reservations in Puerto Escondido. The Budget Rental office was closed, so I'd still need to finalize a car rental from Chicago. But it was time for a short siesta!

That evening I took Gary and Bob to visit the fanciest hotel in Oaxaca, now a member of the Calesa Real chain, previously a member of the famous Presidente chain, originally a 17th century convent. It's a lovely old building which caters exclusively to rich tourists and is always worth a visit.

Afterwards we walked to the Hotel Monte Alban on the zocalo to pick up the airline tickets but, as fate would have it, there was a problem. The flight on Wednesday was tentative. I was advised to check back in the morning.

The distance from Oaxaca City to the coast was not far; perhaps 120 miles but because of the rugged, mountainous terrain, small commuter planes are used. Unfortunately they can be unpredictable.

I really wanted to take my compadres to the coast.

January 31st - Superbowl XXXIII

I got up early and went out for a long walk. It was a beautiful clear day. I met my fellow bomberos at 8:15 a.m. and we went in to breakfast. The main course was huevos rancheros —scrambled eggs with cheese and salsa, a hearty way to start the day.

After another long walk together we went back to the hotel to meet Sister Rosemary, another Medical Missionary nun I've known for some time. We had coffee and rolls on the patio and we gave her a check and a large bag of used costume jewelry which she repackages for gifts for young Indian girls who help her.

We all attended the 11:00 a.m. Mass at the amazing Santo Domingo church and afterwards toured the adjacent state museum; in my opinion one of the finest museums in Mexico. Because it was Sunday, it was free to the public.

At 1:00 p.m. I walked back to the zocalo to check on the plane tickets. No change. Check back tomorrow. Didn't sound good.

Time to make some back–up plans.

As mentioned earlier, the flight from Oaxaca to Puerto Escondido is a short one, but crosses the Sierra de Miahuatlan mountain range — a wild and rugged group of mountains that separate the City of Oaxaca from the ocean. The small planes actually weave in and around the tall mountains. It's a trip I always look forward to, scary but beautiful.

There was a band playing in the zocalo so I stayed and listened awhile and decided to walk to the market and buy a bag to carry back some of the souvenirs I had been accumulating. Afterwards, I stopped at one of the little sidewalk cafes, had a beer, then headed on back to the hotel to see what the boys had been up to.

After a short siesta, Gary and I returned to the church of Santo Domingo for some late afternoon photos. It was lovely out and the plaza around the church was serene and quiet; the majority of natives having returned to their villages. The sun was low on the horizon and shone brightly on the golden face of the church and its blue and white tiled roof.

Super Bowl XXXIII was about to start so we headed back to the hotel to watch it in the upstairs community TV area. During halftime we went to Café Rústica, a small but fun Italian restaurant just a few blocks away. I recognized that by this time my fellow Americans might appreciate a familiar cuisine.

We ordered individual pizzas and glasses of wine, then rushed back to see the thrilling finish. Denver Broncos 34, and Atlanta Falcons 19. But the thing that made it such a memorable game for us was the outstanding performance of the University of Iowa's running back, Tim Dwight, and his 94-yard touchdown run.

We were back in our rooms reading the English language newspaper, *The News*, and in bed by 10:00 p.m.

February 1st - The Blessing of Big Red

A big day today. The blessing of the fire engine. Pancakes smothered with fresh berries made up the main ingredient of today's breakfast. Wonderful!

Then bad news.

I received a call from Hotel Monte Alban — the plane was not flying to the coast in the morning. There appeared to be a problem with the engine.

What now? I'd already purchased airline tickets from Puerto Escondido to Mexico City — and from there to Chicago. If I start changing things now ...

Alberto (private chauffeur of El Presidente Aquino) came to pick us up at 8:30 a.m. and took us straight to Xoxocotlán. He stopped along the way to buy some local newspapers containing an article about us and the fire engine delivery.

We listened to Señor Aquino being interviewed on the radio and mentioning our names — all quite exciting.

I told Alberto the bad news about the plane cancellation to the coast!

"Hey, no problema, amigos," he said. "I, Alberto, driver excellente, will drive you there myself with pleasure! No?"

Really? The mayor would let him do this?

When we arrived in front of the city hall, we found the fire engine freshly waxed and polished. To our surprise it was also adorned with garlands of greenery and large, colorful bouquets of fresh flowers fastened to both the front and the rear! It looked like a million bucks. A large crowd was already gathering; store owners along with a growing bunch of locals trying to figure what was going on.

Soon Señor Aquino arrived fresh from his radio interview, looking very pleased with himself. City officials and the police department began to line up in front of the fire engine. Office employees streamed out to join the fun. It seemed we were going to parade to a nearby church where the actual blessing would take place.

I got in the fire engine with Alberto who insisted on turning on all the flashing lights — no sirens, yet. The police band began playing a martial tune and led the way while we followed. The city officials and curious townsfolk fell in behind.

The trip to the church was only a few blocks. When we arrived I started to panic — the entrance to the church yard was through narrow pillars with only inches to spare on either side and a slight incline to negotiate at the same time. Yikes!

But Bob saw the problem and ran up and directed me through with only a very slight bumper crunching against one of the pillars. No serious damage.

We pulled into a large courtyard in front of a lovely country church followed by a growing crowd. Everyone circled the fire engine. Padre Miguel began to give a speech; only a small part of which I understood but which seemed to cover the expected points: the generosity of the Christian people of Marion, America ... the great use this fine machine will be put to ... the saving of homes and lives ... and so on.

Then Mayor Aquino stepped forward and talked about what a great thing this would be for the community, and how grateful he was to the Medical Missionary Sisters and the Tres Bomberos (us) for bringing such an excellent piece of machinery 2,500 miles, about the new volunteer fire department that would be formed, and so on.

Then they all turned to me. The Mayor handed me the mike. What? No one said anything about me talking. I stared at Sister Magdalen who just smiled serenely. I was on my own.

I can't remember exactly what I said, in fractured Spanish, but it was something about this gift was not coming from me but from fellow Christians in Iowa, and that we hope it would serve the community well, and thanked them for letting us be a part of this wonderful project.

I'm not sure how it all actually came out and how much they really understood but everyone seemed to like it and broke into polite applause and smiled widely at us.

At that point firecrackers and aerial bombs started going off and the good Padre stepped forward and walked around the fire engine, sprinkling it top to bottom from a large bottle of holy water. More applause and horrendous bursts from the aerial bombs. The crowd loved it.

Then, just when I thought everything was over, someone rushed up to the Mayor and handed him two bottles of champagne, one of which he handed to me. I looked at him quizzically. Was I supposed to drink it? No, dumbo, you're supposed to spray the fire engine with it.

So off we went, to the increasing delight of the crowd, circling the truck and spraying it and each other with champagne! What Fun!

With fireworks bursting and people cheering and clapping we backed the holy-water and champagne-dripping fire engine out of the churchyard and headed back around the town square.

"Now, amigo," prompted Alberto. "Turn on the sirens!"

By this time, most of the townsfolk were out in the streets, trying to figure out what all the ruckus was about.

Here we came around the square, the police squad marching, drummers drumming, the fire engine with lights spinning and sirens wailing, followed by the entire city council and office workers of Xoxocotlán walking arm in arm in a wide line, and behind them, a huge group of chattering, giggling locals.

When we all arrived back in front of city hall, I signed the title over to the City of Xoxocotlán and handed it over to Mayor Aquino — our last official act.

Well, not quite.

Just then, out of the city hall rushed ladies carrying trays of what I think was spiked citron which we all used to toast one another. More pictures, *abrazos* all around, and we were through!

Now that was a blessing!

Mayor Aquino was thrilled at how well things had gone. I think he was thinking he had definitely secured a landslide reelection for himself at the very least.

True to his word, Alberto had told him about our cancelled flight and he graciously offered us the use of his personal car and driver not only for the rest of the day, but for the trip to Puerto Escondido in the morning.

We said goodbye to everyone and, taking advantage of Alberto, left to visit a place I had not been before, *Heive de Agua* (The Water Boils). It was a long way out of town and into some rugged mountains.

Heive de Agua is a strange place where bubbling mineral springs run into bathing pools with a spectacular cliff-top location and expansive panoramas. Water dribbling over the cliff edge for millennia has created mineral formations that look like huge frozen waterfalls. It is an ancient place, and a sacred spot to the local indians who were trying to capitalize on it as a tourist attraction. Unfortunately, as fascinating as it was, I think it's far too remote and hard to get to.

On the way back we stopped at the village of Mitla, one of my favorite places in the area to visit. It's a place known for its rug weaving and production of mescal. Nearby we toured a small archeological site, the Miztec City of the Dead, and stopped for some mescal-flavored ice cream! Yum yum – burp!

While in the area it seemed fitting to visit an actual mescal factory owned by Alberto's friends, where we were treated as royalty and given a personal tour. It was a very low key, but interesting, little family operation.

Mescal: First they chop off the leaves of the large aguave plant and use only the cores, which are buried under a hill of sand and upon which a fire is kept lit for several days, slowly roasting them.

They then uncover the smoking cores, chop them up and place the pieces in a bin to ferment. Using burros walking around in a circle harnessed to a large stone wheel, they mash the pieces into a mush.

After an hour or so, the ground-up mush is transferred to a large still. Eventually, out of the bottom of the still drips the warm mescal. We tasted a small bowl full and found it quite flavorful!

If you could overlook the unhygiene appearence of the whole place, and ignore quality control, it was quite an impressive operation.

We headed back toward Oaxaca, stopping in the village of Santa Maria de Tule to visit the sacred 2,000-year-old cyprus tree and then had lunch at a country restaurant, the Señora.

The Señora specializes in grilled and barbecued meats and is a wonderful place. Open on all sides and covered with a large palm roof, it is a local favorite.

The menu was limited: meat or sea food. We ordered beers and the meat tray and soon waiters brought over our own large brazier, filled with hot coals and loaded down with layers of meat; pork, BBQ ribs, young goat, and chicken. We ate our fill and everything tasted delicious.

A small trio of musicians strolled over and we invested 100 pesos in five songs. I know the names of several rather obscure, but famous old traditional Mexican folk songs and surprised the musicians by requesting them. I think they were expecting *La Cucaracha* or *Cielito Lindo*, or something equally touristy.

It was a very enjoyable lunch sitting there, eating good food and listening to our own private musical group. Again, like padrinos, we sat and smiled!

By late afternoon it was time to head back. I had Alberto drop me off at the Mexicana Airline office where I picked up our plane tickets from Puerto Escondido to Mexico City. I then stopped by the Budget Rent-A-Car office and managed to get a car reserved for us when we arrived in Chicago. I was pretty surprised I was able to do all this from Oaxaca — things were definitely changing in Mexico!

I finally stopped by a gift store I had been visiting and picked up a few presents I'd had my eyes on during the past few days. I then headed back to Las Bugambilias.

I hadn't been back very long when Señor Cruz showed up with a lady who wanted to make a presentation to us. I thought this was a bit much, but what could we do except be polite and listen.

She was a founder of a local group that assisted children with cancer. They needed money, of course, and medicine, and were hoping the rich gringos could help them, too. After all, if we could buy a fire engine, we could surely help children with cancer.

It was a sad case — and I told them I would see what I could do when I got back.

Finally to bed at 10:00 p.m. Tired.

February 2 - On to the Sea

After a final lovely breakfast of perhaps a dozen different types of fresh fruit, cocoa, coffee, and pancakes, we were ready to hit the road again. Puerto Escondido, the lovely coast, was calling!

Alberto arrived late to pick us up (or right on time depending on whose time you were using; Gringo or Mexican). The mayor's vehicle was a sleek, black Chevy Suburban with tinted windows, a powerful engine and had been freshly washed.

We stopped to buy a newspaper that covered yesterday's fire engine blessing and we were soon on the highway headed once again toward the mountains. It was around 9:00 a.m. Everyone was in great spirits.

As anticipated, the highway over the mountains to the coast was rough and filled with twists and turns and riddled with potholes. Alberto, our loyal driver, was not fazed and zoomed along as if we were driving on Interstate 80. We had to tell him to slow down numerous times.

At some nondescript village along the way we stopped for a light snack. It turned into a very colorful stop, and a typical small Mexican village eating experience: an open air restaurant covered with thatched palm, crowded tables covered with oil cloth and filled with over-the-road truckers, local field workers, women with children of all ages, parrots and dogs.

Alberto ordered with confidence. Soon, from an open fireplace along the back, came platters of tortillas, chicharon con salsa (deep fat fried pig skin with hot sauce, delicious!), cups of hot cocoa and coffee, fried pork liver with eggs, and diced fried potatoes. Whew! Good thing it was just a light snack.

The route Alberto had chosen to the coast was 150 miles, a little longer than I thought, but a little safer. Unfortunately the Sierra Madre del Sur mountain range was inconveniently in the way. A safer route, perhaps, but still quite rough.

If anything, the road got worse as we climbed higher and higher. Virtually every curve had been reduced to one lane because of mud and rock slides in the preceding months. Occasionally we'd come upon the burned out shell of a vehicle that missed a curve. Of course, Alberto, the mayor's personal driver and old grade school chu, was in his element and soared along, grinning widely.

By the Grace of God we arrived in the early afternoon. The trip took six hours, averaging a blazing 25 mph, not bad considering we made it in one piece. There are many who cannot say that.

Hotel Arco Iris — Hotel Rainbow — was crowded and, as usual, didn't have the rooms we were promised. I had asked for three rooms, all on the second floor, facing the ocean.

Bob and Gary ended up sharing one ocean front room and I took another in the back. I'd been there before and thought those two would appreciate the ocean view. The sign of a benevolent leader.

Before Alberto returned to Oaxaca we treated him to a nice big lunch and gave him several presents to take home to his family including 300 pesos. He was very happy and seemed most reluctant to leave. He was really a nice guy who undoubedly realized his future was limited once his friend, Mayor Aquino, left office.

The pool at the hotel is one of the nicest in Puerto and we spent the afternoon just lounging around and taking it easy. Bob and Gary were thrilled at the place and couldn't believe they had an ocean-facing room for $17.50 each. That evening I took them to the nearby Hotel Santa Fe for dinner.

After eating we walked the beach to town and snooped around looking in shops and checking out what the street vendors were selling. Around 9:00 p.m. we hailed a cab and returned to the hotel where we sipped margaritas on the deck and relaxed to the sound of the pounding surf a couple hundred feet away.

Puerto Escondido is a pretty laid back affair. Known as a surfer's town because of the size of the incoming rollers, there are usually groups of West Coast surfers hanging around waiting for that perrfect wave. It's always been great for a place to relax for two or three days, but after that it can get pretty boring.

It had been a hectic day driving through the mountains, but we had arrived safely and had really started to relax. I went to my room to read and soon fell asleep to the sound of the crashing surf.

February 3rd - Winding Down

A lovely, cloudless day. It was a bit breezy and the ocean looked frisky. Fruit platters, hot chocolate and rolls with jam on the veranda.

Oh the hectic life of the bombero!

I took a four-mile-walk to the end of the bay. Along the way I passed, several topless college students trying to look cool and relaxed as if this were the most normal thing in the world for them to be doing, but who were obviously uncomfortable at the unfriendly stares they were receiving. Mexican women, in particular, do not approve of this type of behavior and let it be known. The men didn't seem to mind.

On the way back I ran into the apprentice drivers sporting new, wide-brimmed straw hats and chattering away as they strolled along the beach: Ernest Hemingway and friend. They told me they'd killed a scorpion in their room that morning and were quite excited about it.

I didn't tell them that the last group of students that stayed there with me actually captured a scorpion in the same hotel so I'd known they were there. Nor did I tell them I'd found one in my shower at Las Bugambilias. There are lots of scorpions in Mexico but I only know one person who was ever stung, one of the Medical Missionary Nuns, as a matter of fact. It made her very sick for several days.

I took my daily ocean swim and went back to the room. Delphina, the maid, was just finishing cleaning and I gave her a few fanny packs and flashlights. She had small children and was delighted to get them. What a neat way of tipping.

We hung around relaxing all afternoon, napping, reading, and swimming in the pool.

Early evening we walked to town again and ate at the *La Pearla Flambete* — The Flaming Pearl — one of my favorite places for dinner. They always feature a dinner special; fresh fish fixed any way you like, a drink, and salad for $7.00. I ordered mahi–mahi grilled in garlic sauce, a margarita and fresh lettuce salad. Just right.

After dinner I bought a silver bracelet for Lois and we headed back to the hotel to get our gear packed and ready to go. It was a lovely, mild evening, our last evening in Mexico.

I know we were all ready to return home — but already I was starting to miss the ocean.

February 4th - Heading Home

I got up at 6:30 a.m. and walked down to the beach to watch the fishing boats come in with their previous night's catch.

I'm always amazed at the variety of fish they bring in, and love to watch the bickering and haggling as the local hotel cooks rush down to make their daily buys.

On the way back to the hotel, I stopped for juice, hot chocolate and sweet rolls at a friendly local restaurant on the main street of town. I left the rest of our flashlights with them.

Four hours to go before time to catch our *collectivo* to the airport. I walked back and checked in with Gary and Bob. They were both lounging around the pool chatting with some folks from Des Moines, Iowa. Small world.

Everyone was packed and ready.

Before we knew it, we were on the plane, circling out over the sparkling blue Pacific as we made a wide turn and swept north toward Mexico City. An endless beach and acres of palm trees grew smaller and smaller. Sigh!

What a wonderful trip it had been. No one got sick. No one got lost, at least for long. We had no problems or accidents with the fire engine and, once again, I believe we left the country better off than we found it. Not a huge difference — but a worthwhile one.

I sank back into the seat, closed my eyes and slipped into a cat nap, already starting to plan for the next trip back.

Hmm. Perhaps another ambulance, this one loaded with cancer medicine for children? Could work. We'll see.

RIDING THE DEVIL'S NOSE

ECUADOR

"Goo' morning. This Maria at Leeen Aul Serbices. Can I help you pleeese?"

"Excuse me?" I said. "Who is this? I thought I was calling Line Haul Services ... in Miami?"

"Yes, ob course. Thees Leeen Aul Serbices. Wad you wan, pleeese?"

Good heavens, I thought to myself. I could barely understand a word she was saying.

"I'd like to make an airline courier reservation? Can you help me? This is my first time doing this and ..."

"Yes, ob course. Where you wan go?"

"Well, I'd like to go to Honduras," I said. "Tegucigalpa, if possible. Can you tell me when your flights are? I'd like to leave on ..."

"We no go more 'onduras."

"Excuse me?" I said, my confidence level slipping. "You no longer go to Honduras? Is that what you said?"

I'd earlier read it was "easy as pie" to make a courier flight anywhere in the world — especially to Honduras and other South American countries.

"No 'onduras," she said. "'ow about *Guataschmeal* ... bery, bery nice."

"*Guata* ... huh ... where did you say? I can't hear you very well."

"*GUDASCIMCALL!*" she shouted. "Bery nice! Bery cheeep! Only $220 American roundtreeep."

"Guadalcanal?" I said. "Did you say *Guadalcanal?*"

"Sí. Ob course. *Guallanikeal*. Ebery day."

Gosh, I thought to myself, beginning to feel a little better about things. Guadalcanal! That would be very cool. I'd never been to Guadalcanal. Isn't that where the Marines landed, or something? I didn't realize it was in South America.

"Well, okay," I said. "That sounds interesting. How about Saturday, September 16th? Do you have a flight going then? And coming back on the 23rd so I can ...."

"Sí. Ob course," she said. "What your address. Weeel sent you papers. You return papers with $220 and weeel take care of eberything."

I gave her my address.

"And you have flights coming back on the 23rd?"

"Sí. Ob course. Ebery day."

"Okay. Great. Thanks, Maria, I'll be sure to return the papers with $220 right away. Is that all there is to it?"

"Sí. Ob course. Adios." (Click)

Well, I guess that *was* "easy as pie."

Too bad about Honduras but what the heck — Guadalcanal! How often do you get a chance to visit Guadalcanal? And for only $220 *roundtreeep*. This'll be great!

And so it was I was headed to Guayaquil, Ecuador.

SATURDAY – SEPTEMBER 16TH

Before I knew it, it was time to leave.

Eventually I'd learned I wasn't going to Guadalcanal after all. The news came when I received the papers from Line Haul Services. It was quite a shock. What I thought Maria was saying as *Guadalcanal* ... was actually *Guayaquil*. Guayaquil, Ecuador, to be specific. What the heck!

Ecuador ... Ecuador ... so where exactly is Ecuador and what's a Guayaquil? Back to the library to return my Lonely Planet guidebook on the Solomon Islands and the elusive Guadalcanal. Time to do a little more research.

Okay, so as it turned out I wasn't going to the South Seas ... but to the Andes Mountains in South America. Close enough. It sounded equally exotic. I also learned I had the option to go to Quito, Ecuador, instead of Guayaquil. I'd heard of Quito so that's what I decided to do.

But first I had to get to Miami.

The morning I left home, the news was full of reports of Hurricane Marilyn bearing down like an out-of-control express train on the Florida coast. It had already done a number on the Bahamas. It had been a busy Atlantic hurricane season and it seemed Marilyn was particularly nasty.

"Are you sure you really want to do this?" asked my nervous wife as she drove me to the airport. "Miami's on the Florida coast, you know."

"Yes, I know where Miami is," I said. "And yes, I really want to do this. It's a little late to change plans now anyway, I've already sent my money and bought my ticket. Besides the news people always tends to exaggerate these things."

The truth was I wasn't totally sure. It's just that after weeks of planning I couldn't back out now. I had too much time and reputation invested at this point.

Earlier in the year I'd read and was smitten with Kelly Monaghan's book, *Air Courier Bargains: How to Travel World Wide for Next to Nothing*.

Wow, I thought. That's for me. It had all the key ingredients in the title: *Travel, World Wide*, and most importantly — *Next to Nothing*. I'm basically a cheapskate.

Of course, I still wasn't totally clear on what a courier's duties were. I did know I'd be limited to one small carry-on. The courier company would then use my checked luggage privileges for one of their own 'packages' ... such as a piece of machinery, or packet of time-sensitive documents. (I was hoping the packages would not be dead bodies, or drugs, or enriched uranium. But the truth was, I didn't know.)

One piece of carry-on was fine by me. I'd only be gone eight days and I traveled light; a change of clothes and underwear should do it. I still had room for 50 mini-rolls of Lifesavers and a supply of balloons to make funny little animals for children.

The plane slammed down at Miami International 30 minutes late and I mean slammed! I don't think I've ever experienced such a hard landing in my life. An audible gasp was heard from all the passengers. The air was muggy — but not the monsoon-type weather I expected.

Maria's instructions were rather vague. I was told to meet a Señorita Blanca at La Carreta Restaurant on Concourse D at 5:00 p.m. That was it.

Up to this point I had received nothing solid from Line Haul Services. No ticket. No confirming reservations. No detailed instructions. Nothing. I was acting on blind faith that a Señorita Blanca would show up and somehow magically recognize me, by telepathy I guess, from among the hundreds of people milling around Concourse D.

I found La Carreta quickly. It was packed with mostly Hispanics eating lunch. It was around 2:30 p.m. — plenty of time before I had to find my "contact" so I wandered around.

Close by the restaurant was an exchange booth where I stopped to get some Ecuadorian money. I'd be arriving in Quito after 10 p.m. and doubted I'd find a place open to exchange money at that late hour.

The exchange rate offered was only 2,200 Ecuadorian *sucres* to the dollar. What? The morning paper showed 2,500 to 1, <u>a 300 sucre difference for every dollar</u>. What's going on here? What a ripoff! I fumed and fussed until I remembered there were 25 sucres to a penny. Hmm, let's see ... so the additional 300 sucres they were socking me would only be ... 12¢. I simmered down a little.

I wandered back to La Carreta and ordered a *cortado* — a thick, sweet and very strong coffee with cream. It was a traditional Latin American refreshment and there were dozens of men standing around chatting and enjoying their cortados. No women, I noticed. Must be a guy thing.

So there I stood, slowly sipping my cortado, my JanSport backpack by my feet, feeling very James Bondish. I was surrounded with people from the Virgin Islands, Jamaica, Mexico, Costa Rico, Colombia and all points south. This courier stuff was pretty cool.

Suddenly I heard someone behind me whisper in a tiny voice, "Meester Bulklee?"

Startled, I whirled around. La Señorita Blanca had arrived! The contact had been made!

Señorita Blanca stood at most four feet tall wearing thick–soled shoes. She reminded me of the quirky-looking actress in horror movies, Zelma Rubenstein. You'd remember her if you've seen the movie *Poltergeist*.

So, as it turned out, there *was* nothing to it. She handed me a one–way airline ticket and told me I was all set to go. Since I had no baggage to check — and nothing to retrieve — she said I could leave the terminal as soon as I arrived. There would be no one to meet me and I was free to do what I wished. Her only instructions were to call their office in Quito in a day or two and make arrangements for the return trip.

I was a little disappointed. I was expecting maybe a leather satchel filled with diamonds handcuffed to my wrists.

I looked at the ticket. The roundtrip price was $567. So, $220 was a definite bargain after all! I started to ask her a question, but she had already melted away in the crowd.

Our plane left at 6:45 p.m, 30 minutes late. It was very crowded and chaotic with people sitting in the wrong seats and trying to stow more carry-on luggage than allowed. But everyone seemed in such a good mood, yelling and laughing, I just sat and watched.

By this time I was starving and was delighted to discover free drinks and a steak dinner were included. Never one to pass up a complimentary Jack Daniels and juicy ribeye I sat back, relaxed and enjoyed a wonderful meal.

Toward the end of the flight there was a large 'bump' as the plane either hit an air pocket or just crossed the equator and entered the southern hemisphere.

We landed at Mariscal Sucre Aeroporto at 10:15 p.m. With nothing to declare, I immediately headed to customs. If anything were to go wrong, I thought, this would be the place. I'd be put in chains. But nothing did, and before realizing it I was walking out the main entrance and into the city of Quito.

Since I didn't have a clue how to get around on my own I took a cab to the Hotel Republica. The driver charged me 10,000 sucres — around $4 U.S., I think.

The Hotel Republica was supposedly a four–star hotel. An Ecuadorian man sitting next to me on the plane had recommended I stay there rather than try to find a place in the old city, which was my original plan. A good suggestion, as it turned out.

Now, I don't know about four-star, but it was okay. The price of the room was a little hazy since I wasn't yet used to dealing in sucres. I thought the clerk said 65,000 sucres, which would have been around $26. Seemed reasonable enough. Two large beds, nice bath with shower, cable TV and phone, and everything looked pretty new. By then it was around 10:30 p.m. I walked down to a small bar in the lobby and ordered a beer.

Ecuador produces two brands of beer: a small 10 oz. bottle called Club, and a large bottle called Pilsner containing 578 cl. I have yet to figure out how much that is; somewhere between a pint and a quart, I think.

The bar was deserted but I was too hyped-up to go right to bed so I drank up and left for a walk around the block.

The area surrounding the hotel could best be described as *suspect*. Everything seemed to be closed or under repair. The streets, of course, were paved but with very sparse traffic. No one was out walking except me, a millionaire *gringo*.

The altitude made any type of exertion seem difficult, but I had expected that. I left Miami at an altitude of six feet and was now at over 9,000 feet.

On the corner I saw a rundown–looking nightclub with swinging doors. I poked my head in and saw several groups of listless men sitting at long tables drinking brandy and Coke. They were halfheartedly listening to a group of young 20-somethings playing an odd mixture of American–type music. They sounded awful. I took a quick look and left, one of the more sensible things I did the entire trip.

I returned to the hotel, took a shower and hit the sack. By this time it was almost midnight and I was exhausted. I was anxious for morning to come so I could actually see the Andes. I must be smack in the middle of them, yet I couldn't see a thing.

SUNDAY – SEPTEMBER 17TH

I left the hotel around 8:00 in the morning and the first thing I noticed was I surrounded by mountains. They were stunning, in particular the snow-clad volcano, Pinchincha — almost 15,000 feet high. The temperature was a crisp 50° and the sky was a clear deep blue.

Unfortunately I already had one strike against me. I'd left all my travel information about Quito on the plane. Drats! All I remembered was the basic city layout and names of several of the main parks and streets.

I walked up two blocks, crossed a very busy boulevard called *The Tenth of August* (my oldest son's birthday), and jumped on the first bus heading toward the old city. My goal was to explore as much as I could before heading to the equator in the afternoon.

I figured that if I planned a route between *The Tenth of August* and *The Sixth of December* (the day before Pearl Harbor Day), I'd be within a fairly manageable area. Now if they'd only had a *17th of March* street (St. Patrick's Day) I wouldn't have needed a map at all.

As it turned out, I got hopelessly lost.

Bus fares quickly became a mystery. The first bus I got on charged 250 sucres, around 10¢. Another cost three times that, another, half. I learned every bus line had a different fare and the fares varied depending on the time of day. Of course there were dozens of competing lines. To complicate things, some buses collected when you got on, and some when you got off.

To make things even worse, I only had sucres in 10,000 denominations ($5). You can imagine how popular I was paying a 250 sucre fare with a 10,000 sucre bill.

The trip to the older part of the city took around 20 minutes. Along the way we passed building after building that wasn't very attractive — not necessary ugly, just very uninteresting and poorly–designed. After a few blocks it dawned on me that none of them looked completed. Kind of like the builder had lost interest towards the end — or ran out of money and just walked away.

I'd read Quito is known as "The Terrible City." I began to discover why. In 1990, the population was just over one million — but I believe it's closer to a million and a half by now. A 50 percent increase in just five years! Urban sprawl at its worse.

I had no specific plan of where to get off so I rode until the area really looked old. No — that would be too kind. It looked absolutely ancient and not very safe.

I guess I was suffering a bit of culture shock and I began to feel a little squeamish. I got off at the first park I saw: The Park of the Virgin's Lagoon. With a name like that I figured I'd be safe.

Wrong. This was definitely not where I wanted to be. Small groups of men were sitting around watching me through slitted eyes. Me, the obviously filthy rich gringo, looking lost.

"I best get out of here," I mumbled to myself.

I spied an elderly gentleman sitting by himself watching young parents paddle their children around a small, algae-choked pond in a leaky boat.

"Excuse me sir," I said in Spanish, "can you tell me the way to the *zocalo*?"

He perked up and looked at me with a puzzled expression.

"The zocalo?" I said. "The Parque Central? The Plaza Central?"

"Ah. The Plaza Principal," he said with a smile. "Of course, let me show you."

He struggled to his feet, took my arm and slowly led me back the way I had just come and pointed to a bus just like the one I had got off.

"The green bus," he smiled. "Take the green bus."

I walked back across the street and got on the green bus. Of course, the fact that all the buses were green or shades of green didn't make me feel very confident. But I got on and sat in the back next to a young man with books on his lap. "Can you show me the way to the Plaza Principal," I asked?

"Certainly," he said, "and I will also show you where to get off." Great, I thought. I was making headway and my Spanish was holding up.

I eventually figured out that zocalo is a purely Mexican term. In Ecuador the main city square is referred to as La Plaza Principal.

The name for this particular plaza was *La Plaza Grande* or *Plaza de la Independencia* depending on who you asked. It was beautiful, with a very large, ornate fountain situated right in the middle with straight gravel paths leading off in several directions, like the spokes of a large wheel.

This plaza served as central gathering place for folk musicians, shoe shiners, tourists, gossip mongers and souvenir photographers. It was definitely the main attraction in the old city. This area alone was enough to keep me busy for the rest of the morning.

On one side of the plaza was the neoclassical Government Palace built in the 1800s. On another was the stunning Metropolitan Cathedral of Quito which houses the tomb of Quito's liberator, Mariscal Antonio José Sucre. (Sucre! Aha! The name of the national currency).

Attached to the huge cathedral was El Sagrario Chapel noted for its flamboyant 17th century facade.

I entered the cathedral and was immediately overcome by the sweet smell of incense and smoke from seemed like a million candles. Tiny native women were everywhere, wrapped in heavy shawls, fedora–covered heads bowed, lips moving a mile a minute in silent prayer. (Where were all the men?)

I stopped at one of the numerous side chapels to attend Mass. It seemed like Mass was going on non–stop throughout the huge building, which felt very old world. Very Spanish. After Mass I left and hung around the fountain area, reading and taking photos. It had been a lovely crisp morning which, in Quito, started out like every other morning at 50°. However, by this time the sun was up and the temperature was rapidly climbing toward a comfortable 75°.

The mountain sky was brilliant blue and crystal clear and the ambiance around the plaza was relaxed and slow. I felt very comfortable just sitting and soaking in the sun.

On the corner of the square I spied a little cafe where I stopped for scrambled eggs, toast, coffee and what I thought was orange juice. At least I'd ordered orange juice — but then I remembered reading they grow another fruit down here similar to oranges but definitely different. The juice tasted a little strange, tart and metallic, but I drank it anyway and it didn't kill me. Breakfast cost $1.75.

Quito, as I mentioned earlier, did not strike me as a very attractive city. I hesitate to say "terrible," but certainly not very attractive. At least this was my initial reaction — and perhaps not totally fair.

After a leisurely breakfast I wandered around taking more photos and finally headed back to the hotel. The temperature was much warmer by this time and I decided to drop off my heavy sweater and take a short rest before heading to the equator.

I tried to call Line Haul Services to get instructions for my return ticket but they didn't answer the phone. Since it was Sunday I decided to forget about it until the next day. Surely they'd be open on Monday, wouldn't they? They wouldn't abandon me in Ecuador, would they? Not sure about anything, I rested an hour and caught a bus going the opposite direction to the *La Mitad del Mundo* (The Middle of the World) as the equator is referred to down there.

It was a wild and woolly bus ride costing around 25¢. The driver looked like he would soon be entering fifth grade, and his helper was his younger brother. Apparently no one had taught him where the brake pedal was, although he was very familiar with the horn. The bus was packed with locals who were also going to visit the equator on their day off. A good sign.

We arrived by 1:30 p.m. at this special spot that in 1736 the French Geodesic Mission determined to be the exact latitudinal center of the earth: 0° 00' 00".

Dominating the area was a 33–foot–tall trapezoidal shaped building with a huge stone globe at the top. For a small fee one could go up and look over the area and visit an ethnographic museum with minimal but interesting examples of the various cultures of Ecuador.

What was particularly interesting to me was the way people reacted to the actual equator, which was displayed as a 4-inch-wide, red-tiled line running in both directions for several hundred feet. Everyone was clowning around: jumping back and forth over it, playing tug of war, or straddling the line and having their pictures taken with legs standing in both hemispheres.

Some more serious folks actually got down on the ground with their bodies dissected by the line. And there they remained spread–eagled — no doubt soaking in some super terrestrial vibrations.

I stopped for lunch at a restaurant overlooking the main plaza. There was a group of teenage boys entertaining the Sunday crowd with music from the Andes played on pan flutes. They were quite good.

It may have been zero latitude, but the 10,000 feet altitude made any form of exertion very tiring and minimized what little appetite I had. After a couple of hours of sightseeing, I jumped on a bus and headed back.

The return ride cost an extra dime. I suppose they figured you had to get back somehow and were willing to pay the price. Several passengers argued at the obvious miscarriage of justice, but to no avail. I kept my gringo mouth shut.

The extra ten cents didn't bother me as much as discovering I appeared to be on a different route. Before I realized it I was in an unfamiliar part of Quito. I sensed I was close to the Hotel Republica but couldn't seem to find it.

Several people I asked admitted knowing exactly where it was and pointed in opposite directions. After an hour of wandering hopelessly around town I got on another bus and stayed on it until I came to a place I *was* familiar with. It happened to be *Parque Ejido* — the main park separating the old district from the new. I knew my way back from there.

All along the front of the park, local artisans had their works on display. Mainly cheesy tourist junk, but a few serious painters and weavers.

Across the street was the hotel where all the filthy rich gringos stayed — Hotel Colon — and where the "ladies of the night," or in this case, late afternoon, were out sunning themselves.

I was told Hotel Colon was one of the few hotels in Quito that exchanged money so I entered like the filthy rich gringo I was, went up to the desk, and was informed the exchange office would not open until 7:00 a.m. the next day.

By this time my supply of sucres was running dangerously low. I'd better watch myself or I'd run out. While I was in the hotel I inquired about the cost of a room and learned that a gringo would have to pay $160 a night. I also learned Ecuadorians were charged considerably less, normally around half.

Hmm, that was interesting, I thought, but didn't say anything. It did surprise me that they really didn't care if anybody knew it or not. I headed back to my hotel. This time the bus fare was a dime less! A different hour? A different company? Go figure.

When I finally got to the hotel, I decided to stay in my room for the evening, relax and watch some of the local, silly game shows on TV. My plans were to leave the next day and head down *La Camino Real* – The Royal Road – an ancient route connecting Quito with the Inca capital of Cuzco in Peru.

Centuries ago a narrow foot road was used by teams of relay runners, known as *chasquis,* carrying messages between the two kingdoms. Following Spanish colonization in the 1500s, the road was paved with cobblestones and eventually converted to what we know today as the Pan American Highway.

Another popular name for this stretch is the Avenue of the Volcanoes. The name says it all. It promised to be a spectacular trip and passed through the resort town of Baños, one of my planned destination stops.

MONDAY – SEPTEMBER 18TH

I awoke at 7:00 a.m. with a stiff neck from the lousy pillow but otherwise quite rested. While I was shaving, all the lights in the hotel suddenly went out. This happened in several other places I stayed and by the end of the trip I was used to it.

When I went to pay the bill I received a big shock. Instead of $26 a night which I expected, my bill was $48! Apparently I was quoted the 'local rate' and charged the 'gringo rate.' I argued about this obvious injustice but got nowhere.

"But Señor, you are not Ecuadorian, *verdad*?"
True, I was not an Ecuadorian. Just a gullible gringo. It was a nice enough room — but not *that* nice. I needed to be more careful in the future.

I took a cab to the Hotel Colon where I changed $100 into a thick wad of sucres and continued on to the bus station. I bought a $2.50 ticket for Ambato where I would have to transfer.

I tried to call Line Haul Services again but no one answered. Perhaps it was too early. I was a little nervous leaving town without clearing up my return ticket business but hoped I could contact them later in the day.

I took a window seat about half way back. Several Indians got on lugging huge cardboard boxes wrapped in twine. They were dressed in brightly colored ponchos, fedoras and woolen pants.

Soon a magazine vendor got on to sell used magazines. Then a candy vendor got on and sold what he could. The crowd was very patient. Eventually we left the station.

The front section of the bus was separated from the rear by a large, side–to–side glass window. The driver and helper sat up front. In the center of this glass partition was etched a portrait of the Virgin Mary. A little overdone for a bus, I thought, but on the other hand we were departing for a trip through some serious mountains. I'd take all the protection I could get.

We quickly left the urban sprawl of Quito behind and immediately the landscape turned greener and greener. I loved the names of some of the towns we passed through — Machachi, Latacunga, and finally — Ambato.

Monday was a huge market day in Ambato. I would have liked to stay awhile but I couldn't find a place to leave my backpack. I thought about asking someone at the station to watch it, but after looking around, reconsidered.

However the bus station itself was fascinating. People in the wildest assortment of native garb were milling around everywhere and selling about everything you could think of. Live goats and chickens and turkeys trussed up and slung over backs. In front of the station were mounds of vegetables, plastic toys, rope, and tape recorders. And this wasn't even the main market!

Ambato was once known as the "City of Flowers and Fruits" until a major earthquake in 1949 completely destroyed it. Today there was nothing around that looked particularly old. Only perhaps a little worn out and bedraggled.

While I was walking down the street, a young school age girl went over to the curb, pulled down her drawers and did her business. A man walked over to a low brick wall and did the same. No one seemed to notice — or care. (You're not in Iowa anymore, Bobby.)

As interesting and colorful as Ambato seemed to be, I pressed on. A bus was leaving for Baños in just a few minutes. I paid 75¢ for my ticket and got on.

Just as we were getting ready to leave, a woman with a baby strapped to her back jumped on and began selling fresh squeezed orange juice in little plastic bags. The bags were tied at the top and had straws sticking out. I saw others buying from her so I figured it would be safe enough. I was halfway finished before I noticed there was an ice cube floating inside. Oh no! I was confident that hunk of ice was not from purified water. *Tourista* — here I come!

I finished as quickly as I could before the ice completely melted. I worried about it for the rest of the day, waiting for the dreaded telltale stomach cramps, but nothing happened. I was lucky this time!

The bus headed downhill out of Ambato in a southeast direction. The countryside was really getting lush at this point as we aimed toward the jungle! We swept down gorgeous valleys covered with unidentifiable vegetables and fruit trees. Everywhere you looked, natives with red wool serapes and brown fedoras were shuffling throughout the countryside.

Shortly after noon we arrived in Los Baños (The Baths).

In spite of the periodic volcanic activity from Mt. Tungurahua, Baños is a tourist area popular with both Ecuadorian and foreign visitors alike.

A popular jumping–off point for adventurers interested in taking trips to the jungle or climbing Mt. Chimborazo, Baños has been the "place to be" for wealthy, vacationing Ecuadorians for centuries.

Hot springs gurgling from the base of the volcano and channeled into three different sets of pools attracted weary trekkers, religious devotees and jungle–bound travelers who relish swimming under an azure Andes sky next to a cascading waterfall.

Sounded like a good place to spend the night.

The bus pulled up to the edge of town alongside stall after stall of sugar cane sellers and college age kids wearing heavy–duty hiking boots.

I stopped at a small shop and bought a map of the city. Baños wasn't very large and I headed out on foot toward the main plaza area, stopping along the way for a cup of coffee and to study the map in detail. I picked out a couple of hotels and went to check them out.

My first stop was my last. Hotel Sangay, at the opposite end of town and adjacent to a very tall waterfall and public pool. It looked perfect but I was a little afraid of what the price might be. I was still a little shell–shocked over the price I had ended up paying in Quito. I was pleasantly surprised to find I could get a little room overlooking the pool for only $25 including tax. I asked about the Gringo-Native rate difference and was told that was mainly a major town thing. Super!

The room smelled musty but had good ventilation if you left the door open. One large shuttered window opened to an interior court yard and outside pool. There was a small but adequate bathroom and a clean, firm bed. It also had a small TV set which didn't work. But it *did* have a TV set.

Oddly enough there was one of those small liquor cabinets filled with all kinds of North and South American liquors, including Jack Daniels, which seemed to be a popular choice. The liquor prices were out–of–sight but it was nice to at least have the option.

I dropped off my pack and left for a walk around town. There were dozens of little gift shops selling a crazy assortment of stuff. One of my favorites was a small cooperative selling items made by women in the nearby Amazon jungle region. A high school-age girl and her younger sister were minding the store. They were happy to have an American visitor. I made a couple of balloon animals for the little girl and bought a few small items for gifts.

Later I stopped at a tiny restaurant for a beer and a steaming bowl of guinea pig stew! Very tasty.

Guinea pig, I might add, is one of the national staples of Ecuador and is sold everywhere. Most homes keep a cage of guinea pigs in their front yards, somewhat in the same way as chickens in rural America.

It was a beautiful afternoon. I was wearing a t–shirt and shorts and felt quite comfortable — quite a change from the chill of Quito. I bought some postcards and went to the post office to buy stamps, which cost 31¢ to send to the U.S.

Back at the hotel, the receptionist helped me place a call to Line Haul Services in Quito. Surprisingly the call went right through.

They instructed me that on my return trip to Miami I was to meet a Señor Orlando Acosta at the airport's American Airlines office at 5:30 a.m. on the 23rd. Ouch, that's early! But I felt so relieved to have that out of the way I soon forgot about the nasty departure time.

Scattered around town were bike shops advertising bike rentals for trips to the jungle, supposedly a downhill ride all the way. Sounded like fun so I reserved a bike for the next morning. I also found a small information office and inquired about trains going to Cuenca.

Cuenca was one of the towns I most wanted to visit on this trip. It was reported to be a beautiful colonial town with amazing architecture and plazas. My hope was to take the train there at the end of my trip, stay a couple of days and fly back to Quito and then home.

I found out there was a daily train that went to Cuenca from the town of Riobamba. But first I had to get to Riobamba and since the train left early, I would have to spend the night there. Okay. No problem.

In this part of the world, except maybe on mountain tops, the sun disappears at exactly 6:30 p.m. every night of the year. Once that happens it gets very dark and cools off rapidly, so I headed back to the Hotel Sangay for dinner.

The large dining room was very formal. All the waiters were decked out in white jackets, black bow ties and black slacks. Right off the dining room was a small bar which exited to a lovely balcony overlooking the mountain, a waterfall and public baths. I headed there first.

I ordered one of Ecuador's national cocktails, the Pisco Sour, which is sort of a dainty little whiskey sour made with local liquors. I sat on the balcony with the cascading waterfall within arm's reach, sipping my Pisco Sour and writing in my log for the day until a table was ready. I felt like Ernest Hemingway.

I ordered the house special, *Lomo Sangay*, a large steak covered with a special sauce, the main ingredient of which was English walnut meats. I thought this a little strange, but it tasted just fine. I treated myself to a cappuccino for desert.

Everything, including taxes and gratuity, came to around $10. The annoying thing was the silly little 5 oz. Pisco Sour cost $3.50, while the complete steak dinner cost $5.35.

After dinner I took a short walk before turning in. I was hoping to spot the Southern Cross, this part of the world's equivalent to the Big Dipper. No luck. The town sat too low in the horizon and the surrounding mountains blocked it from view.

TUESDAY, SEPTEMBER 19TH

On the way to the bike shop I passed a cafe featuring fresh–squeezed pineapple juice, a plate of sweet rolls and cup of chamomile tea, all for $1.25. Wonderful.

It was a cool, clear morning and I was ready for some action.

The cost to rent a bike for the entire day was only $4. The trip to Puyo, at the edge of the jungle, was 48 miles, one way. I was told you could return on a bus with the bike strapped on top. The man running the shop estimated my ride would take six hours. I thought about that for a minute. It didn't sound right.

"If it's all downhill," I said, "why does it take so long? It should only take around three or four hours, at most."

"But Señor, don't you want to stop and take pictures and visit all the pretty places you will pass?"

"Well, I suppose so," I said, feeling a little guilty. And gullible.

The bikes were heavy, 21–speed mountain bikes with fat, knobby tires. I looked them over, picked one that seemed solid enough, and took off.

Of course, the guy had lied like a trooper about the "all downhill" part — but he had told the truth about the scenery. It was stunning. And, for the first five or six miles, it *was* downhill on a fairly well–maintained asphalt road. Unfortunately that didn't last long.

The road soon turned to gravel, then dirt and, finally, dirt filled with deep ruts. And there were several serious uphill stretches, too. In fact, I didn't even argue with them and got off and walked the bike up, something I'd never done in 10 years of riding RAGBRAI. (the Register's Annual Great Bike Ride Across Iowa.)

Even though we were *mostly* heading downhill, the elevation was still around 8,000 feet and made bike riding very strenuous. And I wasn't used to riding a mountain bike with its heavy frame and tires. My touring bike at home weighed half what this did.

The lower I went, the warmer it got. I started passing through areas with temporary rain squalls and at one point, I had to pull over and wait them out as I had difficulty seeing the ruts in the road.

The vistas were truly amazing. The road paralleled the Pastaza river, which was hundreds of feet below me and looked like a sliver of hammered silver. I passed dozens of waterfalls, one of which fell right over the road. I couldn't imagine what it would be like during the rainy season. The drop-offs, with no guard rails, were terrifying.

One side of the road was the side of a steep, heavily forested mountain, the other an abyss.

Every hour or so a bus would come barreling by forcing me to dismount and scurry over to the side of the road which, at best, allowed only inches to spare. It was small consolation to know I would be riding back in one of them.

The road passed very few buildings, and even fewer villages. I only ran into two other bikers the whole day and the only wildlife I saw were some wildly–colored frogs hopping across the road, a few flat possums and one snake with red and black stripes — a deadly Coral snake?

I stopped at one little shack and bought a bottle of water. I made some balloon animals for the owner's little girls playing outside.

Every few miles I would pass by other shacks. At each one, there seemed to be some kind of cottage industry going on: little wooden boxes were being constructed out of the thinnest of materials and stacked along the road. They looked like the kind of boxes used to pack fruits or other local crops.

Usually a couple of teen age boys were nonchalantly running logs through an ancient bandsaw, coming so close to the blade with their hands I could hardly look. Then the mother or an aunt would cut the boards into strips. Finally over in the corner, a bunch of smaller kids no older than five or six sat on the ground pounding in tiny nails and finishing the boxes. Everyone was covered with sawdust, but chatting away and having a grand old time.

About halfway to Puyo I pedaled into the town of Rio Negro. I was getting really tired by this time and debated stopping and heading back on a return bus, but after a short break decided to go on. The road had gotten *very* rutty and I really had to watch where I was going or the front tire would drop into a deep hole. Last thing I needed was a blowout ... or a broken collarbone.

At one spot I came upon a construction crew placing dynamite charges in the side of the mountain. They were widening the road. I stopped to watch a few explosions, but the workers seemed a bit too casual about tossing the dynamite around so I moved on.

Around 2:00 in the afternoon I came to a roadblock. There, in the middle of nowhere, was a guard checking "traffic." He asked to see my passport and we chatted a few minutes before he sent me on. Apparently I was crossing a provincial border. Soon I came to another checkpoint, this time with several guards. They checked me over again and stamped my passport.

Mid-afternoon I finally arrived at *Puyo*, "Garden of the Amazon and Gateway to the Jungle." By this time I was definitely spent. It had taken me a solid 5 1/2 hours — with precious little coasting. The bicycle guy had been correct about the time after all.

I biked to the main "business" district and immediately stopped and guzzled down a large glass of fresh pineapple juice. It didn't appear to be much of a town but then you couldn't tell much from the seat of a bike.

Puyo reminded me of a cow town from the 1800s. There were lots of very "Amazon head hunter" looking people walking around with long stringy black hair, wooden discs in their ears and strange tattoos all over their faces, dressed in jeans. One teenage boy was wearing a Mohammed Ali t-shirt.

In truth this *was* the area of the Jivaros, people who, not too very long ago, were known for head hunting. You saw a lot of fake souvenir heads in the stores, but I'm sure, if you were willing to pay the price and take the risk, you could find a real one hanging around for sale even today.

I peddled around town for a while and found an earthy–looking little restaurant where I ordered a chipped crockery mug of local, frothy warm beer and a bowl of greasy goat stew. I remain convinced that as wonderful an organ as your heart or lungs may be, the stomach deserves the blue ribbon prize.

Although my strength restored quickly it was still a relief to know I'd be riding the bus back up the mountain. We were within a block or so of serious jungle yet the temperature was quite comfortable, and after a nice rest I retraced my route to the main "highway", found the bus station and bought a return ticket for $1.50.

It was 4:00 p.m. and the bus didn't leave until 5:00, so I killed some time making balloon animals for the kids hanging around the station. Before I knew it, there were dozens of natives standing around grinning and laughing. I was a big hit!

The 48–mile bus ride back to Baños took an incredible two hours. But what a trip! It was a traveling road show with people getting on and off every ten feet. Food peddlers were selling everything from slices of watermelon to complete dinners. The teenage driver's helper strapped my bike on top while I settled into a window seat and sipped the cold beer he had also sold me.

We had another visit by the border police as we crossed the provincial frontier and, once again, they checked my papers. And only mine. Everyone on the bus strained to see what would happen. I think they were disappointed when the guard just shrugged, muttered something, and moved on. They were probably hoping I'd try to make a break for it.

As we headed into the mountains all I could think of was how truly narrow the road had been on the way down. I had no hope it had somehow widened itself during the afternoon.

To make matters worse, at this hour, the driver was heading directly into the sun — smoking non–stop, constantly fidgeting with an eight-track tape player above his head, singing and chatting with his "helper", and passing every vehicle in sight. The only safety precaution he took that I could see was wildly honking his horn as he barrelled around blind curves. If he had missed the edge of the road, we'd still be falling.

We arrived back in Baños at 7:30 p.m. Everything was dark by then except my knuckles, which remained white for the rest of the night. I was exhausted. The long tough trip down, the heat and the beer and the crazy ride back had taken their toll.

I returned the bike just under the 8:00 p.m. deadline and limped into the hotel and up to my room for a hot shower.

Feeling refreshed, I tried to place a call home with no luck. The phone system in Ecuador left lots to be desired. There was a central office downtown where you paid in advance for your call. Then you were steered to a numbered booth and went from there. I tried twice that evening and once in the morning and never did get through.

I found an interesting-looking Italian restaurant on one of the side streets and I headed there for dinner. Lasagna (Ecuadorian style), a huge salad, fresh crusty bread and a couple of glasses of chianti – all for $2.75. What a great find.

During dinner I had time to reflect on what I had seen so far and I came to the conclusion that Ecuador seemed cleaner than Mexico — cleaner in the sense you don't see much trash on the streets or along the highways you do in Mexico. I must say this surprised me a great deal. On the other hand, the telephone system was much worse. It seemed similar to Mexico's system ten years earlier. Lately Mexico had vastly improved its phones to the point where you could find efficient long distance offices in almost any village in the country.

Another difference was the difficulty in exchanging money. Mexico, for example, has *Casa de Cambios*, or small money exchange offices, everywhere. Fast and convenient. However, in Ecuador, at least at the places I had visited so far, the bank was still the main point of money exchange and bank hours were spotty at best.

I noticed the people seemed to reflect a strong European influence, especially in skin tone and size. A very handsome group of folks in all. It reminded me of Costa Rica in that regard.

It was my last night in Baños, but I was beat and went right to bed. It was only 9:30 p.m. but I was asleep immediately.

WEDNESDAY, SEPTEMBER 20th

It was very hazy in the morning. I looked out the window and saw heavy, steamy clumps of fog rolling down the side of the mountain. The socks I had rinsed out and hung up by the window the night before were still wet. Great! I had planned to wear them today.

I packed and walked to town stopping for a glass fresh papaya juice, assorted sweet rolls and coffee along the way.

The church bells were keeping the dogs awake in front of the restaurant and they seemed very annoyed. Everything looked damp although it had stopped raining hours earlier. One more attempt to call home — still no success.

It was still a little early to leave town so I took advantage of the extra time to visit the local church — Nuestra Señora del Aqua Santa (Our Lady of the Holy Waters).

Like most churches in this part of the world it was old, huge and under constant repair. Large puddles of water covered the interior floors but Mass was still going on, and no one seemed concerned about such an insignificant thing as a little running water.

All around the interior were large oil paintings depicting the many miracles attributed to Our Lady. Each painting had a hand–printed story along the bottom describing that particular event.

One painting showed a Dominican priest visiting the region in the 1600s who was miraculously crossing a bottomless wild gorge, riding his mule along the top of a thin fallen tree — and not concerned in the least.

Another painting illustrated an incident in the 1700s when, while parading a statue of Our Lady around the town square, one of the local volcanoes starting erupting. The people fell prostrate with fear until the statue came to life and commanded the mountain to settle down, which it did, resulting in perpetual gratitude from the townsfolk. That's what it said.

Adjacent to the church was a special fountain of the blessed water to which a steady stream of people arrived to liberally doused themselves from head to toe.

On an adjacent wall was a large portrait of Our Lady covered with hundreds of *milagros* and photos of local people who had been blessed in some way.

A milagro, or miracle, is a small silver charm usually in the shape of a part of the human body, such as a heart, or leg, to indicate which part of the body a miracle was worked upon. You will find them in churches throughout Latin America.

After Mass I went back to the cooperative that featured hand–made items from the Amazonian women and paid $3.00 each for a pair of tribal necklaces featuring wild boars' teeth, parrot feathers and odd colored seeds and shells. Quite a bargain and perfect gifts for those friends who have everything.

Another store I visited featured "authentic" Ecuadorian artifacts found in mountain tombs. Curious, I went in to look. Even in Baños I knew it'd be very risky to try and sell authentic pre-Columbian artifacts but the man was very convincing. He almost had me until, for some reason — maybe my incredulous manner — he showed me museum books with the identical pieces on display — the same cracks and all!

"See Señor, did I not say the truth? Are they not exactly like these?"

They sure were – exact copies anyway.

When I checked out, my hotel bill came to only $22 a night including tax — less than quoted this time! By then it was time to head to the station for my bus to Riobamba. Don't you love that sound of that — Riobamba!

There was an Otalavo woman selling peaches near the station. They must have been a delicacy because they cost almost 50¢ apiece. I bought one and witnessed the strange spectacle of her blessing my money before she tucked it away. I suspect it was to ward off the evil gringo aura I gave off.

I munched away mostly finishing it before tossing it into a filthy trash can when the bus arrived. Another Indian woman calmly walked up, retrieved it from the bottom of the barrel, wiped it on her apron and cheerfully finished it off.

We left Baños at noon. I wasn't sure how far away Riobamba was but the ticket cost 80¢. We started out with lots of room, but the driver stopped at every corner until we ended up with 40 people and a menagerie of live animals packed in a bus with 20 seats.

We passed through beautiful countryside as we headed southwest and uphill back to the Camino Real. Hundreds of small farm plots dotted the mountainsides, many covered with grape arbors. There appeared to be very little mechanization in this area. It would have been impossible to use tractors on those steep slopes even if they had them.

At 1:00 p.m. we arrived in Riobamba, which appeared to be a much larger town than Baños. I took a cab to the railroad station to find when the trains left for Cuenca.

The station looked like a movie set from a Sergio Leone spaghetti western. It was a huge adobe building with blowing tumbleweed rolling down the tracks. Centuries-old wooden benches lined its crumbling walls, and a wooden, hand–painted illegible sign. I half-expected to see Clint Eastwood gallop by.

I walked up to the ticket window and disturbed two elderly gentlemen who were taking their siestas.

"What time does the train leave for Cuenca?" I asked.

"Cuenca? No Señor, the train no go Cuenca these days. The mountains you know ... ?" he shrugged as if this explained everything.

No, I didn't know. "Does it go to Guayaquil?" I asked with little hope, knowing that if didn't go to Cuenca, which was a relatively calm descent, it surely wouldn't be running to Guayaquil, which had the reputation of being one of the most treacherous stretches of track in the world.

"Oh, sí, Señor. Guayaquil. At 6:00 in the morning. A very interesting trip, no?"

"Really?" I said, surprised. "Then I would like to buy a ticket, please."

"Oh, no, Señor, it would be much better in the morning. At 6:00," he said, turning and heading back to his nap, immediately dismissing me from memory.

Gosh, I thought, getting excited, the train was actually going to Guayaquil ... to the coast. Down the dreaded *Nariz de Diablo* – the Devil's Nose – one of the most famous train trips in the world. An engineering marvel!

I knew about the route but had read the track had been closed years ago. Some type of safety issue. Something about a landslide — or an earthquake — wiping out part of the line. Did I understand the old man correctly? The train still traveled The Devil's Nose?

Of course I still wanted to go to Cuenca. It was supposed to be the most beautiful city in Ecuador. But the trip down the Devil's Nose was the chance of a lifetime ... I wavered. Maybe I could still figure out a way to do both.

There was a hotel directly across the street from the railroad station. It must have been a real beauty in its day. Like in 1805 or so. A perfect match for the railroad station. Taking up a full quarter block, each window on the second floor had a small balcony looking down on the street. I would not have been surprised to see Pancho Villa sticking his head out, huge sombrero flapping in the dusty wind.

It was one of those once classy, Old–World buildings with two-foot-thick adobe walls. The lettering on the outside had faded long ago — and I never did learn its name.

What the heck, I thought. If I took the train, this would be a super convenient place to stay. I walked in to check it out.

The hotel was designed and built in the traditional old way — that is, the interior was open to the elements, without a roof over the center part.

A young woman was tucked in the corner in a makeshift office. She looked up surprised. She'd been sitting on a stool, leaning back against the wall reading a beauty magazine. Above her head was a board with dozens of mismatched keys hanging from pegs. To the side of the board, a sawed–off shotgun leaned within easy reach. Hmm.

"Do you have a room for tonight?" I asked, halfway hoping they were filled.

"Oh, sí, Señor," she sputtered in surprise. "We have many."

I bet.

"How much, please?"

"Six thousand sucres, tax included."

Gee, sixty thousand sucres seemed a little steep. That was $23. Still, it *was* in the middle of town, right across from the station and close to everything. What the heck, why not. It was only for one night.

"OK – I'll take it," I blurted out before I changed my mind.

I started peeling off money. "10, 20, 30, 40 ..."

"No, Señor, SIX thousand sucres! Six ... six...", she said, holding up six fingers. "Not sixty!"

"Six?" I stammered.

"Sí, of course. Six."

I started picking up my money and making lightning fast calculations. How could that be? I know my spanish is rusty ... but six thousand sucres would only be ... let's see ... $2.30? No way. That couldn't be right. Hmm, maybe I'd better look at the room.

She led me up a flight of well–grooved wooden stairs and down a darkened hall to a corner room, then unpadlocked a huge, carved wooden door. Yes, unpadlocked.

It seemed the doors were too old to have actual locks. Each one had a hole drilled through it with a large chain leading out and attached to an outside chain with a monstrous padlock.

The room was massive, perhaps 30' x 30', with two cots, one plain wooden chair, and a pair of large double–shuttered windows looking out over the railroad station.

A single 10 watt light hung down partway from a 20 foot ceiling. That was it. No closet, but there was an ancient-looking wooden chest I suppose one could use to put clothes in. No private bath with sweet smelling soaps and shampoos. No cable TV. No phone. No courtesy bar. The floor was bare wood. A cursory glance told me it had been recently swept.

My window presented an unobstructed view of the Chimborazo Volcano — one of the highest in Latin America at over 20,000 feet.

On the street below, a non–stop stream of cars, buses, taxis, trucks and people passed by. I wondered if things would quiet down by nightfall.

"I bring fresh sheets and the bathroom across hall," she said. "I go now and heat some water."

"Well," I said, "I need to go eat lunch first but I'll be back in an hour." I glanced nervously into the bathroom where I could see a man standing fully clothed in the tub washing his feet and legs. He smiled at me. No teeth. Jeez, I hoped I'd made a wise decision. But, for only $2.30 ....

I left my bag in the room, padlocked the door and walked to the town center. On the way I found a little pizza place and ordered the "House Special" and a beer for $3.75. I had no idea what was on the pizza, but I did note that it cost more than the price of the room! $2.30!

Riobamba is capital of Chimborazo Provincia and I was back up to 9,000 feet altitude. It felt much colder than Quito because of the wind sweeping down off the glaciers of Mt. Chimborazo.

The original city, founded by the Spanish on the site of an ancient Inca civilization, was actually a few miles away having been flattened by an earthquake in 1797. It didn't look like much had changed since the new city was rebuilt in the early 1800s.

I found a makeshift tourist office and discussed my options with the lady on duty. She suggested I go ahead and ride the train — but get off before arriving in Guayaquil at a town called Huigra, then catch a bus from there back to Alusî, a town I would pass through on the way. From there I would catch another bus to Cuenca. That way I could do both things I wanted. Perfect, I thought, if I could only keep it all straight in my head.

It appeared I would, indeed, be riding the Devil's Nose in the morning.

With that out of the way, I walked to the main plazas to watch one of the local photographers at work. It was fascinating. Three Otavalo Indian women, dressed up for a day in the town in all their colorful finery, were debating having their pictures taken.

The photographer looked like he'd stepped right out of a 19th century painting. At least 90 years old, his camera must have been an antique at the turn of the century. It was one of those huge wooden contraptions on a rickety tripod, with a black hood to cover his head.

He placed the Indian women in front of the fountain and fussed around with their fedoras and jewelry, and positioned them in just the right light until he was satisfied. Then he snapped *one* photo, told them to come back in 20 minutes and he would have the picture ready. They left and he started to tinker inside the camera. I couldn't figure out how in the world he was going to develop anything so I sat and watched.

He first stuck his hands in slits in the side of the camera and started to manipulate something inside — all by touch. Pretty soon he pulled out a small piece of paper, maybe 3" x 4" and plunged it into a bucket sitting under the camera.

I walked up to see what it was and was amazed to see he had made a negative image. What was he going to do with that? It was printed on paper, not celluloid, so how was he going to make a photo from it?

He took the print and placed in on a special extension board in front of his camera and proceeded to take a *picture of the picture*! Then he repeated the whole procedure and finally ended up with a positive image. How clever!

The whole process took about 15 minutes, and by then the Indian women were back and absolutely delighted with the photo and giggled over it all the way out of the park. What a show. My only regret was I never thought to have him take a photo of me.

By then it was time to return to my hotel *suite*. Earlier I had noticed the S.S.H.H. (bathroom) had no towels or toilet paper. It didn't have a toilet seat either, for that matter. However, I had come prepared with my own private stash.

Under the assumption there would be warm water by this time, I asked for a towel and was given a homemade one — along with a pair of pliers. It seemed the water faucets had no handles, either.

I asked the young woman what the initials S.S.H.H. stood for and she had no idea. The best she could come up with was holding her finger to her mouth and blowing "shhhh". Nice try. (I later discovered they stood for servicios higiénicos.)

The shower wasn't too bad. Moderately warm water trickled out. It was a little tricky, however, standing in this enormous old cast iron tub, drying off and pulling on your shoes and socks without getting all messy again. The floor was slippery wet and muddy. Kind of like taking a shower at a well-used state park.

I returned to the room and prepared for bed. She had, in fact, put on fresh sheets and pillow cases which made me feel a little better. The mattress, I should point out, was one of those stuffed straw-tick jobs — as was the pillow. Think *Little House On The Prairie*. It was spread over an iron frame with only three or four slats keeping it from falling through.

Remember now, only $2.30.

I looked up and noticed that where the plaster was missing on the ceiling, you could see woven palm leaves had been used in the construction. Neat. I bet this *was* one of the first buildings put up in the new town — close to 200 years ago.

The two shutters were at least 10' tall and each opened to a small balcony. I stepped out to look around. The sun had set long ago but the traffic was still heavy ... and noisy. I set my tiny travel alarm for 5:00 a.m. and went to bed.

The myriad night noises was terrible: heavy traffic with honking and screeching brakes went on nonstop till almost dawn. Throughout the entire evening an unending procession of drunks staggered by at regular intervals, screaming out obscenities at all the injustices the cruel world had heaped upon them.

What a mess. I tossed and turned all night and when I did, the metal bed legs sounded like high school locker doors slamming. I must have slept a little — but it sure didn't feel like it.

THURSDAY, SEPTEMBER 21ST

As it turned out, I didn't need an alarm after all. I was wide awake at 5:00 a.m. lying in bed and staring at the ceiling. I was already packed but had nowhere to go. The station was right across the street.

Outside I could hear rain dripping and the room was uncomfortably chilly. Finally I forced myself out of bed, dressed and opened the shutters, looked out and saw shadowy figures already filing into the station. Maybe I'd better get going. I doubted the train would leave early but you never know.

I padded quietly down the ancient stairs and found the front door locked with a heavy chain. It was now 5:30 a.m. The train was due to leave in 30 minutes and I didn't even have a ticket yet. What now? It was pitch dark in the lobby area and I could barely see what I was doing. I groped through my pack and got a little flashlight and found a heavy lock hanging down on the inside of the massive door. The key ... the key ... I needed the correct key.

I crept back to the office area and started looking at all the keys hanging down from the hooks. And there sat the sawed–off shotgun. Hmm ... probably not a good idea to get caught messing with the keys.

Just then a young man showed up with a backpack. He was a young German *Wandervogel*, unshaven, half-awake and, apparently in a bad mood. He understood some English so I whispered the situation to him.

Without a moment's hesitation he walked over to the counter and started pounding on it with his fist and screaming. I was stunned. He was going to wake up everyone in the place.

But it worked. From somewhere behind the counter we heard a groan and a cot squeak and a man, also barely awake, stumbled out, mumbling obscenities, and opened the door. We rushed across the street to the station.

I paid $10 for my ticket and ran to the train. Although it was still dark out it was getting lighter by the minute. People were pouring into the station by this time — and you could hear a steam engine hissing somewhere up the track.

The first car I came to was an ancient old coach, painted red, and already full. I should say it was loaded with Germans who, upon asking, told me the few empty seats I saw were already taken. I didn't believe them for a minute — but decided not to argue.

There were three other rail cars and they were basically boxcars. Open doors and windows, and long benches lining the walls with one row running right down the middle. I climbed on and grabbed a spot by the door next to an Ecuadorian family.

The car reeked of fish although I was apparently the only one who noticed. Three Belgian ex-pats sat across from me. They were very nice and spoke good English. They told me they now lived in Quito and absolutely loved the country.

The car soon filled with a few assorted tourists, but mainly Ecuadorians returning home after a weekend in the "big city."

The train left close to 6:00 a.m., slowly screeching its way out of town in jerky side–to–side movements. Everyone was disappointed by the clouds as we passed Chimborazo Volcano. On a clear day it would have been a spectacular sight.

It was getting lighter and warmer as we rocked along. I had put on all the warm clothes I could muster; long sleeved shirt, heavy wool sweater and windbreaker — and I was glad I had them with me.

The trip to Huigra was five hours.

Our first serious stop was at a little market town called Columbe. The train pulled down the middle of main street and stopped in the city square when all hell broke loose. Natives began climbing on board selling food and drinks and handmade souvenirs. At the same time people poured off the train and started bartering in the square. It was absolute pandemonium.

Just when I thought I was catching on, the Belgians poked me and said, "C'mon. It's time to get on top."

"Excuse me?" I asked, startled. "What you mean, *on top*?"

"On top of the train," they grinned, already jumping down on the platform. "It's great ... you'll love it. Everyone does it. Grab your stuff. Let's go."

And so it happened. And they were right. From inside all the cars, giggling people came clamoring up for a place to sit *on top* of the three boxcars. It was like a circus, and before long the roofs were covered with travelers staking out spots for the remainder of the trip. I grabbed a spot between two large Ecuadorian families.

Before we left I climbed back down and purchased a hand–woven wool bag I had been watching an Indian woman unload from a pack on the side of a mule. It was beautifully made and I paid her $12 without bargaining. I scrambled back on top just as we took off.

It was a wild and joyous trip to Alusí, passing through the colorful mountain villages of Guamole, Palmira and Tixán. And at every town, local children would climb up selling all kinds of things. One pair of shy young girls were selling little bags of doughnut–like sweets drizzled with honey. I bought some to munch on.

When we arrived at Alusí, the excitement mounted as everyone knew the infamous *Nariz del Diablo* — the Devil's Nose — was dead ahead. This spectacular stretch of track plunged 3,000 feet within a few short miles.

Engineered by Americans in the late 1800s, the narrow gauge train negotiates the descent via an ingenious system of hairpin turns, switch backs, span–bridges and tunnels.

By now most of us were spaced out on the corrugated metal of the box car's gently rounded roof, a slightly uncomfortable but incredible perch with 360–degree visibility. We lurched along barely faster than a walking pace.

There were few firm hand holds, and just a narrow steel rail welded along the edge for your feet to brace against and keep you from sliding off. Sliding off? What was I thinking?

My chest tightened as I noticed the distance between the edge of the track and the edge of the cliff become considerably narrower — in places less than two feet. In fact, if you leaned over even slightly, and many brave souls did, you could look straight down into a terrifying abyss.

For the life of me I couldn't see what was holding the train on the track. I stopped taking pictures at this point and tried to figure out if I could leap far enough to reach the side of the mountain should the train start to topple over.

All this time, the conductor wove his way in and around passengers who were paralyzed with fear, punching tickets and chatting with anyone who would listen. I thought to myself — you'd never see such a spectacle in America. Can you imagine American lawyers getting their hands on something like this?

The Devil's Nose is a sheer granite cliff face. Picture it like this: the train comes out of a head of unruly hair and proceeds across the forehead and has to maneuver itself down the length of the nose, around the mouth, and on to the chin — without falling off. Kind of like descending the face of Mt. Rushmore in a Model T Ford.

It does this by a series of switch–backs whereby the train comes chugging around a steep curve, screeches to a stop and backs around the next steep curve, screeches to a stop ... and heads forward again. All this time you're hoping the engineer has had a good night's sleep.

If I'd had the nerve to use my camera, the pictures would have been spectacular. But like everyone else I was using my hands and feet to hang on for dear life. I wasn't about to let go.

This torture kept up until the train finally came around a final curve and chugged into the town of Pistishi. After this the track flattened out, the train picked up speed and everyone breathed again. We were now much closer to sea level and the temperature had climbed at least 30 degrees. The vegetation suddenly got quite lush.

I finally relaxed and looked back up — and up and up — and had a hard time believing the train actually came down that cliff face without falling off. The next town was Huigra, my exit spot.

We pulled down the main street of town around noon, and I got off. Almost immediately the train started off again, continuing to the coast. I waved good–bye to my Belgian friends.

A bus was sitting on the corner. I rushed over and asked if he was going to Alusí.

"Certainly, Señor, and very shortly."

Great I thought, buying a ticket and placing my bag by a window towards the back. I then made the mistake of running across the street to buy a bottle of drinking water.

By the time I got back, the bus was full of Germans and my bag was sitting up front on the floor by the driver's seat.

"Wait a minute," I said, "I had that seat by the rear window."

"But where are you going?" asked a German tour operator, a coarse–looking little troublemaker who came rushing up to me.

"Alusí," I replied, "and I've already paid for the ticket."

"Ahh ... but this bus is going directly to Riobamba," she said with a sneer.

I turned to the driver who shrugged and gave me my money back. She had filled the bus with her group and paid off the driver to go another route. I couldn't believe it.

"If you hurry, you can catch the train back to Alusí," he said, looking a little sheepish.

Without time to argue I turned and looked. Sure enough, another train had pulled into town from the opposite direction so I ran and climbed on top just before it started pulling away. Somehow I knew I'd just been had but really didn't mind too much as I got to ride The Devil's Nose once again — this time going up. No one had said anything about a return train, so I was actually quite excited.

Going up was as unnerving as going down, only it lasted longer. Early in the afternoon we pulled into Alusi — a sleepy little mountain village time had passed by. I got off the train and learned the bus to Cuenca didn't leave for two hours. Darn. It was a four-hour trip. That wouldn't get me there until almost dark — but what could I do? My well-laid plans were unravelling.

I paid $3.00 for my ticket and went into the Hotel Panamerico for a glass of some kind of fruit juice and a bowl of "meat soup." The juice was great, but the soup was just hot water poured over some bones and vegetables — no meat.

Although I had a seat reservation, when the big Mercedes bus finally pulled in it was packed and my assigned seat was occupied.

A mistake had been made. I was given the option to stand or wait for the next bus in three more hours.

"I'll stand," I said.

I was forced to stand crouched over until people started to get off along the highway. Eventually, enough people got off that I found a seat.

Again, the scenery was spectacular. We were riding right along a steep ridge trail that ran down the middle of the Andes. On both sides loomed gorgeous snow–capped mountains dotted with tiny towns. At one point during the trip we were stopped for around half an hour while a religious procession wandered down out of the hills, across the highway, and into a tiny village. Hundreds of Otavalo Indians, in colorful outfits, carrying crosses and statues and all kinds of other religious objects, were singing and playing pan flutes all the while. It was fascinating.

But as with the train trip, I must say I never did feel entirely relaxed. Periodically the bus would drive into pea soup thick fog and the driver hardly slowed down. I swear you couldn't see one foot ahead of the windshield and all the time we were driving around hairpin curves on very narrow roads.

Later, a rather ugly incident occurred. I was sitting in the back surrounded by a dozen or so Indians who had gotten on somewhere along the road. As the ticket seller worked his way back there was a heated argument about the price of the tickets.

I thought there was going to be a fight after lots of screaming, pushing, and shouting. I think the driver wanted to kick the Indians off, but was afraid to do so. I didn't blame him. They all carried machetes.

Apparently a recent increase in ticket fares caused by an increase in taxes was infuriating them. Every once in a while, they'd glance over at me to see how I, the millionaire gringo, was reacting — but I just kept my eyes pointed straight ahead.

We didn't arrive in Cuenca until almost 7:00 p.m. It was an exhausting ride but the scenery made it worthwhile. I immediately grabbed a cab and went to Hotel Presidente, which had a very comfortable room for $29.

Out of curiosity, during the cab ride from the station, I had asked the driver what I should expect to pay for a room in one of these hotels.

"$11.50, Señor, perhaps $12.00, certainly no more than that."

The room, however, had a lovely, Old World look with lots of dark wood and a large double bed. It was on the top floor and looked out over the street which was, thank God, very quiet. It also had a private shower and cable TV. Very comfortable and a very good value, I felt. Over ten times what I had paid in Riobamba but that was okay.

I cleaned up and decided to eat in the hotel at the restaurant on the top floor, which I had read had a panoramic view of the city. First I checked on airline flights with the friendly clerk at the front desk. And disaster struck!

She told me there were only two flights to Quito — and both most likely would already be filled.

What? Only two flights? And both most likely already filled? I was under the impression there would be several to choose from. I planned to catch an evening flight so I would have a whole day to explore Cuenca.

She advised me to go to the airport early and try to buy a ticket there. If not, she mused, you could always take a bus. They leave much more frequently and are very reasonable, she added.

Reasonable, perhaps, but also a 12-hour trip through the mountains. And as scenic as that might have been, I really didn't want to spent an entire day on the bus.

But what could I do? I had come all this way to see the one city I was really interested in and it looked like I'd be leaving first thing in the morning. But I had to get to Quito the next day!

Feeling rather dejected I went up to the restaurant with my complimentary drink ticket in hand and ordered a rum and Coke. Feeling a little better I treated myself to the "Meal of the Evening," which began with an appetizer of cold ceviche — raw, pickled fish and a generous serving of pork cutlet served with freshly–made French fries. For dessert they served a wonderful fruit salad. All together, including a glass of wine, cappuccino and gratuity, the meal was $10. Four times what my hotel had cost in Riobamba.

During dinner I had a nice conversation with the waiter, an elderly gentleman who displayed a great deal of sympathy for my current travel predicament, but offered little helpful advice. The dining room had large windows and after dinner he led me around and pointed out some of the sights I could still visit this evening ... and dozens of others I would miss.

Cuenca is a lovely city. The capital of the Azuay Provincia, it is the natural jumping off place for what is referred to as the Southern Sierra part of Ecuador, and the least visited by tourists.

It may be Ecuador's third largest city, but isolation has saved it from the effects of industry and mass tourism. Paved roads between Cuenca and Quito were not even laid until the 1960s. It boasts 52 colonial churches and cathedrals, as well as numerous parks and plazas. Most of the ancient architecture is still in place and cobblestone streets run everywhere. It made me sick to think I would miss most of it.

After dinner I went outside and took a long walk, taking in as many sites as possible within just a few blocks of the hotel. But it had been another exhausting day and by 10:30 p.m. I returned to my room and turned in.

FRIDAY, SEPTEMBER 22ND

When I got up at 6:00 a.m., there were neither lights nor hot water. I skipped the shower — but tried as best I could to shave in the darkened bathroom.

By the time I got to the airport at 7:00 a.m. there was already a long line at the ticket window. Soon everything got quite confusing as it quickly became apparent there weren't going to be enough seats. People got panicky and started shoving and yelling.

The flight was scheduled for 8:30 a.m. and by 8:00 the clerk hadn't show up yet. By the time she arrived at 8:15 things were almost out of control.

Finally a piece of good fortune: a very nice attendant, to whom I had earlier explained my situation, took me under her wing and somehow quietly managed to get me the *last seat* on the plane. There was a moment's panic when I was told they didn't accept credit cards. Luckily I had enough sucres — 90,000 ($35) — to pay for the ticket. Whew, that was close!

I had no sooner boarded than we took off and in a short time landed in Quito. TAME airlines doesn't fool around. A man sitting next to me was an Ecuadorian who had graduated from Boston College and now worked for Visa and spent all his time traveling around the country visiting their various offices.

I told him how much I hated to miss the sights of Cuenca but this was certainly better than a 12-hour bus ride. He quickly agreed. And in reality I really didn't have any choice. Therein lies one of the problems with courier flights: you had a strict schedule to adhere to. If I had been on my own, I would have arranged an additional couple of days in Cuenca.

I stopped at the CETUR office at the Quito airport. CETUR is the national tourist agency and is always very helpful. We decided a better lodging choice than the Hotel Republica would be the Hotel Savoy — which was fairly close to the airport and only cost a gringo $35, including taxes.

As it turned out, Hotel Savoy was a great find. A very nice four–star hotel that catered to businessmen and middle–class Ecuadorians. My room had a huge picture window with a lovely view of the city and was very comfortable.

I took a quick shower and headed to town for a final flurry of shopping and sightseeing. It was only 10:30 a.m. but I hadn't eaten a thing, so I stopped at a little ice cream shop up the street from the hotel: La Heladeria Pink Floyd. I ordered a toasted ham and cheese sandwich and a mara (red raspberry) milkshake. It was here I finally discovered why I had been having so many problems ordering sandwiches. In Mexico, sandwiches are called *tortas*. In Ecuador, they are called *sanduches*.

Feeling much better, I took a bus back to the fascinating Parque Ejido where I strolled around and watched a terrific music act, followed by a mime act. All free for the people to enjoy.

La Avenida Amazonas is the main drag through town. I found a comfortable-looking sidewalk cafe, sat and ordered a beer and watched the world pass by. It was quite a sight. Lots of street peddlers hustling to make a living, interesting curio shops and a non−stop parade of shoeshine boys working the crowd. It was during the noon hour and the avenue was filled with business people out shopping and visiting.

The women of Quito, like in downtown Mexico City, were all extremely attractive and dressed in what Americans would consider very provocative clothing. Very tight fitting — at least two sizes too small. All the men were dressed in very expensive Armani suits and looked very elegant as they smiled and shouted greetings at one another.

I stopped by several shops and bought some wood carvings; an Otavalo Indian doll for my granddaughter, Taylor, a woven rattle for grandson, Benjamin, and other miscellaneous gifts and souvenirs.

I spent the rest of the day wandering around and taking it easy. There wasn't much that could go wrong at this point and I started to relax. I still hadn't found a gift I liked for my wife. Unlike in Mexico, the jewelry I had seen looked poorly−made and I was hesitant to buy any woven goods.

At 7:00 p.m. I stopped at a small sidewalk cafe with a huge sign advertising cold American beer and hamburgers. The eternal sucker, I stopped. The beer was Old Milwaukee. The hamburger was awful. I would have loved to know what the meat was. Unfortunately that would be my last evening meal in Ecuador. I would have much preferred a tasty bowl of guinea pig stew but I was in the big city now and that kind of "country fare" was not considered chic.

Along the busy streets families were out in force, strolling arm in arm. The local "hippies" were spreading their drug paraphernalia out on blankets to sell. In front of the fashionable hotels, the ladies of the night were beginning to appear.

By this time the sun had disappeared below the majestic mountain peaks and it was starting to cool down. It was time to return to the hotel and pack.

On the way to the bus stop, I saw something I hadn't seen before: teenage entrepreneurs selling single cans of cold beer to people in traffic. They were boldly standing in the middle of busy intersections and would run up to a car that slowed down or stopped at a traffic light and sell cans as fast as they could replenish their supplies, which were stacked on the curb on top of blocks of ice. The local traffic police stood by watching and didn't seem to mind in the least.

Back in the room I watched *60 Minutes* while I packed for the last time and went to bed. Tomorrow was going to be a long day.

<u>SATURDAY, SEPTEMBER 23RD</u>

It seemed like I'd been asleep all of ten minutes when the alarm went off. It was 4:30 a.m. Time to get up. I was very groggy. Of course there wasn't any hot water or lights. Not a great way to start the day, but I cleaned up as best I could.

There were a few balloons left in my bag, so I made some animal figures for the maids, left them with the rest of the Life Savers and headed for the deserted lobby.

A cab was parked in front of the hotel — with the driver sprawled out fast asleep on the front seat. I tapped on the window and got in the back. I must have irritated him because he charged me $4.00 for the trip to the airport — less than a five minute drive. Oh well, I had a few thousand sucres to get rid of anyway — and it *was* terribly early.

The American Airlines office was by the main entrance of the terminal. The cab dropped me off and I knocked on the door. An English–speaking employee opened up and I told him I was an airline courier and was supposed to meet Señor Orlando Acosta at 5:30. It was then 5:20. I received a blank stare and was told he knew of no Señor Acosta.

"Really?" I said as a twinge of panic passed through me. "Perhaps I'll just wait out front."

5:30 a.m. came and went. 5:45. I returned to the American Airlines office thinking he had somehow sneaked in when I wasn't looking.

"Sorry. No Señor Acosta works here," he said, looking a bit irritated this time.

At 6:00 a.m. I really started to panic. The plane was scheduled to leave in less than an hour and by this time the terminal was packed with people. And I didn't even know what this character looked like. Was I a victim of some cruel international trade scam?

I asked the clerk at the information booth to page him — no success. What was I going to do if he didn't show? I had no idea. I checked with American Airlines ticket counter and was told a one–way ticket back to Miami was $450. Should I go ahead and buy a ticket (assuming they had space) and argue with Line Haul Services to reimburse me when I got to Miami? Fat chance. Should I stay or go to their downtown Quito office and raise gringo wrath? I started pacing back in forth in front of the American Airlines office.

Just as I was starting to hyperventilate I noticed, out of the corner of my eye, a pudgy little man nonchalantly entering the terminal. He was wearing a sweatshirt with the initials LHS on the front. I watched him go in and look around. Could that be him, I wondered? LHS? It must be Line Haul Services. But why wasn't he going to the American Airlines office?

I walked up behind him and spoke out, "Señor Acosta?"

He turned around, all smiles, and said, "Oh, Meester Bookleee. How be you?"

"Where have you been?" I croaked. "The plane leaves in 30 minutes and I haven't gone through customs or anything, yet."

"Oh, no problema, amigo. There plenty of time, no?"

"No," I replied, more than a little irritated.

"Com wit mee, but we muss hurry, no?"

"Yes," I spat, wanting to slap the silly grin off his face.

But to his credit, he charged up to the head of the line of angry-looking officials and whisked us through in quick order. I say 'us' because I was surprised to find another courier standing by the ticket counter, also waiting for our dear Señor Acosta.

I found out later that she was from Quito originally, but now lived in Miami and she and her entire family are 'on call' for last minute flights to Ecuador.

Under that kind of arrangement, the entire family gets to travel quite frequently. 'On call' means one must be ready to accept a flight at the last minute, usually within 24 hours. The sweet part is the flight was usually free!

After we had checked in and boarded the plane — with 10 whole minutes to spare — I asked her what would have happened if Señor Acosta hadn't shown up.

"Occasionally that happens," she said. "When it does, you just have to wait around for the afternoon flight and someone will usually come then."

"But why didn't he go to the American Airlines office?" I asked. "That's where I was told me to meet him."

"Oh, they don't like each other," she said.

Great! Nothing like a little breakdown in communications. If he hadn't been wearing that LHS sweatshirt, I might still have been standing in front of the airport waiting. On the other hand, he hadn't asked me to carry on any kind of "contraband" (that I knew about), so I guess I was again fortunate in that regard.

By 8:30 a.m. we were well on our way back the 1,750 miles to Miami. I was hungry and when the plane filled with the smells of breakfast I was more than ready to eat. We were served orange juice, an omelet, ham, fruit slices and coffee. It tasted marvelous.

Afterwards I sat back, relaxed and reflected on the trip. I found myself comparing differences between our two countries. As I thought about it I realized that in the short time I was gone, I had actually begun to miss such things as schedules you could count on, hot showers, an easy–to–use phone system, and electricity. It sure is easy to become slave to simple comforts. We really do take them for granted.

I recalled the conversation I had with the man on the flight from Cuenca who blamed "the complacency of the people" on the lack of progress in Ecuador. I suspect the terrain had more to do with it than the people. The topography was much more severe than Mexico. Stretching electric distribution lines, for instance, across Ecuador must present vast challenges.

I couldn't help thinking about the faith these people have in each other — and on common sense. There was very little room for error, for example, when riding on top of a train. Should an accident happen, as did from time to time, there's no possibility of a lawsuit down there. They'd laugh you right out of the country.

I imagine they figure that if you're foolish enough to climb on top of a train, that's your choice and your responsibility, and you would be expected to live by the results of your own actions. All in all, not a bad philosophy.

The other major difference I thought about was the mature attitude of the young children; particularly the Indian children. I suppose they have to grow up quickly just to survive. Everywhere you went you saw little children taking care of even smaller children. And everywhere, youngsters were hustling to make an buck — or sucre in this case.

After breakfast I sat back and began to really relax for the first time in several days. The movie *Legends of the Fall* was being shown on those little TV sets: the tragic story of Colonel Ludlow and his three sons living in the Montana wilderness. I'd seen it before but, for some reason, I didn't remember it being so sad.

It made me think about my own three sons, and I wasn't comfortable watching much of it.

I was feeling maudlin. I guess I really was ready to return home.

THE TURKEY TROT
IS NOT A DANCE

TURKEY

PART ONE

Which records my shaky departure from America to the Muslim empire of Turkey ... where I boldly set out to explore a strange and mysterious land.

SEPTEMBER 4

I'd arrived at the Cedar Rapids Airport in plenty of time. I checked in, received my seat assignment and said goodbye to my wife. I went through security, walked upstairs to the departure gate and sat down. I was a bit nervous and decided to check my tickets one last time.

Check the tickets. The tickets. Now where did I put the tickets? I remembered placing them in my special, pickpocket-proof packet along with my passport, $600 cash, my driver's license and everything else that was valuable and irreplaceable. Where were they?

"Don't panic now," I muttered to myself as I started to panic. "Check all your pockets. They've got to be here somewhere. You have almost 10 minutes before boarding. Take it easy. Slow down. Take a deep breath. DON'T PANIC!"

But I didn't have the tickets. In fact I didn't have the pickpocket-proof packet. And I panicked. Barely starting on a three-week trip to Turkey and I'd already lost everything?

"You aren't going *anywhere*, you idiot," I said to myself.

My heart pounding I stood up, took a deep breath and mumbled the St. Anthony prayer. He's the patron saint of lost objects and he's never let me down. I quickly retraced my steps to the lower level, going down to a seat where I had sat and read the paper — nothing. On to the bathroom — nothing. I rushed along, my eyes wildly sweeping the floor like a madman. Alarmed people moved aside to let me pass.

"Oh please, *please* St. Anthony, help me find my pickpocket-proof packet. Please. Please. *PLEASE*!" But nothing. I found nothing. My chest tightened, my life started to flash before my eyes as I thought of all the weeks of careful planning, all the preparations made in vain. I was not going *anywhere*.

Just as I was about to rush out of the terminal to see if I could possibly catch my wife, I heard an announcement over the loudspeaker.

"Would Mr. Robert Buckley please return to the American Airlines ticket counter. Mr. Robert Buckley, please return to American Airlines."

I froze and whipped around. "Oh please, dear God, let them have my tickets. Please, please St. Anthony *and* God I will be SO good. Forever and ever and EVER. I will never do anything even remotely wrong for the REST of my life."

Yes, they had my pickpocket-proof packet. Some lovable, honest, bless you wherever and whoever-you-are-person had found my packet somewhere and turned it in at the ticket counter — intact — tickets, cash, passport, everything.

The grateful look of relief on my face kept the airline official from admonishing me for being so careless as I mumbled a word of sincere thanks and turned and rushed away — back through security, up the stairs, arriving barely in time to board the plane. That was close.

It was not what you'd call a very cool departure. But the important thing was, I was on my way.

—o—

It was late in the afternoon of the next day when I finally arrived in Istanbul, Turkey. I was totally wiped out.

The flight from Cedar Rapids to Minneapolis had gone smoothly enough, but when I arrived I learned my flight to Amsterdam was not only delayed but *overbooked*. People were milling about and very unhappy. Some of us were not going to leave.

I was among the last three they found seats for. Whew! I was safe again and began to relax.

We arrived in Amsterdam at 6:00 a.m., where I had another long layover before proceeding to Istanbul Atatürk Airport, finally landing at 3:00 p.m. I was groggy by this time and fading fast.

I exchanged $150 for more than 200 million Turkish Lira! How in the world was I going to keep all that straight? Suddenly I was a multi-millionaire.

Fez Travel, true to its word, had a man waiting for me. He seemed very upset that it had taken me so long to appear.

Fez Travel was a travel organization I had earlier researched that offered a wide variety of group trips. It turned out to be an excellent choice.

Although the tour didn't begin for a few days, Fez included a free airport transfer as part of the agreement. The hotel where I was staying *also* offered free airport transfers, so I had arranged with them to use *their* transfer on my return trip.

I finally arrived at the Hotel Pierre Loti. By this time I was so exhausted I barely noticed the room when the clerk let me in. After tipping him a cool million, I threw my bag in the corner and myself on the bed. I desperately needed a short rest.

It seemed just moments had passed before I was brusquely awakened by the evening call to prayer as it drifted into my hotel room from the nearby Blue Mosque. I staggered out of bed and over to the window to better hear those strange discordant notes sung in a language so foreign to my Western ears. Soon, chanters from a dozen other mosques joined in, filling the still evening air with ancient prayers.

From my upper window, the ancient city of Istanbul was bathed in a lovely warm sunset glow. Dozens of gold-tipped minarets dotted the skyline. Off in the distance, the Sea of Marmara was already turning deep purple as it joined and followed the Bosphorus Strait up to the Black Sea. And just across the strait was the continent of Asia.

I stood at the window until the singing ended. It was a million dollar moment. I was so glad I'd come.

I turned back to inspect the room; it was rather small, but clean and comfortable, and cost only $40 a night, including breakfast. The bed was built on a raised platform, as were all the other beds I encountered on my trip. No bed springs, just a thick mattress resting on wood. No covers at this time of year, just a heavy cotton sheet was all you needed.

A tiny german Grundig television sat on a small desk alongside a phone. There was a sitting chair, a tiled bath with shower and that was about it. The room faced a main street which, with heavy pedestrian and trolley car traffic, turned out to be a bit noisy. For a short stay, it would do just fine.

Feeling refreshed, I went out to explore. I was staying in the old part of Istanbul, an area called the Sultanhamet where most of the popular tourist sites are located. It was dusk and the temperature was a comfortable 70°.

I hadn't walked two blocks before I came upon a sunset view of the Blue Mosque itself. The fading light was perfect — lighting up the golden minarets so they dazzled! My tour package included a full day's tour of Istanbul, so I decided I'd wait until then to visit.

I next found myself in a large park-like area called Sultanhamet Square. With its lovely fountains and flowers it separated the Blue Mosque from the equally world-famous Hagia Sophia, or Church of Holy Wisdom. Dating back to the year 536 it is considered to be one of the finest architectural creations in the world.

Street vendors were scattered everywhere, selling rugs, roasted chestnuts, package tours to Syria, hotel rooms, restaurants — you name it. As hectic as it may sound, it was all quite orderly and friendly and I never did feel pressured into buying anything.

I finally stopped at a sidewalk cafe for a large glass of fresh-squeezed orange juice. It was my first financial transaction since arriving and I was a bit nervous. Cafes in this part of the world have well-posted menus listing prices so I knew the cost should be two million lira. Let's see, 2,000,000 Turkish Lira at 1,365,000 lira to the dollar makes it $145? No, maybe $14.50? Still too much, let's see, slip the decimal over one more space … $1.45.

So far so good. I finished and kept walking. Soon I came upon a very striking-looking old hotel that had been converted from a large Ottoman-style house: Hotel Valide Sultan Konagi. I went in to check it out and was offered a short tour. It was truly a marvelous place in amazing condition; very, very fancy in an Old World type of way. A double room cost $60 and the rooms and the views were spectacular. Maybe next time?

I was getting a bit hungry by now so I headed back to where I'd earlier spied an outdoor cafe. I ordered a mushroom and pepperoni pizza and a beer, both of which were very good and quite reasonable. The local beer is called Efes. I kept track of its cost during my trip and found it ranged in price from 750,000 to 2,000,000 lira … or around 50¢ to $1.50 … depending on how fancy the restaurant was.

For you students of biblical history, Efes is also the Turkish word for Ephesus.

A half block down the street was an internet cafe. I went in and sent a flurry of messages home. The cost was only 60¢ an hour, which had to be one of the best bargains in town. It was my first experience using an internet cafe and I found it very user friendly. In fact I was able to continually keep in contact with friends and family throughout my trip.

I found internet cafés everywhere. The biggest challenge was the odd characters on the Turkish keyboard. It took a few days to sort them all out. In the meantime, my messages must have looked a little bizarre.

It had been a busy, busy day. Back at the hotel I forced myself to stay awake as long as possible to overcome jet lag. Tomorrow I planned to take a cruise up the Bosphorus.

SEPTEMBER 6

The call to prayer at 6:15 a.m. The call was so loud it woke me up. For a second or two I couldn't figure out where I was and covered my head with my thin pillow.

Soon several other mosques joined in. Same prayers, but always out of sync with each other. Within a minute or so, there were dozens, perhaps hundreds of different mosques all blaring out the first daily call to prayer. There are five calls in all during a 24-hour period. There are over 3,000 mosques in Istanbul.

It reminded me of Sunday morning in Oaxaca, Mexico, when the city's ancient church bells begin chiming for early Mass, never at the same time.

I must have drifted back to sleep because the next thing I knew it was 7:00 a.m. ... and then 7:30 a.m. I finally struggled out of bed, my biological clock quite upset with me, and stumbled into the shower. I should have waited until I'd at least had one cup of strong coffee.

The shower was not made by American Standard, I can tell you that. It was shaped like a quarter of a circle and had a door that slid open and shut. I waited until there was hot water and slipped inside.

There were three shower heads from which water spurted. There was one at a normal height, another half way down, and finally a hand-held spray with a mind of its own. The problem was they seemed to alternate automatically and although I looked for a switch or lever that would select one or the other I never did find it.

The other problem was the square foot space of the shower was so limited that if you were unfortunate enough to drop the soap (as I did on several occasions), you had to turn off the shower, slide open the door and get out before you could reach back in to pick it up. The good news was there was plenty of hot water.

A buffet breakfast was served on the terrace rooftop, a delicious choice of juices, coffee and tea, bowls of black and green olives, platters of fresh feta and Gouda cheese, hard rolls, sliced tomatoes and cucumbers, some type of sliced meat, and finally bowls of yogurt with honey. What an odd selection to my American taste buds, I thought, but authentic Turkish fare I was told. A bit foreign to my palate, but I'll get used to it.

The terrace offered a grand view of the city — as well as some sinister-looking dark clouds rolling in from the west. Before too long it did start raining and ended up doing so on and off throughout the day. Strangely and happily enough it was the only rain on the entire trip.

By 8:00 a.m., or midnight back home, I felt ready to face the world again. I grabbed my camera and a rain jacket and jumped on an electric tram that ran down the center of the street in front of the hotel. The routine was quite simple. You went to a small kiosk by each tram stop and bought a *jeton* or token, costing around a quarter, inserted it in a turnstile and entered the train platform.

The tram was automatic and had a diagram inside so you could tell where you were going and when to get off. I headed toward the end of the line where the docks were located; the area is called Eminönü (pronounced like AMEN-en-new).

The geography of Istanbul can be complicated. The old, original section of the city, where I was staying, is part of a peninsula surrounded by the Sea of Mamara on the south, the Bosphorus Strait on the east, and a body of water called the Golden Horn on the north.

Across the Golden Horn is the newer, more modern part of the city. Both of these sections are in Europe. There's a third part of the city across the Bosphorus; in the continent of Asia. Istanbul is the only city in the world that spreads across two continents.

I knew to look for Pier 3 and bought a round trip ticket on the next ferry for $2.00. The route was from Istanbul up to the mouth of the Black Sea and back; reportedly a lovely trip.

It was still early, so I wandered around the dock area watching men (never women) lined up along the edge of the water fishing with long, thin poles. All they ever caught were skinny little fish, smaller than a sunfish, but these seemed to please them very much.

The dock area was like an outdoor department store with lots of street vendors selling clothes, snacks and tea. One young man caught my attention as he was selling fortunes!

He had a small stand with three white rabbits sitting on top. You paid a bit of money and one of the rabbits would select a piece of paper with your fortune written on it. I was promised a long life and a rosy future. Cool.

Men and children loved to have their pictures taken, but it was still polite to ask permission. Women always shied away and avoided cameras. Turkey is almost 100 percent Muslim and the adult women all dressed very conservatively, with hair completely covered and bodies enveloped by long, full dresses.

More traditionally-dressed women were completely covered in black with everything concealed except their eyes and nose. However, in the urban areas, they were the exception rather than the rule.

As departure time neared, there was a rush for the best seats on deck. I had been watching carefully, figured out what was going on, and took off with the best of them.

Top deck, end seat by the rail. That's where I headed. A Japanese tourist beat me up there and was upset with me as I ignored his attempt to reserve the entire section of 20 seats for himself and his 11 friends. How gutsy what that?

The route is always the same: crisscrossing the Bosphorus Strait between Europe and Asia, stopping briefly at colorful villages along the way to take on or let off passengers. The entire trip takes 90 minutes to reach the last village, Anadolu Kavagi, on the Asian side, where the ferry stays for a while before returning the same way. It's a marvelous cruise and the scenery is fascinating.

Not being familiar with the route, I got off early by mistake. It wasn't a problem as I found I could catch the next ferry using the same ticket, so I decided to explore.

It was all fascinating to me: the colors, the smells and the friendly hustle and bustle of the people.

I entered a small grocery store and bought a banana and a bottle of ayran, a popular yogurt drink (half water, half yogurt with salt added). It may not sound very appetizing, but it was actually quite refreshing and healthy.

With my ayran and banana I went out to the waterfront to eat.

Afterwards I wandered up and down narrow side streets where vendors had set up stands selling an amazing variety of fresh farm produce; huge heads of cabbage, grapes by the crateful, olives, cheeses, stacks of eggs, mounds of onions, potatoes, tomatoes and bunches of fresh-cut flowers of all types. The organized confusion reminded me of the weekend markets of southern Mexico.

When the next ferry arrived, I jumped on and proceeded to the end of the line. Along the way I struck up a conversation with a young journalist from Sweden who wanted to practice his English. We got off and climbed a steep path to the top of a cliff where there was an old 14th century fortress overlooking the Black Sea. It was a wonderful vantage point from which to see fishing boats displaying Russian, Bulgarian or Turkish flags, all saluting each other as they entered or left the strait.

By the time we left on the return ferry, cold beers in hand, the sun had come back out and the water color changed from drab gray to deep blue. The picturesque, shore-side villages sparkled with wet, red tile roofs and golden-tipped minarets.

Tourists and locals alike lined the rails on the boat and seemed mesmerized by the breathtaking scenery as we glided past on the way back to the city's main docks.

I finally arrived back in my hotel room around 5:00 p.m., ready for a short siesta. All that fresh air and climbing had taken their toll.

The Sultanhamet area, where I was staying, smelled overwhelmingly of tantalizing food. By 8:00 p.m. I was back out prowling the streets and alleyways looking for the perfect place to eat. Cafe Evin seemed ideal. It was a traditional Turkish restaurant where I went a little crazy: a huge mixed salad, a basket of hard rolls, a main dish of baked lamb and vegetables, all washed down with a couple glasses of the local wine. Hot apple tea and baklava for dessert.

Marvelous and under $10 for everything. At the time I thought it was a great bargain but it later proved to be one of the more expensive meals I had.

As a bonus to the wonderful food, eating in a Turkish restaurant is great theater all on its own. My waiter, for example, announced that he spoke German, English and French. I tried to slip into Spanish to trip him up. No dice. He spoke fluent Spanish, as well.

As far as I could tell there are no female employees in Turkish restaurants — at least outside the kitchen. It was definitely a male-dominated trade. And there was only one man assigned to do just one task. For example, one man emptied ashtrays, another took drink orders, another took your food order, while a different one served the food or beverage. Finally, an entirely different group cleared tables, and brought your bill. It was like a cast of thousands.

Across a narrow alley from the restaurant was a outdoor hookah parlor. Here one could go with some friends and smoke scented tobacco out of three-foot-tall water pipes while sitting on a raised platform covered with carpets and strewn with fancy embroidered pillows.

The whole thing looked very illegal. I nervously watched them during dinner expecting the "narcs" to come rushing in at any minute. It turns out it's all quite legal and harmless.

While all this was going on, cars would pull up and stop in front of the restaurant to review the menus and discuss with the waiters what was fresh.. Meanwhile other cars pulled up behind them and waited patiently until some type of decision was made. All very civil and friendly.

After dinner I walked back to the internet cafe where I had earlier struck up a friendship with the proprietor. I checked my messages and left him with a couple of flashlights as a gift. It was a smart move as I was treated with wide smiles whenever I returned.

Back in bed reading by 10:30 p.m., the last call to prayer had come and gone and everything was peaceful. It had been a wonderful day, full of strange new sights and sounds and smells.

SEPTEMBER 7

Not a cloud in the sky this morning, and a balmy 75°.

There were mostly Germans at the breakfast buffet this morning and the food selection was the same as yesterday. I filled my plate with olives and cheeses, tomato and cucumber slices, hard rolls and honey.

After breakfast I walked up a half-block to visit the famous Çemberlitas Turkish Bath. It was built in 1584 by the legendary Turkish architect Mimar Sinan and is among the most beautiful in the city. I walked in and snooped around a little having read about these places, but wondered if I had the nerve to try one. It seemed rather reasonable, just $15, but I was still a little timid. Perhaps later.

Further up the street I came to the famous Kapili Çarsi, better know as the Grand Bazaar, a rabbit burrow of over 4,000 shops under one roof. I wandered around and was reminded of a combination yard sale, antique shop, shopping mall and grandmother's attic all rolled into one. They say if you can't find what you're looking for there, go home, it doesn't exist. I spent a couple of hours wandering up and down the maze before the noise, massive crowds, and nagging kids drove me away.

Next I came upon the main campus of Istanbul University, founded in 1453. I have to say the place looked more like a collection of reform school cell blocks than a university.

I'd never seen so many drab-looking buildings in my life. Very bleak! I was amazed to learn the university has a teaching staff of 2,000 professors and associates, and 4,000 assistants and younger staff. More than 60,000 undergraduate and 8,000 postgraduate students follow courses offered there every year.

The students were still out on summer vacation and not scheduled to return until the first of October.

A few blocks further down the hill was the Sülemaniye Mosque, the second largest mosque in the city and reportedly the finest in the world. Built by Sinan for Süleyman the Magnificent in 1550, it was absolutely huge.

Removing my shoes, as you are obliged to do, I entered its mainly vacant interior. It was my first visit to a mosque and I learned as I went that most mosques tended to look alike with their high domes from which multiple brass chandeliers hang almost to the floor, providing light and elegance.

The floors were carpeted and there was a section in the front facing Mecca where infidels such as myself were not allowed. Outside I strolled its vast gardens where Süleyman and his wife, Roxelana, are buried. It was all quite lovely and peaceful.

Leaving the church grounds I noticed I was very close to the dock area so I continued down the hill to revisit.

The dock area was as bustling as it had been the day before, and I visited yet another very famous mosque, Kutucular Caddesi which was also designed by Sinan in 1561 for the husband of Suleyman's favorite daughter, Mihrimah. This particular mosque is famous for its abundance of priceless Iznik blue tile work.

By this time I was quickly reaching the limit of my sight-seeing abilities so I took the tram back to my hotel to rest. I was planning to connect with a good Cedar Rapids friend of mine, Duane, who I knew would be arriving in Istanbul sometime that day. He and Mae were at the end of a cruise tour and staying at the Hotel Marmara. I called and he answered on the first ring. We agreed to meet for dinner and I told them I'd come over to meet them around 6:30 p.m.

I play golf with Duane every week and when we had earlier discussed our upcoming trips, we were surprised to learn we'd both be in Istanbul at the same time; he on his way home, me just getting started. Perfect! I looked forward to getting together with a friendly face and comparing notes.

The hotel clerk informed me the T4 bus headed across the Golden Horn right to the Taksim area of town where the Hotel Mamara was located, a 20-minute ride.

Luckily the bus stopped right in front of the hotel! I entered and called his room.

"Come on up!" he said.

The Hotel Mamara was very fancy and expensive (at least by my standards). Mae had to change first, so Duane and I headed down to the lobby. And then a very strange thing happened. The elevator door opened and out stepped Kay, a totally unexpected friendly face.

Now I have to tell you that Kay was the last person in the world I expected to see in Istanbul. Kay is another friend of mine and serves as program chairperson for our local library.

Several weeks earlier she had called and asked me if I'd be willing to give another travel presentation. Of course I agreed and shortly before I left the country, she called back to set up the details for the talk. Unfortunately I wasn't home at the time. She left a message to call her back. I called her back a number of times but never did reach her. Finally the time came for me to leave and I forgot all about it.

So you can understand my amazement when we literally bumped into each other at 7:00 in the evening on the 6th floor of the Mamara Hotel in Istanbul, Turkey!

Her mouth dropped open, her eyes widened and she stopped dead in her tracks. I stared at her a moment and the first thing I could think of to say was, "Kay, I've been trying to reach you."

She just happened to be on the same cruise as Duane and Mae. It was all too bizarre and after the initial shock wore off, we both had a good laugh. What's the chance of that happening?

Still reeling from the episode, Duane and I continued to the lobby to wait for Mae. We had a beer and discussed where to go for dinner. Neither of us had any idea so when Mae joined us, we left the hotel and hailed a cab.

Of course the one time we needed someone to speak English, our cab driver didn't know a word: no English, German, or Spanish, either. During my unsuccessful attempt to communicate with him, Duane and Mae, who had been sitting in the back, got out, assuming we were going to switch cabs. Just about that time, I somehow got through to the driver what we wanted and we sped off. I turned around to "high five" Duane only to discover an empty back seat.

"Halt!" I shouted. The driver understood that and stopped immediately, I opened the door and they came running back, laughing, and jumped in.

Driving like a mad man, the driver took us to a restaurant right on the banks of the Bosphorus. Oddly, the restaurant had two floors; one served only seafood and the other only meat. We chose seafood and were led upstairs to a lovely table overlooking the water.

It was a traditional Turkish restaurant with white-coated waiters and lots of silverware and linen. Soon waiters began bringing over trays of hot and cold appetizers to choose from. I selected a serving of stuffed mussels. Duane and Mae selected something different and we shared.

For a main course I ordered skewered halibut which was served with fresh vegetables and a salad. I also ordered Raki to sip with my meal. Raki is a traditional and popular Turkish anise-flavored drink cut two to one with water. Similar to Greek Ouzo.

For dessert I ordered coffee and rice pudding. What a wonderful meal!

We took a cab back to their hotel, said our goodbyes and I had the cab take me down to the Golden Horn and let me out at what I thought was the Galata Bridge. Since it was a balmy night I thought it would be fun to walk across the bridge and catch a tram back to my hotel.

The cab dropped me off at a bridge and rushed away before I discovered it was the *wrong* bridge. Confused, I looked around and had no idea where I was. What the heck! Where am I? I was lost again.

There wasn't a soul around. A little creepy. I walked across the vacant bridge and followed the river bank a few miles up a dimly-lit and sinister-looking waterfront area.

It was a stupid mistake on my part, but luckily I had no problems and eventually, found my way back to the hotel.

Pay attention to what you're doing, Bobby.

SEPTEMBER 8

I needed to check out of Hotel Pierre Loti by noon and into a different hotel, Hotel And, by 2:00 p.m. The Fez Tour was to begin there with a group breakfast the next day.

Up at the terrace buffet for my last breakfast, the green and black olives, Gouda and feta cheese, sliced tomatoes and cucumbers had somehow lost their luster and I concentrated on juice, a bowl of cold cereal and hard rolls.

After breakfast I went out for a long morning walk and stopped at another hotel I had spotted a few days earlier, The Hotel Hali. I knew I would be needing a place to stay for a couple of nights when the tour was over and I thought I might try someplace new.

The Hali seemed very nice and only cost $35 for a much larger room. Another positive was the view from its rooftop was even more spectacular. I reserved a room for when I returned from the tour.

I next went to visit the Mosaic Museum which was highly recommended for its 6th century display of tile works dating back to the Emperor Justinian. It was interesting, I guess, but ... tiles? I mean, how many tiles can one absorb so soon after breakfast?

In front of the museum is a lovely park-like area area called the Hippodrome of Constantinople, an ancient sporting and social center of the city dating back to the third century.

Speaking of Constantinople, it was becoming very confusing keeping all the names of this city straight.

It started off with the name Lygos eons ago before it changed to Byzantium in 667 B.C. In 193 A.D. it became Augusta Antonia and shortly thereafter, when Constantine came along, changed again to Nova Roma or New Rome. That didn't stick and it soon became Constantinople, or the City of Constantine. That lasted until 1453 A.D. when the Ottomans conquered the city and changed it once more to Istanbul.

So there you have it, fascinating facts you can amaze your friends with at your next cocktail party.

I tell you, it was very difficult to keep all this stuff straight; thank heavens I had invested in a decent guidebook.

Temporarily steeped in history, I stopped for tea in peaceful little garden cafe to rest and let everything sink in.

I should also talk a little about tea, which is the national drink in Turkey. Everywhere you go tea is served; on the streets, in parks, cafes, stores, and homes. It's a national institution and a ritual that takes place several times a day. The Turkish word is *Çay*, and is pronounced *chi* as in china.

The Turks drink their tea plain. Flavored apple teas are pretty much a tourist thing. It's served piping hot in a small tulip-shaped glass delivered on a small metal dish along with two sugar cubes and a small spoon. Always the same, all the time and everywhere.

Professional tea sellers swarm the streets adorned with huge copper containers strapped on their backs and carrying trays of glasses, sugar and saucers.

If you'd find yourself waiting for a bus, for example, or sitting on a bench reading a paper, you could wave your arm around a bit and before long a tea server will come running. Amazing.

Before checking out of Hotel Pierre Loti I reminded the desk clerk of our prior agreement of a free airport transfer when I returned from my tour.

"Yes, of course, kind sir," he said. "Have a best trip."

Hotel And was just a few blocks away. My room wasn't ready yet so I left my pack in the lobby and walked across the street to Restaurante Medusa for lunch. I ordered a small bottle of local Doluca wine and platter of assorted cold appetizers. It was a vegetarian restaurant and I was curious what I'd get. It turned out to be a large selection of potato salad, egg plant, sliced tomatoes and cucumbers, marinated string beans, assorted cheeses, salsa and hard rolls plus a few mysterious things. An excellent value at only $5.

After lunch I returned to the hotel and checked in. My room was tiny, but clean and comfortable. It was on the fourth floor and looked out on the world-famous landmark, Hagia Sophia. The view filled my window ... wow!

First thing I did was check out the shower. It was a bit strange; a very small, two level space with a hand held sprayer. It took a few minutes to figure out you must sit on the top level and place your feet on the lower level and spray yourself the best you could. Quite different, indeed. (I can understand why the typical American tourist might opt for more expensive but recognizable surroundings — but I found it all fascinating.)

Down in the lobby I found the Fez Tour sign-up sheet. There were 20 people listed. I appeared to be the only American. The majority were from Australia and New Zealand. There were two from England, one from South Africa and one from Honduras. Quite an international group, this should be interesting.

This was my last day by myself so I slipped out to visit yet another museum, the Museum of Turkish and Islamic Arts, reportedly one of the best museums in the country. It's housed in the finest Ottoman residential building in Istanbul, built in 1524 for one of Süleyman the Magnificent's grand vizers, or counselors.

The museum specializes in religious artifacts and antique carpets, with some pieces dating back to the 1200s. It was really interesting and I could happily have spent more time there but by late afternoon I was starting to fade and headed back to the hotel to rest.

On the way, I spotted a fascinating-looking Muslim man sitting in the park knitting. He was wearing a turban, had a white beard, and a very friendly face. I stopped and asked if I could take his picture.

"Yes, of course," he said in broken English, "but perhaps you could present me a small coin?"

What an interesting character, I thought as I dropped a few coins in his hand and snapped off a couple of pictures. Somehow he looked vaguely familiar ...

When I got back to the room I glanced down at my *Insight Guide For Turkey* guidebook and there he was, staring at me from the cover. The same great face.

That evening I returned to Cafe Evin for dinner as it was just around the corner from my new hotel. I ordered a beer, a bowl of tomato soup, an entrée of baked chicken and a helping of their marvelous baklava for desert. All that wonderful stuff for $5.40!

After a brief stop at my friendly internet cafe I returned to the hotel. By 9:00 p.m. I was sitting on the roof top café sipping a Raki and enjoying a million-dollar, night-time view of Istanbul. I was the only guest there.

Echoes of the final call to prayer had long since faded away. The waiter was watching a basketball game on a small TV set in the corner. In a few minutes he came to my table all smiles.

It seemed Turkey had just beaten Germany 79-78 in the semi-final round of the All Europe Basketball Tournament. He was so overjoyed, he insisted on buying me a drink. I stayed longer than planned as we sat and visited like old friends.

It was all too great. How many times has an American waiter insisted on buying you anything?

SEPTEMBER 9

The Fez Tour was on. I was up and showered by 8:00 a.m. A full day tour of the city was planned before we left town the following morning.

The breakfast buffet consisted of what you may wonder? Need I say ... black and green olives, sliced tomatoes, sliced cucumbers, feta and Gouda cheeses, hard rolls, juice, tea and coffee. But instead of cereal, there were hard-boiled eggs.

"Well," I said to myself, "Hard boiled eggs ... there's a welcome change." I decided to skip the olives and feta and Gouda cheese and tomato and cucumber slices for awhile.

Everyone met in the lobby at 9:00 a.m. No introductions were made which I felt was a little awkward — just a few words of welcome from our Turkish guide, a 20-something young man named Ken who appeared a trifle nervous.

Soon we were out the door. First stop: Topkapi Palace.

Topkapi Palace could easily have been a day's tour all by itself. The palace grounds occupy several acres entered through a massive guarded gate. It was the palace for over 400 years' worth of Sultans, and oozed of obscene excess.

The grounds themselves were meticulously manicured with shrubs, trees, and flowers. There were several courtyard areas and we visited them all.

In one courtyard, the entire brick building along one side was made up of three huge kitchens. One for the Sultan, one for the rest of the family, friends, palace guards, and army of employees (50, 000 strong), and one for the poor.

The entire complex is built on a high hill at the confluence of the Sea of Mamara, the Bosphorus Strait and the Golden Horn. As you might imagine, the views from the palace grounds were stunning with ships passing by below and the continent of Asia in clear view off in the distance.

We visited the Sultan's Armory with its vast array of weapons, the Sultan's Portrait Studio with a full-size oil painting of every Sultan that ever was, and the Sultan's Official Treasury which housed an amazing collection of jewels, costumes, furniture, and miscellaneous items (such as bird cages) made out of solid gold and silver and studded with diamonds, emeralds and rubies. It made you dizzy. The wealth of the Ottoman Empire was staggering!

I was particularly impressed to see the actual Topkapi Dagger, shimmering star of the 1962 movie, *Topkapi*, starring Peter Ustinov, Melina Mercouri, and Maximilian Schell. When I returned home, I rented the movie, which I hadn't seen for years, and was surprised to see the dagger actually did resemble the real thing; it was obvious many of the scenes were filmed in Istanbul, and, in fact, at the palace.

Around noon we moved on to the nearby Hagia Sophia, or Church of Holy Wisdom. This internationally-important building is now a museum but was originally built as a Christian Church in the 6th century, during the reign of Justinian. It was originally filled with decorative mosaics which were later destroyed by the Iconoclasts in the 8th and 9th centuries. Eventually new mosaics were added and were preserved by the Muslims, who whitewashed over them to hide and protect them. The images were rediscovered during the 1930s, at which time the immense building was converted into a museum by the famous Atatürk; more about him later.

For lunch we went to a very nice restaurant with the quirky name of Doy-Doy. I ordered a glass of aryan and a mixed kebob, a large platter of grilled meats and vegetables along with some pizza-like snacks that reminded me of tostadas. It was more than I could possibly eat and cost around $3.50! (In case you're not getting the picture yet, Turkey is a real bargain when it comes to eating.)

After lunch we walked through the Hippodrome where our guide Ken pointed out all the significant points of interest, and then on to the adjacent Blue Mosque.

Ken was very knowledgeable about the history and points of interest on the tour. His English was very good although you had to listen carefully. Of course, I had just as much problem understanding the Kiwis and Aussies, as the New Zealanders and Australians referred to themselves.

The Blue Mosque is not only huge, it is also architecturally significant. It was constructed in the early 1600s by a student of the great architect Sinan, of whom I have written before. It was built as a tribute to the superiority of Islam and today maintains that symbolism for many Muslims. It gets it name from the exquisite blue Iznik tiles which line its interior. It has 260 windows, an associated religious school, a hospital, a soup kitchen, and a caravansaray (shelter for caravans).

Of course, by this time I was an old hand at entering mosques and whipped off my shoes like a native. However some of the 'liberated' female members of our group had a little attitude problem covering their bare legs, heads and shoulders. In the end, they all did but grumbled about it.

Our last stop of the day, The Basilica Cistern, happened to be right across the street from our hotel. To tell the truth I wasn't expecting much but I was amazed at what we found.

An ancient military tactic in this part of the world was to lay siege to your enemies until they starved to death, or died of thirst. To prepare for such a possibility, the Byzantine emperors constructed several large cisterns around the city. The largest is the Basilica Cistern, the one we were entering. With an 80,000 square meter capacity, it's immense, and includes 336 twenty-seven-foot-tall columns supporting the ceiling.

Built about the same time as Hagia Sophia, aqueducts brought water from 12 miles away. Two huge Roman Medusa heads act as pedestals in one corner adding to the unique atmosphere of the place. 7,000 slaves reportedly died while building this cistern which fell into disuse after the Ottomans came into power. At that point there was no need for it; no one messed with the Ottoman Empire.

Today it still holds around three feet of water and you can walk through it on raised walkways. It was very eerie walking around down there realizing we were directly below the main business section of Sultanahmet.

By 5:30 p.m. the tour was over and everyone was ready to call it a day. It had been very informative and well-organized. I was feeling good about my decision to join the group considering I usually like to travel alone. I'd gotten to know most of the people by this time; Katherine and Simon from Birmingham, England, Dee and Ron from New Zealand, and Sancia and Ashley from Australia.

Returning to the room I took a short rest. I didn't feel all that "brilliant" as my new travel mates would say. Not really sick, just a little "dodgy."

Early evening I went up to the terrace to talk to my friendly waiter and sip a beer hoping that might settle my stomach. Showing little improvement, I went out for a walk and purchased a glass of aryan, reportedly a miracle drink. Still no improvement. Back to the room for a hot shower. No hot water. Drat! I wasn't going to get sick was I? We were leaving in the morning. What would happen if I were to really get sick?

I knew the answer — they'd leave me behind. Better go to bed and get some rest!

PART TWO

During which time I walked battlefields and climbed mountains — rode wooden horses and caressed marble statues – stood and gazed in wonder at some of mankind's finest achievements – and froze in shock at its absolute treachery!

SEPTEMBER 10

I had a miserable night. I was up several times to use the bathroom and, to add insult to injury, I had chills. I feared   I was beginning to suffer from the dreaded Turkey Trots I'd heard about. With every cover piled on top of me I only managed a few hours of sleep before the morning call to prayer rousted me out of bed. It seemed unusually loud this morning.

Thank God there was plenty of hot water — I soaked myself awake and afterwards felt a lot better. I got dressed and headed down to breakfast. I was going to make it after all.

Oddly, I didn't feel really sick, but definitely "out of sorts"; a little dizzy and weak in the knees with a nervous stomach. One thing for certain, I knew there was no way I could face another breakfast spread of green and black olives, tomatoes, cucumbers and feta and Gouda cheese.

Steering clear of that section of the table, I concentrated on hot tea and a hard roll with honey. I wasn't really hungry anyway, but knew I had to eat something. Ron had eaten the same thing I had the day before and I asked how he felt.

"Smashing!" he said with a wide grin. Showoff.

We finished breakfast and piled into a large Mercedes Benz diesel bus; it looked brand new. There were too many of us to fit into the 15-passenger vans they normally used, so we were assigned this ultra-fancy bus instead. It came complete with driver and assistant. Very nice, I thought. Off we went in plush comfort.

We left Istanbul heading due west towards the Greek and Bulgarian borders before turning south onto a narrow peninsula toward Gallipoli, our first stop of the day. We arrived around noon, picked up sack lunches in town and went right up to a national park.

I'd read about Gallipoli in high school, but really didn't remember much about it. I recalled it was the site of a World War I battle and terrible defeat of the Allied forces. I didn't realize how terrible.

After nine months of fierce hand-to-hand combat, 86,000 Turks and 160,000 Allied troops, mainly Australian and New Zealanders, lay dead. As you might imagine it was a spot especially meaningful to the group I was with.

When I returned home I rented the 1981 movie, *Gallipoli*, starring Mel Gibson in one of his earliest movie roles. And just recently I saw the 2015 movie, *The Water Diviner*, starring Russell Crowe. Both dramatically illustrated the horror of that terrible battle.

We visited a museum and several key battle sites; very reminiscent of a trip through the battlefield of Gettysburg. Oddly enough, it was probably the one major victory Turkey enjoyed in the war and it marked the beginning of the rise to power of a junior officer of the Ottoman armies, Mustafa Kemal, aka Atatürk, the father of modern Turkey.

The Turks may have won this battle, but along with the rest of the scoundrels with whom they had cast their fortunes, they lost the war, and afterwards the Ottoman Empire came crashing down. In the aftermath, the country was mercilessly divided.

At the Turkish memorial at Anzac Cove, site of some of the battle's heaviest fighting, there's a large plaque that bears an eloquent message of reconciliation written by Atatürk:

"There is no difference between the Johnnies and the Memhets to us, where they lie side by side here in this country of ours. You, the mothers who sent your sons from far away countries, wipe away your tears; Your sons are now lying in our bosom and are in peace after having lost their lives on this land, they have become our sons as well."

We spent almost four hours there ... quite a long time but considering the keen interest of the group, most of whom had relatives buried there, I understood. Part of my problem was I didn't feel that great and needed to sit and rest.

Half-way through the afternoon, my stomach felt funny. I rushed to one of the park's brand new restrooms, charged in, and was confronted with ... THE HOLE IN THE FLOOR.

My heavens, I hadn't seen that type of toilet since I was in Yugoslavia in the '70s!

Assuming they'd all be outlawed by now, I was surprised to learn they're still the toilet of choice in most of rural Turkey. For those readers who have no idea what I'm talking about, picture a bathroom with no toilet but instead, a hole in the floor beside which stood a bucket of water.

After my initial shock, I managed to do just fine and even took a photo for the folks back home. (I couldn't wait till the Aussie and Kiwi ladies discovered it.)

We caught the 6:00 p.m. ferry across the Dardanelles Strait to the lovely little harbor town of Çanakkale where our hotel for the night stood facing the waterfront. My room was very nice, faced the harbor, had a small balcony, a modern bathroom with shower and plenty of hot water.

Still not feeling 100% I skipped the group dinner and strolled up and down the colorful harbor promenade, sipping a Coke, enjoying the balmy night and colorful scenery. I even found a wonderful little internet cafe and managed to send and receive several messages before returning to my room.

SEPTEMBER 11 - The day the World Trade Center was attacked.

I was grateful for a fair night's rest, although I was still bothered with chills. Same old, same old breakfast again. No thanks! I concentrated on a couple of slices of toast, a hard boiled egg and hot tea.

We left town around 8:00 a.m. and in a short time arrived at the famous city of Troy. There stood this funky wooden horse you could climb into and wave to friends and get your picture taken from. Pretty cheesy but a photo-op nevertheless. The adjacent museum, however, was wonderful.

Many years ago I'd read *The Greek Treasure*, by Heinrich Schliemann. He was a German businessman and advocate of the historical reality of places mentioned in the works of Homer. He eventually discovered Troy by reading Homer's *Odyssey* and believing it to be true. He followed the clues in the story and *voilà* — to everyone's amazement, he actually found the city.

He also found an astounding treasure of gold, silver and precious jewels, which were all shipped to Germany, later stolen by the Russians during World War II and subsequently disappeared. To this day the treasure remains lost.

The ruins themselves are very confusing and confined to a small area. Built layer upon layer (seven of them) you have to be an experienced archeologist to make much sense of it. It appeared the Turkish government didn't want to invest much money in fixing the place up. Instead, they were putting their money in the archeological sites of Pergamon and Ephesus.

We stopped for lunch near the city of Bergama at a large and popular truck stop. It was time to fill up the bus and ourselves.

Fez Travel seemed to have favorite places to stop for gas, and when they did, a small army of station employees would rush out and scrub and wash the bus so it sparkled!

My stomach was absolutely empty so I was ready to eat something. Other than a very meager breakfast and lots and lots of water, I'd consumed very little solid food in the last two days. This rest area, like others we stopped at during our travels, featured a lovely buffet where, for $3.00, you could eat as much as you wanted.

There was no way I could identify all the dishes; lamb and chicken for sure, and there were a variety of various vegetables including egg plant. Of course, rice pudding was always welcome.

Back in the bus we motored up to the ruins of Pergamon, over 1,000 feet above the city and the second highest point in Turkey. We parked and walked up a steep path to where the ruins began.

It was about this time the ladies first became aware of the local bathroom facilities and were not pleased at all.

Pergamon was a thriving city in the third century B.C., and a proud rival to Ephesus, Alexandria, and Antioch. It was here that parchment was invented, and Alexander the Great came to visit. Its spectacular amphitheater had seating for 10,000 and faced the cliff edge, offering an amazing panoramic view of the entire valley below.

The library was once filled with 200,000 priceless volumes written on parchment, which were given as a wedding gift to Cleopatra by Marc Anthony. Tragically they were later lost in a fire with the rest of the huge Alexandrian collection.

We still had over a three-hour ride to Selçuk, our evening destination. Around 4:30 p.m. we piled back on the bus and shortly thereafter stopped for gas on the outskirts of Izmir, Turkey's third largest city.

It was there we learned of the terrorist attack at the World Trade Center.

It was quite surreal and I'll never forget it. I got off the bus to purchase a bottle of water when one of my Kiwi friends yelled at me to come join them in a small office. There, crowded around a tiny black and white TV, we watched the attack being broadcast live on a very grainy screen. With the eight hour time difference, it was sometime around 9:30 a.m. EST.

At first I couldn't understand what was going on; people moved aside and motioned me up front for a better view.

"Is that the White House?" Ken asked me. "It's under attack!"

"What?" I said unable to make very much sense of what I was seeing. "The White House is under attack? By whom?" I asked, confused.

"The Japanese Red Army," replied Ken, looking at me as if this would make perfect sense.

"I've never heard of the Japanese Red Army," I replied in bewilderment staring at the small screen, trying to figure out what was going on.

"Well, they're bombing New York and Washington!" he said. "At least that's what they're saying. What's that building?"

I stared at the tiny set. I was looking at what turned out to be the twin towers of the World Trade Center just as the second plane smashed into it.

"I'm not sure," I said with alarm. " It's not the White House, I can tell you that."

"No wait," he interrupted. "It's not Washington ... it's New York City and that's the World Trade Center, but they've bombed the Pentagon, too."

"What? Who?" I stammered.

"The Japanese Red Army!" he insisted.

Try if you can to imagine the confusion of the moment with everyone crowded into this one small room and not being able to tell much from the TV set and people shouting and screaming in Turkish and English. It was quite mad. We all stood there frozen in shock and watched the horrible video being replayed over and over and over. It was wretched.

We stayed there mesmerized for 30 minutes before we left, thoroughly confused, alarmed and frustrated.

Later that evening we were told that the terrorists were not the Japanese Red Army after all but most likely the thugs of Saddam Hussein.

I checked my map to see where we were in relation to Iran and discovered we were just a few hundred miles away. In fact, Iran, Iraq and Syria all border Turkey on the east! Not good.

We checked into Hotel Akotel in Selçuk and I was assigned a very simple room; quiet, clean and functional. Dinner was on Fez Travel tonight, and by the time we arrived it was time to eat. It was a simple, but filling meal: a garden salad, a platter of rice and meat/rice balls, potatoes and melon for dessert. I ordered a beer to wash it all down.

There was not much talk about anything but the attack. Everyone was concerned and frustrated, not knowing what was really going on regarding the bizarre events of the day. Telephone lines had been jammed all day long so no one was able to call out of the country.

I ate quickly and walked down the street to a much larger hotel I'd noticed when we drove into town; Hotel Canberra. Since our hotel didn't have a television set, I was hoping they did.

In its small lobby a group of locals were, in fact, watching the news reports on a local channel. When I entered, they sensed I was either Australian or American and immediately switched over to the English-language BBC channel so I could understand. They motioned me to a seat up front. By this time someone called Bin Laden, not Hussein, was being identified as the person responsible for the attack ... but still no one really seemed to know for sure.

Later I tried to call home again and this time I finally got through. My wife did her best to fill me in on the news and told me that our son Brennan, and his wife Sarah, who were scheduled to fly home from Budapest, Hungary the next day, had been grounded.

I assured her that everything was quite calm where I was and not to worry. I was telling the truth; it appeared the Turkish people, who are 99% Muslim, seemed as shocked and disgusted at this as we were.

I was still losing all nourishment rather quickly so had been careful to drink lots of aryan, water and other liquids. Although I felt okay I feared dehydration. At dinner I noticed a couple of other people in our group were just picking at their food and thought they may be coming down with something as well. Although I felt sorry for them I took perverse pleasure in the fact that it wasn't only the Yank who was feeling dicey.

In fact one member of our group came down with something serious during the afternoon tour. She became so ill she was admitted to the local hospital and put on IV fluids. That didn't help our collective mental state.

With the madness going on at home, coupled with the fear of getting really sick, I went to bed feeling quite apprehensive.

SEPTEMBER 12

It had been a full week since I arrived in Turkey, although it seemed much longer with all that had happened. Our guide, Ken, confirmed that the majority of our group was under the influence of the wretched Turkey Trots. But, he hastily added, everyone gets them and we were not to worry. It would all pass soon.

One look at the breakfast table confirmed the worse; the dreaded lineup of olives, cucumbers and cheeses stared back at me — daring me, taunting me. I skipped breakfast entirely and had a cup of coffee instead. Probably not a good idea since I can assure you my stomach was totally empty.

Two Australian chaplains had joined our group the night before, Peter and Andrew. The three of us hit it off pretty well together and left after breakfast to visit the nearby Basilica of St. John.

They were very interesting chaps, always dressed in wild batik-print shirts and wide-brimmed Outback hats. They were both assigned to the New South Wales Police Department and were on vacation visiting various religious sites.

The Basilica was within walking distance of our hotel and contained the burial chamber of St. John the Apostle, who spent the last years of his life in this area. The Bible tells of his banishment to the Greek Island of Patmos, only a short boat ride from Selçuk.

When we returned to the hotel it was time to board the bus for our visit to Ephesus.

Before we left, Ken came to me and quietly told me it would be best to keep my American passport out of sight. "If we get stopped along the way and checked," he said, "just say you're from Australia and you've lost it. Don't worry, it will be good. I will stand up for you."

I wasn't sure what that was all about, but I can assure you, it made me feel a little nervous.

Ephesus is a blast if you have any interest in history at all. Judged on sheer size alone it's awesome. I was amazed to learn only two percent of the ruins had been excavated. It was obvious the Turkish government was putting a lot of time and money into making the site tourist friendly.

According to popular legend, Ephesus was founded by the tribe of Amazons, those great female warriors. By the 6th century B.C., it was already a thriving population center. Its Temple of Artemis was one of the seven wonders of the ancient world, but today is so deteriorated it's hardly worth seeing. The rest of the site, however, is quite impressive.

Ephesus entered a golden age during the Roman era when it was declared capital of Asia Minor. By the time St. Paul arrived in A.D. 53, he attracted enough followers to establish the first Christian Church of Ephesus. He, as well as St. John, spent several years preaching in and around the city.

The surviving ruins are mainly Roman and we visited most of the famous ones, including the magnificent Library of Celsus and the Arch of Hadrian.

I paid an extra fee to visit an area currently under excavation and completely undercover; a hillside of homes of the rich and famous, filled with colorful and detailed tiled floors and fresco-covered walls. It was fascinating and I could have spent more time there, but after a few hours the group left to visit Meremana, the home of the Virgin Mary.

According to tradition, the Virgin Mary came to Ephesus with Saint John in A.D. 37 and lived there until she died in A.D. 48

when she ascended into heaven. Situated in a lovely wooded area high on a hilltop a few miles outside of Ephesus, Meremana is a popular pilgrimage for Catholics as well as Muslims, who both of whom hold Mary in very high esteem. In 1967, Pope Paul VI visited the site and confirmed its authenticity.

We stayed until early afternoon and then returned to Selçuk for a late lunch. I hoped to partake of something very bland; a glass of aryan, a bowl of lentil soup, bread and tea, but didn't have much luck.

At lunch we learned that our hospitalized Honduran comrade, Dee, had been suffering from a combination of stomach problems complicated by a kidney infection. They took her off IV fluids, gave her some strong medication, and sent her back to the hotel. We all hoped she'd feel okay in the morning, otherwise she'd have to stay behind and somehow try to catch up with us later.

At 4:00 p.m., those who were interested met in the lobby and drove 15 miles to the coastal town of Kusadasi. This is the main harbor along this part of the southeastern coast of Turkey, and the place where all the big cruise ships come in from Greece and Israel to dock while passengers visit Ephesus and other world famous archeological sites in the area.

We had three hours to shop, stroll, and just sit and relax. I walked the colorful harbor front, bought some postcards, and found a comfortable little sidewalk café where I could sit, sip a glass of chilled wine, and write notes to family and friends. It was a nice respite from the rather hectic pace we had been keeping the last few days and I enjoyed the break in action.

Dinner was on Fez Travel again this evening: rice and chicken, potatoes and a dinner salad. I didn't have much of an appetite, but I felt fine so ate as much as I could; but I was still not able to retain it for very long. This was getting tiring.

Afterwards I walked back to the Canberra Hotel and caught up on the BBC reports, although there didn't seem to be much new\. Still lots of misinformation and confusion.

I found a small internet café nearby and sent and received several messages before returning to the hotel and turning in around 11:00 p.m.

SEPTEMBER 13

Another lovely, sunny day which, if there had been hot water would have started off *brilliantly*, as my Kiwi and Aussie friends would say.

I cleaned up, shaved as best I could in cold water, then went downstairs and approached the dreaded breakfast table. Oh good God! It was absolutely *loaded* with green and black olives and sliced tomato and cucumber slices and feta and Gouda cheese. Is that all these people knew how to eat?

I gave the room a wide berth until I finally found some peach slices, yogurt and honey.

Food in hand I looked around the room and spied Dee, our sick Honduran, off to the side, a brave smile on her face, sipping a cup of hot tea.

"Just feeling a little dodgy at the moment," she said in a weak voice, "but don't despair, I'll be on the bus." And she was.

After breakfast, we piled into the bus and left to visit the two famous sister sites of Hierapolis and Pamukkale.

We stopped at Hierapolis first; a fascinating ruin that dates to A.D. 17. The thing I remember best about it was its vast graveyard, supposedly one of the largest in the world, sprawled out in every direction almost as far as the eye could see. Most of the crypts were above ground, and because of the many earthquakes that have occurred in Turkey over the centuries, they were all piled up and tilted over one another. It looked like many had been pillaged. Very bizarre!

But the real drawing card at this site is the unusual limestone-laden hot springs of Pamukkale that have flowed down from the top of the hill for thousands of years.

Over time the mineral waters have created stalactites, potholes and a series of hot water pools amidst a surreal landscape. You can see the site from miles away as the hardened calcium shimmers a brilliant white against the surrounding dull and barren landscape.

The area was once overrun by hotels, but recently the Turkish government had them all removed leaving just one or two that were lucky enough to be set back far enough from the cliff edge. One of these hotels featured a large outdoor pool through which the hot waters flowed before cascading down the hillside.

The pool, very popular and filled with tourists, was clogged with ancient Roman statuary and other architectural ruins that once stood on the site.

We left early afternoon, stopping along the way for lunch and to drop off our two Australian chaplains at a train station. Their vacation time was almost up and they were headed home.

We continued our journey south toward the coastal town of Köycegiz, which was situated at the far end of a beautiful, large lake that emptied into the Aegean Sea. I was surprised at the steep mountain roads we had to negotiate, very twisty and full of sharp turns. Our poor driver spent all his time manually shifting gears up and down.

We arrived at Kounos Hotel by early evening. Once again I lucked out and was assigned a large room with a balcony and breathtaking view of the lake and mountains. The hotel was at the end of a very quiet and sleepy street ... actually the whole town was very quiet and sleepy, probably our most off-the-beaten-path stop yet.

Dinner was again on Fez Travel and we all walked to a restaurant with the wacky name of the Tango Passion.

A large group of people were already there when we arrived. I sat with Ron as Dee was still recuperating and had decided to stay in the room and rest. I noticed there were several others who only ordered rice so I was sure they, too, were having some stomach challenges.

My appetite, prompted by a couple of glasses of wine, was a little better this evening, and I actually enjoyed the meal. Over dinner I learned that Ron was a physics instructor in a Brisbane private school for 14 to 18-year-old boys. A physics instructor! Boy, you could have pushed me over with a feather when I heard that.

After everyone was finished eating, an attractive and energetic belly dancer suddenly showed up — whirling around to loud Turkish music, clapping and shouting, finger bells clanging like crazy. It was quite a sight. Later, much to everyone's shock and surprise, the 'she' turned out to be a "he".

By the time the mischief was discovered I'd already left and was spared the details. I walked the few blocks to the downtown area, found an internet café and sent off some messages, and found a phone and called home. My wife told me things on the world front hadn't changed much, and Brennan and Sarah would soon be heading home from Europe.

By 10:00 p.m. I was back in my room, reading and catching up on my log. The moon was bright and full and shining down on the lake, turning it the color of melted pewter. Everything was so still and very, very peaceful.

Tomorrow we'll be taking a boat trip out to the mouth of the bay to visit some ancient rock tombs along the way; sounded very interesting.

SEPTEMBER 14

Although I was convinced I was on the mend, I was still up during the night. The bathroom had a Western style toilet which featured a water supply in a large holding tank up by the 10-foot-high ceiling. Every time you flushed, which you did by pulling on a long cord with a handle, it sounded like the entire lake was draining. Then a diesel pump kicked on and a fresh supply of water pumped back up from somewhere (I'm thinking the lake) to fill the tank up again; it was a rather noisy operation.

Up early I showered, dressed, and strolled down to the dining room for breakfast. There they sat waiting, those ever-present, awful platters of stinking olives, cucumbers slices and cheeses.

Not even bothering to enter, I turned around and walked the few blocks to town. I needed some aryan in my system. I needed *anything* in my system, but certainly not olives and cheese. I was a little concerned my digestive system was so slow adjusting to the local foods. But as long as I felt okay and kept hydrated, I figured I'd be fine. Of course, by this time, everyone in the group was having similar problems, yet no one seemed overly concerned.

Back at the hotel I sat on the open veranda, wrote some postcards, and waited for the group to assemble for our day's outing. It was a lovely morning with a perfect temperature, a clear, bright day. To pass the time, I perused the hotel's bilingual tourist pamphlet and was delighted to discover the following introductory paragraph:

> *Come to Köycegiz and unite with the unrivaled nature, stride on the roads dated to 3000 B.C., and taste to romantic scenes that inspired Homeros. All the stress, tiredness and heartaches of the year will be vanished on the second day here. Best of all, get the rest you deserved and find your human self away from the nois crowds. We will be honored to see you in our hotel by the lakeside. You will have corely and superior service for your comparts. Hotel Kaunos*

At 10 a.m. we piled onto a chartered gület and headed out across the lake toward the mouth of the bay. A gület is a traditional type of diesel-powered boat you see everywhere in Turkey: a wooden affair, open on the sides, but covered with a solid roof. Gülets are large enough to walk around in and as comfortable as they are colorful. Halfway on our trip we stopped so we could take a swim break in water that was half salt, half fresh.

Soon we passed by an area where the Lycians carved huge tombs out of the solid rock face of the mountain. It was near the ancient city of Kaunos. We slowly motored by the cliff and marveled at the workmanship.

The Lycian people lived in this area of Turkey dating back to 1400 B.C. Strangely they remained independent and isolated from the rest of the country until only 20 years ago. It has only been very recently that people have been prohibited from climbing the cliff faces and damaging the tombs where Lycian nobility are buried.

We continued out to open water where we had time to swim, hike, or do whatever we wanted before we anchored the boat in calm water just off a wide stretch of beach.

I rented a lounge chair and umbrella and sat and read. It was very hot in the sun and I didn't feel like swimming in the salty water without the chance to rinse off afterwards.

The beach was crowded with tourists of many nationalities; there seemed to be more Germans than any others. I remember one rather heavy German woman, I'd guess in her 40s, with dyed bright red hair strolling topless down the beach. Yikes!

We headed back mid-afternoon, stopping along the way at a small village famous for its hot-mud, medicinal baths.

If you can visualize an odorous pig wallow, you'd be close to what we found at these baths. There were shallow, swampy-looking depressions where, if you were so inclined, you could walk in, sit down, and smear hot, smelly, green, radon-saturated mud all over yourself.

Then you could wait till it dried and wade into an icy cold stream to rinse yourself off. Theoretically, if you had previously suffered from male impotency, gynecological problems, rheumatism, or a host of other ailments, you would now be well on the road to recovery.

Having evaluated the situation, I volunteered to be the official photographer for any of my travel mates who couldn't wait to slither into the foul mess. Most of them did and I captured the magic event for them on film; it was quite comical.

Back in our gület we continued, again stopping halfway back for another swim. I decided I was lucky to have joined up with such an agreeable group. Everyone seemed to get along with everyone else, and managed to handle the ups and downs just fine. It was a beautiful evening and we were treated to a fabulous sunset view as we quietly motored back to shore.

Back in the hotel I showered, changed clothes and quickly headed out by myself for dinner. I'd been with the group the entire day and needed a little alone time.

It was a lovely evening as I walked along the promenade towards town. I soon came upon an attractive little hotel right on the lake, with a outside restaurant surrounding a softly-lighted pool. It looked perfect! I entered and was led to a table.

The young waitress (the first female I'd seen working in a restaurant) only spoke Turkish, but motioned towards an older man circulating among the few tables. He came over and introduced himself as the owner/manager; she was his daughter. He had recently retired after 40 years in the Turkish navy and spoke several languages, including excellent English.

At his recommendation I ordered a freshly prepared casserole of lamb mixed with rice and several different vegetables. It was spicy but delicious, one of the best meals of my entire trip. With a couple of glasses of the local wine, a wonderful pastry and Turkish coffee, the meal cost only $5. Wow!

This is a good time to talk about cats. You see them everywhere you look and everyone seems quite taken with them. I don't recall seeing any dogs but cats definitely ruled!

One of the places you often saw them is in and around restaurants. You might, for instance, be sitting quietly enjoying your meal and suddenly hear a soft, pitiful meow come from under the table. You look down and see one or two polite cats or kittens staring up at you begging for a morsel. This restaurant was no exception.

But a funny thing happened this evening. One cat in particular, a rather large tom, seemed quite bold indeed. It not only sat and meowed, it weaved its way in and out of the legs of everyone sitting around the table. It had no intention of being ignored.

There was one unfortunate couple sitting at a table directly in front of me who made the mistake of trying; the cat did not like this.

All of a sudden (and I saw the whole thing coming), the cat leapt up from the ground, sank its claws into the tablecloth at the very edge of the table, pulling everything onto the floor. Wine glasses, salad plates, rolls, and entire entrees. It then grabbed a whole grilled fish, and dashed off into the darkness. All of this took place in a matter of seconds!

The couple jumped up screaming. The manager and his daughter came running over, and the cook came charging out of the kitchen with a broom — but alas, it was too late. The damage had been done and the dinner, last seen in the cat's mouth, had disappeared. Somehow, I got the idea this particular cat had pulled this trick before.

Everyone turned to see what the American's reaction would be, and when I burst out laughing, so did everyone else. It was great theatre and soon the whole restaurant was roaring.

After dinner I walked back to the internet cafe and sent off a few messages before heading back to the hotel.

On the way back I passed by another small restaurant and spied Dee and Ron listening to a group playing and singing traditional Turkish folksongs. I joined them for a drink and comparison of meals. Dee was feeling much better and assured me she would be 100% by the next day.

SEPTEMBER 15

I got up just in time to witness the departure of the hotel's remaining hot water. No problem. By this time I was used to tepid showers.

Today we headed down the coast to Olüdeniz and the nearby town of Fethiye. This area of the country is very mountainous and famous for its spectacular coastal scenery, and is one of the main reasons I decided to come to Turkey.

Along the way we stopped at a rural cooperative carpet factory, where we watched women combing out wool and spinning it on large thimble-like pieces of wood. We watched how silk is harvested from the actual silkworm cocoons and woven into thread. Finally, we were ushered into a large display area where hot tea was served and a very well-spoken salesperson started explaining the entire process, and the differences in the various kinds of carpets.

As he spoke, three assistants were constantly picking up rolls of carpets and, with flourishes, unrolling them and layering them around the large room. We were all sitting on benches around the perimeter watching, fascinated.

Many of these carpets were silk and cost thousands of dollars, and they were all gorgeous: rich and very well made. Even I could tell that. But surely he didn't think any of us were going to buy one, did he?

Then came a very interesting sales pitch. He invited us to take off our shoes and walk over them before they began rolling them back up again.

"If anyone wants to take a closer look at one of these excellent carpets," he said, "simply raise your hand and it will be dropped at your feet for closer inspection."

If anyone was foolish enough to raise a hand, another salesman (translate that as "high powered closer") would take them and the carpets they had shown interest in into a private room.

At this point I beat a quick retreat and found a comfortable waiting room with a large platform covered with soft rugs and pillows, and enjoyed another cup of tea. I gave the attendant's young son one of the small flashlights I had brought along, and he enjoyed it immensely.

As it turned out, several members of our group *did* buy carpets, and I believe they were treated fairly. But the key question was, "How would you ever know if you weren't?"

Early afternoon we arrived at a place called the Saklikent Gorge where several country restaurants were built on decks over a shallow, but fast running river. There were no chairs, just lots of rugs and pillows strewn everywhere. We ate lunch and those who wished could take an hour-long tube ride down the icy cold river. Those that didn't could relax and just take it easy. I elected to stay and catch up on my log. It was all quite peaceful and soothing sitting with the rushing water just a foot or so beneath me and I soon fell asleep.

Later several of us decided to hike up the gorge which is the second-largest gorge in Europe. It is a spectacular place, with sculpted walls soaring high above. We had to wade through thigh-deep, ice cold river into the narrow and steep canyon.

Since it was late in the year, the water level was much lower than normal. I still thought it was still quite dangerous, involving some hard scrambling over boulders and occasionally wading through neck-deep pools.

We went in quite far before turning back to rejoin the others. I got thoroughly soaked and only just managed to keep my small camera dry. My travel packet with all my documents and money was a dripping mess. Later I spread out everything in the hotel room to dry.

We arrived at Hotel AtaPark in Fethiye (FEY-teh-hay), tired and hungry. It was a lovely location right on the inside bend of a large bay. Olüdeniz (oh-LOU-den-knees) was a few miles away. My room was very comfortable and, more importantly, featured a shower with plenty of hot water. Yes! My legs were still half numb from wading though the ice-cold water in the gorge.

For dinner I joined Susan, an expatriate living somewhere in Honduras, and Rex and Diane Humphrey, a New Zealand couple, around an open-air pool adjacent to the lobby.

Rex and Diane were both professionals in the medical field, specializing in the area of bacteriology. I found this rather comical as Diane was one of the first ones in our group, other than myself, to came down with what everyone was now calling the Tragic Turkey Trots.

Diane explained we were not actually *sick*, but just adjusting to a different type of bacteria used in milk products in this part of the world. Whatever ... my stomach had been adjusting way too long.

Susan, I learned, was an Iowa native! She'd graduated from the University of Iowa and for many years has been living on a sailboat in Honduras, but was now a widow. She was very nice and these days spent a great deal of her life traveling around the world visiting old friends.

The four of us were probably the senior members of the group and over dinner decided we'd rent a Jeep in the morning and go and visit some of the local sights.

The rest of the group were going to go swimming at a nearby beach. We checked at the front desk and made all the necessary arrangements.

I was chosen to be the designated driver as Susan confessed she was a horrible driver, and the Kiwis were only used to driving, in their words, on the "correct side of the road" ... or the left side, of course.

After dinner I walked up the road to find a pay phone and tried to call home to get a report on the state of the world. None of us were really up-to-date on the World Trade Center attack. We all knew something terrible had happened, but still were not clear on exactly what, and by whom. The line was busy so I walked back to use the hotel's computer to check for messages but it was jammed.

It was late when I finally returned to my room to read. It had been a very pleasant, comfortable day although I was a bit frustrated in not being able to obtain any concrete news.

SEPTEMBER 16

Of course you already know what breakfast consisted of, but today there was a new item to make it interesting. I never thought I'd get excited over Kellogg's Frosted Flakes, but I did that morning. Yay! Good old Tony the Tiger to the rescue.

Our promised rental Jeep turned out to be a well-used Suzuki Samurai that had either been manufactured without shock absorbers or had lost them along the road years ago. Our goal was an abandoned Greek village called Kayakoy around 20 miles out of town and up in the mountains. Built in the 1700s, the town is called Karmuylassos in Greek and was home to as many as 20,000 Greek Orthodox residents until World War ll came along.

After the war began, the Greeks were forced to vacate and return to Greece. The Turkish people, however, believe the town to be cursed because of religious differences and refuse to occupy it. Today it still stands empty.

Driving there we almost ran into a very large Lycian sarcophagus (huge burial vault) sitting in the middle of the road. We drove around a corner and, without warning, there it sat on a column around four feet higher than the rest of the road. It had been found while they were grading the road and left untouched while the earth around it had been lowered and leveled.

I swerved sharply to avoid running into it and having it crash down on top of us. I'm not sure why it was left there, but I suspected the locals felt it would be bad karma to move it so they just worked around it.

Eventually we arrived at the village, parked the car, and split up, planning to meet again at noon. I immediately headed up into the ruins, which were built into the side of a large hill facing the sea. It was very eerie. There was not a soul around — just hundreds of buildings, most with the roofs collapsed — and a rabbit warren of abandoned pathways.

It was hot as I scrambled and snooped my way through stone houses and other buildings. I climbed up and up and reached an old church along the ridge, where I ran into my friends who had just arrived by one of the few streets that were still being used, mainly by curious tourists like us.

We headed back to the car and were invited to join a friendly family for tea on the porch of their home. The woman showed me a box of artifacts and coins, including one old Roman coin her husband had found up in the village. She was hoping I'd buy it. I was interested but she wouldn't budge from a price of $100. I wasn't about to pay that and hoped I hadn't passed up a priceless item. I didn't think so but will never know. I wish I had taken a picture of it.

We left and drove to a small seaside village where we stopped and had fresh-grilled fish on the beach. We drove on to another beach packed with sunbathers, swimmers and paragliders.

This is the place to go if you want to have a Turkish teenager strapped to one's back and then leap off a tall cliff. We were approached several times by the local entrepreneurs who could spot a filthy rich American, Honduran or New Zealand tourist from a half mile away.

Although it looked quite exciting, we all declined. I later talked to some of the younger members of our group who had done it, and they reported it was "absolutely brilliant" — which meant we definitely made the right decision.

We stood and watched them soaring around like big colorful birds, swooping down, catching updrafts and rising up, out and over the ocean. When they finally came down after 30 or 40 minutes, they glided over the tops of hundreds of sunbathers and landed within a very small target area, certainly no more than 20 square feet.

I had to admit, it looked like fun and the young Turkish pilots seemed to know what they were doing. But for a little more money, I planned go hot air ballooning over Cappadocia.

We drove back over the mountain to Fethiye, and returned the car. We were scheduled for our first Turkish bath experience after dinner and needed to change and get mentally prepared.

In this part of the world, Turkish baths, or *hammams,* are an important ritual of life. They're not only places to get "really clean", but places to gossip and visit with friends. They don't necessarily replace a daily bath, but once you complete the session, which lasts approximately one hour, you understand why once a week is plenty.

The bath we were visiting was in the lower level of our hotel. We were greeted at the door by an attendant and given sandals and large bath towels, called *pestemals,* all sewn from an identical, traditional red plaid cotton cloth. We were led to individual locker rooms where we disrobed, carefully wrapped our frail bodies in the towels, and were escorted into a large, hot central room. Really hot!

This inner sanctum was handsomely constructed entirely of marble and featured a large, round, raised circular area in the middle and marble benches around the perimeter. It was very hazy inside, but you could tell there were lots of Greek columns and fancy statuary placed around the room, which was lined with large basins overflowing with warm water. Buckets stood by each basin so you could dip into them and pour the water over yourself.

The idea was to sit and relax and let your pores open so that, according to our attendant, the *poisons* in your body could escape naturally. Sounded a little loopy to me but I went along with it. After 30 minutes of purging, we were told to lie on our stomachs on the warm marble in the middle of the room while our skin was pounded and scraped clean of impurities by attendants wearing what felt like #2 sandpaper mitts.

First one side of your upper body was scraped, then the other, then legs, arms and necks, hands and feet. I was about ready to throw in the towel, so to speak, when, mercifully, the scraping stopped and my ultra-clean, purified body was dosed with bucket after bucket of hot water. This was almost as bad as the scraping and a little like drowning and, I'm guessing here, the precursor of water boarding.

Next, we were heavily dosed with hot suds and given another massage, more pounding, a final drowning and eventually excused to the side of the room while another person was pummeled.

The end of the session came when we were all clean and I mean REALLY CLEAN. We were led into another, much cooler room and wrapped up, including our heads, with a number of warm towels, then led to lawn chairs where we lay whimpering while our red, raw bodies recovered. In about an hour we were allowed to dress and escape to our rooms.

And that, dear reader, is what a Turkish bath is. Sounds lovely, doesn't it? Well, it actually was lovely and we all felt marvelous despite the pain and punishment and, for only $7, I was sporting a new body as pure as the driven snow.

That evening a group of us hailed a couple of taxis and went to town for pizza and beers. We found an out-of-the-way outdoor cafe which was quite wonderful. The pizzas were Turkish pizzas — quite different than ours. Strange combinations of meat (probably lamb) and vegetables prepared on paper thin, crisp crusts, delicate and delicious.

The beers arrived from another location, camouflaged in large Coca Cola cups. Apparently our restaurant had no liquor license, but this didn't seem to slow them down, as they just sent a couple of runners out to another restaurant to buy it and bring it back.

Everyone in our group agreed Fethiye was a wonderful stop. The weather was a balmy 70° and clear as a bell as we all walked back along the bay front to the hotel.

However, the really BIG news of the day was not the car trip to the deserted Greek village of Kayakoy with the Lycian sarcophagus in the middle of the street. It wasn't the fresh fish dinner under swaying palms, or the Olüdeniz beach with its bevy of lovely bathers and wild-eyed paragliders. No, it wasn't even our fascinating adventure at the hammam – or the $2 pizza and beer.

The REALLY BIG NEWS was the fact that when I turned in for the night my stomach finally felt normal! That's right, after an eight-day bout with the Tragic Turkey Trots this pilgrim finally came out the victor.

SEPTEMBER 17

I awoke at 7:00 a.m. after a solid, uninterrupted night's sleep. The first in over a week. Yay! I was finally back in the game!

A casual glance around the full breakfast room and it appeared most everyone else appeared to be well on the road to recovery. Lots of smiles. Everyone was raring to go to Olympos where, if one were to believe our tour leader, we would be spending the next two nights sleeping in tree houses. That's right, tree houses — like in secret codes and passwords and all the neat stuff you did when you were a kid.

We stopped at Kos for lunch, another picturesque fishing village along the Mediterranean. Kababs and Cokes in a small restaurant on the waterfront.

Originally known as Myra, our next stop was another small coastal town called Demre, the alleged birthplace of Santa Claus. Born in the 4th century, St. Nicholas of Myra was known for his legendary habit of secret gift-giving which gave rise to the traditional of Santa Claus.

There we boarded another boat and headed out to visit an ancient submerged city. We stopped at some sea caves along the way and everyone jumped in the water to investigate. The day was brilliant and clear.

Later we motored past several islands inhabited centuries ago by the Lycians. Eventually we glided over the submerged 1st century city of Kale. Over the side of the boat you could clearly see ancient houses, wharfs, churches and roads, all through 15 feet of crystal clear water. It was eerie and beautiful at the same time.

Everyone jumped over the side again and swam down to explore the underwater ruins. I found numerous pieces of decorated pottery and asked Ken if I'd get into trouble if I took one or two home with me. He found that very amusing and assured me I should feel free to help myself.

By late afternoon we were headed back to shore, sipping beers and enjoying the lovely scenery.

That evening we arrived at Beydaslari Olympos National Park. It was far out on a peninsula and down a narrow road that eventually ended at an archeological site bordered by a very secluded beach. Along the road we came to our night's lodging ... Kadir's Yorük Tree Top Houses.

My first impression of the place was that I'd gone through a time warp and had been transported to some wacked-out hippy hangout; a throw back to the '60s. I looked around for Janis Joplin and Jimmy Hendrix.

As it turned out, I wasn't that far off. We entered through a large gate and saw ... well, tree houses scattered everywhere around a large central lodge. They were reached by climbing up rickety-looking stairs. I stood for a moment amazed at the place.

Several young people of indeterminate nationalities met us at the bus and took us to our assigned rooms.

As it turned out, my little house was on the ground level. At first I was a bit disappointed, but after thinking it through I decided I ended up with a pretty good deal. The room was small, with a night stand and queen-sized bed. It even had a private bathroom with hot water.

People assigned to the treehouse units had to climb up and down every time they wanted to go to dinner or take a nap, use the toilet, or shower. I figured that could be a bit of an annoyance — particularly at 3:00 in the morning.

As soon as we got squared away, we gathered for dinner in a combination mess hall-bar TV room. The meals were all vegetarian; lots of beans, rice, potatoes, and egg plant. Okay, I thought ... healthy I suppose, and for a couple of days I'd survive.

I took a closer look at the clientele. The place seemed to be filled with a large tribe of 20-something, bearded, tattooed, metal-studded and lost-looking misguided youth. Fire pits were scattered all around the grounds and groups of young people were sitting, staring vacantly into the flames. What in the world is this place, I thought? And why are we here?

After dinner I had a chance to watch a little British TV, the first English speaking coverage I had seen in several days, and was shocked to see the Dow had dropped 650 points! The world news seemed bleaker and bleaker and, of course, all the talk was about the World Trade Center and progress made tracking down the terrorists.

I remember thinking if there were another World War, the bad guys, whoever they were, would *never* find this place, although we were as close as we would ever get to Iraq and Syria.

Ironically, of all the places I had stayed so far, this one had the best reading light and the bed was quite comfortable even though it looked like it had been made by beginner Boy Scouts using willow bark and discarded tree branches.

SEPTEMBER 18

What a bizarre night! I fell asleep just fine ... but was jarred awake around 1:30 in the morning by very loud, throbbing, thumping sounds coming from outside. What in the world was that racket? I got up, opened the door and looked out. There was a lot of noise coming from someplace nearby, so I went out to investigate.

Nearby I found several groups of young people sitting around large fires. The noise was coming from a bank of large, loud speakers emitting a sort of primitive, wailing, mournful sound.

It reminded me of a clan meeting on the TV series, *Survivor*. Or a reenactment of some ancient druid ceremony taking place at Stonehenge. No one was doing much more than sitting around, swaying to the primitive beat. It was obvious a large volume of beer had been consumed. And Lord knows what else. I returned to my hut and went back to sleep.

I awoke too early for breakfast, but there were hard boiled eggs and rolls set out so I grabbed a couple of each and headed down the road toward the ocean.

I soon arrived at a gate where I had to pay five million lira — approximately $3.50 — to enter the archeological site of Olympos. It was not only the shortest way to get to the beach, but I had wanted to visit the site anyway.

It turned out to be several acres spread out on both sides of a shallow river. It had been explored by archeologists long ago because you could see a few very faded informational signs here and there, but for the most part the place was pretty much the way they must have found it.

It was hard to tell much as the area was overgrown with large plants, trees and shrubs. It was very similar to walking through a jungle. I came upon an an amphitheater, public baths, houses, and lots of large first and second century buildings in various stages of disarray and decay. It was fascinating! It reminded me of a scene from *Planet of the Apes*.

I continued on until suddenly, spread out in front of me, was the ocean and a vast sand beach running for miles and miles. It was almost empty. I walked about a mile up the beach until, in the middle of nowhere, I came to a small, very rustic restaurant and stopped for orange juice. The waiter/owner offered me a cup of tea if I'd sit and talk with him awhile. Of course I was delighted to do so and soon learned he just wanted to practice English.

Before returning, I climbed up to the Acropolis of the ancient town and found a spectacular view of the entire beach. I quickly snapped some photos and carefully worked my way back down; it was quite steep and dangerous.

On the way back I hunted around a small grove where the ground had been tilled up and found several artifacts, mainly first century pottery shards; excellent souvenirs.

Kadir's Treehouses was pretty quiet when I got back at mid-afternoon, so I took advantage of the scarcity of people and used the community computer to send some messages.

That evening a group of people had signed up to go to a mountainous area where flames constantly burn, an area called Chimera.

We boarded a small bus and headed up the mountain. The leader suggested that we bring torches (flashlights) along. I had two tiny emergency pen lights which I felt would be sufficient. I was wrong.

After a 30-minute trip we arrived and unloaded. There were a couple dozen of us. A local guide quickly started off into the dark and we hurried to keep up with him. The path was easy to see at first but after a short while, when we entered a heavily-wooded area, it got pitch black and people started to trip over rocks. My pen lights pooped out after 10 minutes and I stumbled on trying to catch up to a small group that had a decent flashlight.

On and up we went, scrambling over rocks and boulders, a task that would have been difficult to do in broad daylight. Finally, after a half hour, we arrived, out of breath, and slightly bruised, at the top of a small mountain. I was amazed no one had turned an ankle.

Flames were belching out of fissures in the rock, the result of escaping methane gas. The site is thought to be the origin of the Greek myth of the Chimera, the fire-breathing monster with a lion's head, a goat's body and a serpent's tail that was finally destroyed by Bellerophon. The people of Olympos constructed a sanctuary here, dedicated to Hephaestus (Vulcan), the god of fire.

It was strange all right, but I'm not sure it was worth the effort of struggling up here. We sat around for 30 minutes and finally headed back down.

This time I was careful to position myself as close as possible to the group with the brightest flashlights. Next time I'd pay more attention to instructions.

I was back in my room by 10:30 p.m., packed for tomorrow's departure, showered and lying in bed reading and catching up on my log. We'd been told we had a long bus ride ahead of us tomorrow. We were heading to Cappadocia.

PART THREE

Which lead me into the Ali Baba land of camel caravans and fairy tale cities – over which I soared in a colorful balloon and later descended into its very depths like a mole – an encounter with an odorous church – and the clickety-clack of a train that could.

SEPTEMBER 19

6:30 a.m. – a sharp rapping on my door. I sat up straight. Where was I?

"Time to get up, dear sir," called out a heavily-accented female voice. Well now, wasn't that special ... my own personal wake up call.

It had been a quiet night. Apparently the 20-somethings had gotten all the nonsense out of their systems the night before, because the revelry had come to a halt around midnight. Either that, or I had been too tired to notice.

It was cold down in our wooded ravine, surely no warmer than 50°. Need I mention what was set out for our farewell breakfast? Ouch! Mountains of black and green olives, feta and Gouda cheese, sliced tomatoes and cucumbers. I settled for hard rolls and a cup of hot tea.

We loaded up in the bus and were moving in an hour, the earliest we'd left yet. As we wound our way out of the valley, the sun peeked over the top of the ridge and ever so slowly moved down through the trees. It would still be a long time before it reached Kadir's Yörük Tree Top Houses ... definitely one of the strangest places I'd ever visited!

We drove up the coast and passed through Antalya, one of the larger towns in the area. How clean and organized everything looked as we motored by mile after mile of lovely pebble beaches.

Mid-morning we stopped at one of the country's huge truck stops to fill up with gas, snacks and water. Again I was impressed with the efficiency and cleanliness of these places. It seemed each one offered an enormous variety of snacks from which to choose: American candy bars and chips, nuts, ice cream, soft drinks. And not just a few brands, but literally dozens of choices in each category. There were even several brands of gasolines from which to choose from. The cost here was around $4.00 per gallon.

From Antalya we turned north and headed up into the mountains — and for the last time, left the lovely Mediterranean shore far behind us. After an hour of twisting and turning we finally reached the high plateau which characterizes the middle part (and the majority) of the Turkish landscape.

Honey stands appeared along both sides of the road, all competing for the motorists' business.

By early afternoon we arrived in Konya, the capital of the Selcuk Empire between 1071 and 1308. Long a very important regional center, the city was visited by St. Paul several times during his epic travels bringing Christianity to the Gentiles.

Located right on the ancient Silk Road, it's an extremely old city, its roots going back to the days of the Hittites. As a Roman city it was known as Iconium. Today it's known as the most religiously conservative city in Turkey.

Its main claim to fame today is that it's home to the mysterious *whirling dervishes*. You may remember these are the guys who dress up in long white capes and red fez caps and with arms outstretched spin themselves into a religious frenzy for *Allah* and, I suppose, for tourists who have the time and money to watch.

We were on a mission to get to Cappadocia before dark, however, so we only had time for a quick lunch.

The place we picked was one of the best restaurants we'd been to yet, featuring a magnificent buffet of a staggering variety of salads, main dishes of lamb, fish and chicken, and many platters loaded with fresh fruits and pastries. If I recall correctly, there were five different types of *baklava* from which to choose!

This was definitely not your ordinary truck stop buffet and featured table cloths, lovely china and silverware, and uniformed waiters. Eat as much as you want for $2.80!

You can imagine my surprise, therefore, when their brand new, spotless Turkish restroom featured the traditional "hole in the floor." How great is that?

We were on our way again at 3:00 p.m., stuffed and happy. It felt wonderful knowing I was over my shaky stomach episode and I physically felt much stronger.

Late in the afternoon we stopped at a fascinating 13th century caravanseray at a remote, high-desert spot called Sultanhami.

In the era of the sultans, caravanserays were large fortress-like buildings, around half the size of a football field, spaced out about every 40 miles across the high-desert countryside. They were places you would find hospitality and safety for your camel caravan for the night. One had to arrive before sundown, after which time the huge doors were locked tight until dawn. This particular building was very well-preserved, with sleeping areas spaced along the eight-foot thick walls, and a large open grazing area for the camels.

We arrived at Hotel Surban at sunset. It was in the town of Ürgüp, right in the middle of Cappadocia. The entire hotel was carved completely out of stone, matching the rest of the buildings in the area.

Although the building was only 12 years old, it was designed to look much older, and featured winding hallways, relaxation rooms and secluded terraces, including a roof terrace overlooking the town. The lounge was laid out Turkish-style including a large reclining platform with lots of pillows and rugs strewn around. And all carved out of solid rock.

Like the rest of the hotel, my bedroom was also carved out of solid rock. I'm not sure how they got the piping in there, but the bathroom was spotless and had plenty of water. Large, colorful tapestries covered the walls which, of course, had no windows.

I sat with my travel mates at the lounge bar and ordered a glass of excellent local wine. Dinner was on Fez Travel this evening and consisted of a large tray of cold appetizers, barley soup, a main course of lamb or chicken, rice and dessert.

After dinner I walked about a mile into town to look around. It seemed a friendly place and the local shopkeepers were polite and spoke surprisingly good English; apparently this was a favorite tourist area. There was an abundance of gift shops and antique stores which had an amazing array of items for sale, from old jewelry and ancient armaments to musical instruments. It was too late to do any serious shopping, so I planned to return the following night.

Back at the hotel I placed an early wake-up call. Several of us had signed up for a hot air balloon ride and planned to meet in the lobby at 5:30 a.m. Lift-off at 6:00!

SEPTEMBER 20

Cappadocia is internationally famous for its eerie lunar landscape and one of the best ways to see it is from a hot air balloon at dawn.

At 5:00 a.m. the phone by my bed jangled quite loudly.

"Ooomph! What's that noise? Where am I?" I muttered as I fought my way out of a sound sleep.

"Good morning, my sir," a female voice chirped happily. "It will be 5:00 a.m. and your most preeeety balloon awaits you."

Of course. It's Thursday. I must be in Orgüp, Cappadocia, Central Antolia, Turkey ... the very day I foolishly signed up for a most preeeety balloon ride.

What in the world had I been thinking? I'd passed up paragliding in broad daylight because I felt nervous about safety issues. Now I was leaving in the dark to go ballooning? I'd never been in a balloon in America. Why would I do so in Turkey of all places?

A young lady from Snowball Balloons was waiting for us in the lobby. Six of us had signed up. None of us was quite awake yet as we piled into a small van and joined two middle-aged French women. A balloon basket-full.

We drove through the dark countryside to the launch site. There were three balloons spread out on the ground, slowly being filled. It was very chilly and everyone was wishing they had dressed warmer.

While the balloons filled, some cellophane-wrapped snacks were spread out for us on a small table, along with a thermos of hot water and tea bags; our complimentary continental breakfast.

As the propane burners began to lift the balloons off the ground, we edged closer. The heat from the flames felt soooo good. Soon we were motioned into the gondola. It had two main compartments, one on either side for passengers, and a small space in the middle for the pilot.

I studied the pilot in a last minute attempt to access his hot air-ballooning knowledge. I was unnerved to see he looked a little goofy, showing a tendency to twitch a lot for no apparent reason.

"Günaydin. I Murat Yildirim," he said, stretching out his hand with a huge grin and a twitch. I assumed he was introducing himself, although for all we knew he could have been saying he'd been to all night party and was still "dead drunk". I would have bought that.

Just as we were about to lift off, a cab came roaring up and two people jumped out. They were waved towards our balloon as the one they were originally assigned to had just floated away. Oh no, I thought, we were already filled. They were German, and when they were directed to separate side, of our gondola, they became very upset.

"*Nein, nein, zusammen!*", they yelled. (Together, we must be together.)

So we had to shift people around so the Germans could hold hands. Finally we took off.

Up to this point I had been pretty cool with the whole thing. I was a bit nervous, sure, but was handling it okay. But as we started to actually lift off the ground I started to panic.

What was I thinking? Putting my life on the line with a drunken hot air balloon pilot and two crazy Germans ... in Cappadocia!

We rose silently, except for the periodic rush of flames inches from my head, and were soon 50, 100, 150, feet off the ground. I couldn't look down for fear of passing out so I studied the ropes tied to the gondola for signs of wear. They seemed quite skimpy.

The gondola itself looked homemade and sort of "loose." *What if it was made by Murat's almost blind grandmother*, I thought with a rush. *My God, what if the bottom came apart*? Quickly I slid my feet to the corners where I thought I had the best chance of finding a solid footing when the floor disintegrated.

Meanwhile Murat, the pilot, was looking off into space, smiling. Was it my imagination, or were his eye lids starting to droop?

I found it very hard to look down and had visions of tumbling over the side. Relax, I had to relax, and eventually I did, a little, but never enough to fully enjoy the ride.

As the sun came up, it was indeed a spectacular sight watching the glow race over the surreal landscape. Millions of years ago Mt. Argaeus, the third highest mountain in Anatolia, convulsed, smothering the surrounding landscape with a torrent of lava stretching hundreds of miles in every direction. They say it must have been one of the greatest upheavals on the planet. For eons since, floods, rain and wind have worn away the table of lava, creating deep valleys and fissures, while the slopes were carved into astonishing cones and columns.

We drifted silently, occasionally dropping down into some secluded narrow canyon and rising up again, just barely clearing the ridge before sinking down into another fissure. I have to say my confidence in Murat rose with the sun and I almost felt comfortable by the end of the voyage.

As it got brighter we could see pathways winding through the crazy landscape, leading to melon patches and long lines of grape vines spread out on flat rocks. Many paths led to rock cliffs where rooms had been carved out of the living rock and where people live to this day.

They're known as troglodytes, a Greek word for cave dweller because they live in holes, clefts, and labyrinths. The structures look like huge, overgrown toadstools and they're spread out all over the strange landscape.

Other than one insane stunt at what seemed to be a million feet in the air when our crazy Turkish pilot climbed out of his center space to pose with the equally crazy Germans — and while doing so frightfully tipped and shook our frail gondola causing the rest of us to shriek in terror — I guess it was a normal flight.

After about an hour and a half, and to my immense relief, we gently touched down on a barren plateau. Murat had stayed awake the whole trip and somehow kept the balloon steadily in place until a support crew of five arrived and helped us climb out.

We were served 'survival' glasses of champagne while our faithful pilot signed and handed each one of us an official Flight Certificate, one of which now adorns my office wall. It may have been only 7:30 in the morning but I gulped my champagne in one swallow and cried tears of joy. I had cheated death another day.

Soon I was back at the hotel awaiting breakfast, and getting ready for another full day of sightseeing. Unfortunately I already felt exhausted.

Our first stop was the underground city of Derinkuyu, which means Deep Well in Turkish. The city has eight underground levels, reaching a depth of 180 feet! Amazingly it's just one of many underground cities in Cappadocia.

Many of these cities were used at various times by Christians escaping from invading Arabs and Turkic hordes. Erich von Danniken, author of *The Chariots of Heaven*, believed they were constructed by extraterrestrial beings!

In fact, we now know the tunnels were probably used as early as the Bronze Age. As many as 20,000 people could live and hide in them. And we were about to enter their ancient domain!

Well I'll tell you right now, I don't know which was worse — floating hundreds of feet over this crazy landscape in a homemade hot air balloon or climbing down hundreds of feet underneath its surface via ancient wooden ladders and worn-away stone steps.

Before we entered, I knew something unusual was up when our guide, Ken, warned us very sternly not to wander away from the group or lag behind or, heaven forbid, stray off the approved route which was lighted by (I swear) flickering ten-watt bulbs. Up to this point he hadn't seem fazed or the least bit concerned by what anyone did. Now he was deadly serious!

"It very easy to be losted," he said, "and probably not to be founded for a long time ago!"

We got his drift and entered the narrow entrance tunnel single file. It was very eerie indeed. Miles and miles of tunnels zig zagging and branching off in every direction leading to churches, residential areas, huge store rooms and (watch your step) bottomless cisterns. And all of this dug by hand out of solid rock over centuries.

We went down five floors — around 100 feet — which was as far as they let people go.

"Why can't we go further?," someone asked.

"They not cleared from last earthquakes," Ken replied.

"My God, that's right," I muttered to myself. "Turkey has earthquakes, lots of them!"

At that point everyone thought it would be a dandy idea to head on back to the surface to see if the sun was still working. We were all getting a little claustrophobic. It was very creepy. I could't imagine hiding down there from anyone. I'd be the first one to give myself up!

Next stop was Göreme, where over 30 of the finest churches in Cappadocia are clustered together in the Göreme Open Air Museum. They are all carved out of the rock mountain and date from the 9th and 11th centuries.

We didn't have time to visit all of them but did go to the most famous: the Church of St. Barbara, the Church with the Apple, and the Church with the Snake. The ancient frescoes were magnificent and as bright as any I'd seen.

The next town we visited was Avanos, famous for its pottery thanks to the rich clay found along river banks in the area. We visited a pottery collective and were treated to a well-run tour and had a chance to visit several rooms filled beautiful hand painted bowls and platters.

I would liked to have bought one of the more intricately designed ones but I didn't want to be hampered carrying it with me as baggage. I did buy one smaller ornate plate which was tiny enough to pack. It hangs today on my office wall.

On the way back to the hotel, we stopped several more times to inspect the strange landscape. Üchisar was one such stop, a place famed for its immense fist-shaped tower of volcanic rock, honeycombed with chambers. This citadel, the highest point in Cappadocia, offered a spectacular view of a typical Anatolian village below and a wide expanse of the otherworldly rock formations in the Göreme Valley.

It was here that Steven Spielberg filmed scenes from the first *Star Wars*; the episode that featured the mysterious sand people.

We arrived back at Hotel Surban in time to clean up and relax before dinner. Most of the group had elected to go to a nearby town and partake in a typical Turkish nightclub experience with belly dancers and all you could drink for one small price. The bus was scheduled to leave at 6:00 p.m.

I wisely passed the event thinking the pace these people were keeping was insane. Instead I decided to walk back to town and have a nice, quiet dinner by myself. I'd been up for 15 hours by this time and was fading fast.

After the group left I climbed up to the roof terrace with a glass of chilled wine to relax and catch up on my log. I sat and pondered if my wife, Lois, would have enjoyed this trip and decided she probably wouldn't have. The noise, the hectic pace, the dust, the long bus rides, and especially the bathroom facilities would have not sat well with her. On the other hand, I think she would have enjoyed the people, food and scenery as much as I.

It seemed to me that Turkey was economically in pretty good shape. At least tourism seems to be well-developed here. Everything seemed very organized and made easy for the semi-adventurous traveller. My decision to use Fez Travel was definitely a good one. Their schedule may have been a bit frenzied at times, but it was definitely worth the money, especially for the first-time visitor to the country.

It was hard to believe the trip was almost over. Tomorrow we had a long hike to look forward to, and then the night sleeper on a train back to Istanbul. I was looking forward to heading home, and concerned about the international situation.

It was a lovely, soft evening and I had the entire roof-top terrace with all its rose-filled flower pots to myself. Ürgüp was spread out below me, beautifully tinted in a red-golden glow as the sun slowly set. The only sounds were a bell-laden ox pulling a heavy cart of straw down the cobblestone street and, off in the distance, bleating goats, most likely hungry for dinner. As was I.

The bell clerk exchanged $100 into lira. The exchange rate seemed to be getting better and better — I received 1.48 million lira to the dollar compared to only 1.35 million the day I arrived. He recommended a restaurant and I headed off.

The restaurant was wonderful, although almost empty when I arrived at the awkwardly early hour of 7:30 p.m. I ordered lentil soup and hard rolls, a of glass of wine, rice and lamb kebabs, hot tea and a serving of baklava. A marvelous dinner for less than $7.00.

Restaurants in this part of the world all seemed to have several things in common. First, as I mentioned earlier, all the waiters were male. I rarely saw a female anywhere except for brief glimpses into the kitchen where they were cooking or washing dishes.

Almost every restaurant I visited had marble floors and a fountain somewhere near the dining area. The lights always cast an attractive amber glow and the walls were stone and featured carved reliefs. You could be served terrible food, but in surroundings like that, you didn't notice. I relaxed and lingered over my meal.

Afterwards I strolled around town, and eventually entered one of the antique shops I'd seen earlier. The owner spoke excellent English and I ended up buying myself an old Ottoman silver ring, and a silver necklace and amulet for my granddaughter Taylor.

He had several old Turkish stringed instruments hanging in the shop, and when I admired one, he took it down and proceeded to play a song so lovely and sad we both almost cried.

He showed me a tray of Russian army medals he'd acquired in the nearby Black Sea area. Russian peasants — old war veterans, desperate for money — had sold them. I was sorely tempted, but didn't buy any.

Pleased with my purchases, I started back toward the hotel and found a little pastry shop open. I stopped for some hot tea and dish of their delicious rice pudding. Later I flagged down a cab — too tired to negotiate the hill.

SEPTEMBER 21

The buzz around the breakfast buffet was all about the previous evening. It seemed the "traditional" Turkish entertainment turned out to be a ripoff. "Absolutely desperate," was the universal feeling of my Aussie and Kiwi friends. They said the food was mediocre and the belly dancer had more disco moves than *Saturday Night Fever*.

However, there was plenty to drink and they enjoyed that part a great deal. Have I mentioned how much these people enjoyed their beer? From the looks of the lot of them, they'd taken full advantage of the evening's "All You Can Drink" feature.

Not only that, it appeared that Ken, our intrepid Turkish guide, was now sick. He looked terrible! "Like death warmed over," as my mother used to say.

"Something I ate," was his feeble excuse. Hmm, where had I heard that before?

We piled in the bus and headed towards Ankara with the promise of a challenging hike along the way. By mid-morning we reached Ihlara Vadisi, a six-mile-long, 262-foot-wide gorge which runs along the Melendiz River.

It was a surprise when we arrived! We'd been driving through a flat, barren landscape and suddenly, without any fanfare, a deep gorge appeared out of nowhere. We parked the bus and those who were so inclined began to descend a very steep stone stairway down into the canyon. We were told to return within a couple of hours. Ken and several others elected to stay behind (I suspect to sleep off their "evening" off in the bus.)

The gorge was famous for a grouping of 11th century churches built in caves along its rock face. I enjoyed reading their names as I hiked along: the Church Under the Tree, the Church of the Serpents, the Church with the Crooked Stone, and my personal favorite — the Odorous Church, a bad translation which should have read the Fragrant Church.

When we reached the floor of the gorge we hiked a couple of miles before we came upon a family of local wood gatherers resting in a shady grove.

Dressed in colorful peasant garb, the adults refused to have their pictures taken, but the kids were delighted. One small boy even insisted I climb upon his donkey to have my *own* picture taken.

It was a fun break from a long bus ride, but all too soon we were loaded up again and heading toward Ankara via "the most dangerous highway in the world," according to my guide book.

Ankara was chosen to be the capital of Turkey by Atatük in 1923 because of its central location in the country, and also because it had absolutely no association with the hated Ottoman Empire. It was a flourishing trade center in Roman times, and was supposedly the place where King Midas was born.

These days, it's a major political and business center, but not the tourist destination you'd suspect. Still, it's a place you can go out and eat in style, visit a private club, or tour elegant art galleries and antique shops, definitely a modern city. However for us, it was a place to kill four hours before our train left for Istanbul.

Our driver dropped us off at the entrance of a shopping mall with instructions to be waiting by the entrance in four hours. Then Ken disappeared!

Why he ever thought we'd be interested in walking around what turned out to be a very boring and very small (by our standards) shopping mall for four hours was beyond any of us. But it was too late. He'd vanished.

Leaving the group to sit and grumble, I walked down the main street for few blocks, found a busy outdoor cafe and ordered a beer. It was a fascinating experience to sit and observe the highly-westernized Turks gather after work. After several days of traveling "off road", the contrast was startling.

Both men and women were dressed very stylishly. It was like sitting at an outdoor cafe in any large U.S. or European city. Everyone was sipping wine, chatting up a storm and constantly using cell phones. I could have been in Chicago or New York except for the teenage street merchant who came by selling stuffed clams. I flagged him over and bought a plateful. Wonderful!

Later I was surprised to spot a Kentucky Fried Chicken! I went in and ordered chicken strips! I couldn't help myself. They tasted soooo good! I only hoped they paired well with stuffed clams.

On the way back to the mall I passed a large Best Western Hotel, and stopped to use the restroom. Not so fast. I had to negotiate a barbed wire security gate and get past a pair of suspicious armed guards. I don't know if it had anything to do with the recent terrorist attack, or if it was just normal precautions in that part of the world.

Everyone was bored silly by the time the bus finally pulled up, and we were taken to the central train station. Along the way we drove by the tomb of the great Atatürk himself. It was absolutely huge — three stories high and covering an entire block. We all wished we'd have been dropped off there instead of the mall.

The train station was immense. All marble, it reminded me of New York's Grand Central Station in its heyday. At 9:00 p.m. we boarded and were led to a set of sleeper coaches.

My private compartment was plushly elegant, with a large comfortable couch, which was later turned down into a bed, a sink and dresser, and a toilet and shower next door. On the elegance scale, I'd guess it was somewhere between Amtrak First Class and the Orient Express.

I was thrilled, and had soon stored my bag and walked to the dining car to join some of our group in sharing a bottle of wine and a tray of cheese and crackers.

By the time I returned to my private compartment, we had left Ankara and were well on our way to Istanbul. My bed had been turned down. I climbed in and spent some time catching up on my log but was soon nodding off to the gently swaying train and clickety-clack rhythm of the rails. Gosh, I just loved traveling by train. And this train was a beauty!

A good night's sleep. Next stop, Istanbul.

PART FOUR

During which time I return to my beloved Istanbul to revisit favorite haunts and prepare myself mentally and physically for the long voyage home!

SEPTEMBER 22 - The Fall Solstice

A train attendant knocked on my door at 7:00 a.m. to alert me that we would arrive in Istanbul in one hour. Already packed, I went to find a cup of tea. I really didn't want to leave the train, it had been a fun experience.

We pulled into the station, got on a bus and were transported to the Sultan Hotel where we gathered on the rooftop for a farewell breakfast.

"Order what you want," said Ken, our guide, "It's on us."

I sat with Dee and Ron, who were by this time my solid Australian friends. Dee ordered the featured Sultan's Breakfast, stating if she had to face one more olive or hunk of cheese she would absolutely scream.

Of course, when her breakfast arrived — we all howled! It was a monstrous platter of (you guessed it) green and black olives, sliced tomatoes and cucumbers, and two very large hunks of feta and Gouda cheese! The look on her face was priceless! It was one of the funniest moments of the entire trip.

After breakfast we said our goodbyes after making outrageous promises to get together again, and I left. I walked the few blocks to the Hali Hotel and checked in. It turned out to be a great choice. My room was spacious, super clean, had a color TV with BCC, a marble shower and two beds ... plus it overlooked the Blue Mosque and Sea of Mamara! What a wonderful location and at only $35, a great bargain.

I took a short nap and got up feeling like a million lira, maybe even bucks. The weather was clear and the temperature a perfect 76°. I went out and ordered a beer and pizza.

While eating, Susan happened to stop by. She wanted to tell me the group was planning a farewell luncheon tomorrow at the Doy-Doy restaurant, the place where we had all eaten the first day. I told her I might join them, but if the weather was nice I planned to retake the Bosphorus Cruise trip.

More gifts needed to be purchased, so I walked to the Grand Bazaar to shop. I was used to the way things worked now and wasn't as intimidated as I was during my first visit, when I'd only been in the country for a short time. Now I figured I was a seasoned veteran and was able to turn a deaf ear to their cries ...

"Hello, dear sir, may I ask you a question please?"
"Pardon me, kind man, may I show you this?"
"Excuse me, sir, I see you are from Chicago!"
"Oh sir, have you ever seen anything like this before,
I trust not."

The Bazaar was still overwhelming and I found myself walking through at a brisk pace. I knew if I stopped, I'd be instantly surrounded. Finally, I found an interesting shop and entered. The proprietor was a nice, soft-spoken man who spoke excellent English.

I ended up buying four Fez hats; one each for me and my three sons, and four purses for my wife and daughters-in-law. The purses were handmade from leather and parts of nomad carpets that were very old. It was a complicated transaction involving a combination of Turkish Lira and American Dollars and ended successfully with a flourish and a cup of tea.

The owner almost "cried at the price" he had to let them go for. It was great theatre. He didn't fool me in the least, but the deal was done before I gave it a lot of thought and in the end, we were both satisfied.

I'd heard carry-on luggage would not be permitted on the plane, so I was being careful that everything could be checked. As it turned out, this was not true, but I didn't know it at the time. As a matter of fact, I wasn't even sure my flight was leaving. I had been trying to reach KLM for several days, with no success.

On the way back to my hotel I passed by the Hotel Pierre Loti, where I'd stayed upon arriving in Turkey, and stopped to remind them of the free transfer to the airport. They seemed very foggy about their earlier commitment, leaving me a little nervous. I decided I'd better stop by the next night just to be sure.

SEPTEMBER 23

My last full day in Turkey! I went to the rooftop terrace for breakfast and was treated to a stunning view of Istanbul; a panoramic 360° of the city under a deep blue sky. Wow!

Breakfast was as you might expect, but with an exciting twist: a basket of delicious sweet rolls. Back I went for seconds, then thirds. Marvelous.

KLM airlines was still not answering the phone. This really started to worry me. Since my room has its own TV, I'd been able to follow the bleak BBC news quite closely, and felt it was about time to get out of the country while I still could. But I couldn't tell if the airline was running or not! Many weren't.

The weather was ideal so I decided to take the wonderful ferry ride up to the Black Sea again. Before leaving for the docks, I stopped one more time at Hotel Pierre Loti to reaffirm my free taxi delivery in the morning. The assistant manager nodded his head, but still seemed a bit vague. I saw danger signs on the horizon.

The docks at Eminönü were packed with hundreds of fishermen. I watched for awhile but all I saw them catch were the same tiny fish. I think they must sell them to small markets in the area.

It was Sunday and the dock leading to my ferry was packed with visitors. As usual there was a huge rush for the best seats. But as this was my second go round, I knew the best route to the top deck and arrived in time to reserve a prime spot by the railing.

I enjoyed the trip as much as I did the first time, maybe more so, because the weather was gorgeous. When we reached the end of the line I got off and walked through the town, stopping at a small cafe for a cup of tea.

Later I was lured to a local seafood restaurant and ordered a mixed platter. Out of the kitchen came a fresh vegetable salad, a platter of fried mackerel, calamari and clams, a basket of hard rolls and a beer. Halfway through my meal I began wondering if this was the smartest thing to eat on my last day — all fried seafood. It'd be disastrous if I picked up something and got sick at this stage of the trip. I looked around and was relieved to see mainly local families eating there so I figured I'd be okay. And I was.

The ferry took me back to Istanbul which, at that time of day, was bathed in a golden glow. Rather than rush back to the hotel, I walked from the docks to one of the old mosques and watched people purify themselves from the sacred fountains. I sat and pondered their Allah and my God, and that was as close to Mass as I ever got. I'd yet to see any churches other than mosques anywhere in the country. I'm sure there were some around, but they must have been scattered far and wide.

To be safe I stopped by one last time at Hotel Pierre Loti — a good thing I did. The staff had decided they would *not* provide a free hotel transfer after all! What? I hit the roof! I got very angry. After a long, loud argument right in the lobby (with people staring), the manager was summoned on the phone and eventually agreed to honor his promise. The clerk was surprised that I, infidel millionaire American that I was, would raise so much fuss for a free cab ride, and he ended up all smiles and handshakes.

Back in my room I laid everything out and repacked one final time so I could speed off the morning without a struggle. One last trip out to send a last minute email message home and I treated myself to a final apple tea and rice pudding.

I set the alarm for 2:30 a.m. and went to bed to watch more bleak BBC. I was concerned I'd either oversleep or there'd be no cab waiting for me in the morning ... or both. My flight, assuming it was still leaving, wasn't until 6:30 a.m., but I was told to be there at least three hours ahead of time because of all the extra security. Better early than sorry.

SEPTEMBER 24

I woke at 1:30 a.m. and couldn't get back to sleep. With only one hour before my alarm went off, I stayed in bed and worried about the cab, and then I worried about the airline, but at least I hadn't overslept.

When the alarm finally did go off I quickly got up and showered. Since I'd already packed and checked out the night before, I left as quietly as I could and walked around to the Hotel Pierre Loti.

Saints preserve us, they were waiting for me, all smiles. In fact, the clerk insisted on carrying my bag to the cab, which was parked just up the block. The driver was sound asleep in the back.

I got in and woke him up; he wasn't happy and drove like a madman, making the 30-minute trip in 15 minutes. Obviously he wanted to get back home and go to bed. Other than a white knuckle ride through mainly deserted streets, the only odd thing I noticed was a bunch of teenagers playing basketball in a park along the way. At 3:15 in the morning?

We pulled up to the departure gates in plenty of time. I got out and froze. They were passing all bags through X-ray machines before even letting them enter the airport. I figured I was in for trouble. After all, I had cameras, an electronic door alarm, a GPS and other devices packed away, all of which had an abundance of wires and batteries. Surely this is where I will be detained.

Wrong again! No problem at all, I passed right through. Either they didn't notice all the electronic gear, or they just didn't care, but they waved me through with a smile.

I immediately checked to find out if my flight was scheduled and on time. It was. What a relief!

I had a half hour to kill before I could check in so I spent the rest of my lira on coffee and sweet rolls. The airport was tomb quiet and much larger than I remembered when I'd arrived earlier in the month.

When I finally did get to check-in, I noticed many people had carry on luggage. Hey, what's going on here. I was told this would not be allowed. Not fair! That also bothered me and started a cycle of worry that the airport personnel were much more lax in their security than they should be. Why, those passengers could be carrying anything in those bags.

I went to the departure lounge and sat, fighting to stay awake until I at least boarded the plane. I figured I'd be able to sleep on the way to Amsterdam, and that would be something.

Less than two weeks had passed since the horror of the World Trade Center and here I was sitting in Atatürk Airport, Istanbul, Turkey.

The difference in my attitude had drastically changed. A month earlier I was excited and full of grand expectations. Now, I sat in fear studying the diverse bunch surrounding me. My imagination, stimulated by too many Turkish coffees, was running wild.

As I looked around it became obvious I was the *only* non-bomb carrying terrorist in the room. I stared at a young man sitting across from me. He had dread-locks, baggy soiled pants and worn-out sandals. They were like signals flashing: "Warning! Warning!" But wait — stop and think a moment, I'd seen others just like him in Minneapolis the day I left. Still ...

And what about the three bearded men seated quietly off by themselves in the corner? They looked *exactly* like the photos of the terrorists that were being flashed almost daily on BBC! Too obvious perhaps? ...

Then there were a pair of Muslim women, draped head to toe in black, with only their eyes and noses showing. Or at least I *thought* they were women. They were dressed like women! But for all I knew they could be men, and they had enough room under those bulky burkas to conceal an arsenal of weapons. Of course, how clever ...

Or how about the Australian couple seated besides me? Nah, too elderly. The woman could barely walk to her seat and she seemed so friendly — perhaps too friendly?...

Then I thought, hey, what about me?

Could their furtive glances at me mean they thought *I* could be a terrorist? And why not? Talk about clever. A trained international counter-spy-terrorist, resourceful, very James Bond-looking, speaks passable English, dresses sort of like an American, but with *no* carry on luggage? Of course!

STOP IT! I was getting ridiculous. Just relax. At least *try* to relax.

By the time our flight was finally called, I was a nervous wreck. The mood in the waiting room had been quite somber, with no one talking or smiling. No eye contact was being made.

One by one we were called up to another set of security guards. And the questions began:

"Passport please."

"Where did you go while you were in Turkey?"

"Why did you come to Turkey in the first place?"

"When was this photo taken of you?"

"Why do you have no carry on luggage?"

I stumbled my way through the wretched questions and was finally allowed to board the plane. My seat was next to a Muslim man, one of the three who had been sitting off to the side whispering to themselves: full beard, dark complexion, sinister-looking. Where were the others, I wondered? Scattered strategically throughout the plane, I assumed. We didn't say a word to each other but sat quietly and waited for the flight to leave.

The worst moment was when our plane finally lifted off and banked away from Istanbul, headed north over the Black Sea. This is where it would happen, I agonized. The plane would explode in full sight of millions of Europeans and Asians, a statement of some kind. Turkey was, after all, on the brink of letting America reoccupy its abandoned air bases in the country. What a meaningful way to warn them. I closed my eyes, sat back and whispered to Saint Christopher.

Of course, nothing happened. We landed in Amsterdam quite routinely and on time. Was it my imagination or did *everyone* on the plane breathe a collective sigh of relief?

I wasn't quite home yet, but I was getting closer, step-by-step. Minneapolis next. Cedar Rapids after that. I started feeling a bit more relaxed.

But I sadly realized international travel would never be the same again.

WHAT'S A NUBIRABYDAEWOO?

THE MARITIMES

Sunday, September 15

The plane shakily dropped down through a dense mattress of clouds — the seat belt sign overhead blinked wildly and with good reason. Slowly, bumpily, we descended, down and down. Finally we broke out of dense clouds and slipped into a rainy afternoon sky somewhere over northern Maine.

I peered out the window. All I could see for miles were the tops of dense green pines, broken periodically by the grey sheen of boggy ponds and the flash of small upland lakes. Occasionally a gravel road criss-crossed below us.

It was 2:30 p.m. and according to Captain Nelson and his good buddy, Assistant Captain Watkins, the Bangor airport was less than 50 miles straight ahead. It looked like we'd arrive right on time.

I quickly grabbed my bag and beat the crowd to the National Rental window to pick up my car.

"Good afternoon, Mr. Buckley," said the perky young clerk. "Welcome to Maine. Sign here please and you're all set to go."

"Great! What kind of car do I have?" I asked, scribbling my name hurriedly on the rental form.

"Hmm, let me take a look here," she said, checking her records, "... ah, here we are ... a nubirabydaewoo!"

"Excuse me?" I said.

"A nubirabydaewoo," she repeated.

"I'm sorry," I said. "I'm afraid I don't understand you. I was wondering what kind of *car* I'll be driving."

"A-N-U-B-I-R-A-B-Y-D-A-E-W-O-O," she repeated slowly and loudly while looking closely at me, possibly checking for a dangling hearing aid. People lined up behind me were growing impatient with the delay. I decided to give up.

"Thank you," I said, taking the keys and heading to the parking lot. What language was she speaking? French maybe? I knew they spoke French in Quebec, which wasn't that far away.

I found space 39 and aha! Mystery solved. A Nubira by Daewoo. That's what she'd been saying. I was stunned. I'd never heard of a Nubira, let alone a Daewoo.

It was about as ugly as a car can get. A dull gold, two-door compact with a very small, un-powerful engine and teensy-weensy little foot pedals. I almost went back to find out how much more a different model might cost, but I was anxious to get going. I had to find a place to set up my tent before dark.

The Canadian border is less than 100 miles north of Bangor. Crawling along in my underpowered little Nubira by Daewoo, I arrived there around 5 p.m.

St. Stephens, New Brunswick, is the entry point into Canada and the western part of the Maritime Provinces. The Maritimes were a place I'd always wanted to visit and had finally decided to do it.

I coasted up to the international entry window.

"Who are you visiting in New Brunswick?" asked the officer.

"Well - uh - actually, I don't know anyone," I said.

"Well, you soon will," she replied stamping my passport and waving me through. Hmm. That was it? Apparently so. I was in Canada.

My destination for the night was Island View Campgrounds, an additional 20-mile-drive on the way to the Bay of Fundy.

My ingenious plan was to camp out *every other* night alternating with stays in B&Bs and small hotels. Unfortunately this particular night probably wasn't the best to begin camping. It wasn't raining yet ... but seriously threatening.

I found the campgrounds easily enough but the office was closed. GONE FOR AWHILE read a handwritten note posted on the door. I peered in. It looked to me like they may have been gone for a good while already. A stack of do-it-yourself payment envelopes were in a box on the outside wall. I took one, inserted the required $12, and slipped it under the door as instructed.

I drove into the campgrounds, which sloped down a narrow gravel road toward the St. Croix River. Other than a couple of empty trailers parked nearby, no one else seemed to be around. The place looked pretty deserted although it wasn't supposed to close until the end of October. Odd ...

I was looking for the tent camping area, not to be confused with the RV area, which featured running water, electrical hookups and level ground. That was for the softies, the wimps, the people who cherished a good night's sleep. I would be housed in a small tent — my back-to-nature survival unit.

It seemed like I drove around in circles forever until I finally found a small tenting site, barren of grass and severely sloped — and with very few trees scattered around to slow down any rain when it came.

I figured what the heck, it was only for one night so I pitched my tent on the flattest patch I could find. I then got back in the car and headed back to the office to ask a few questions.

It was still closed.

By this time it was beginning to get dark so I decided to drive on into St. Andrews and have dinner. There was no sense staying in the campgrounds since there wasn't a soul around to talk with anyway.

The Harbor Front Inn was in the middle of town and looked like a solid choice. Cozy and warm, with lots of old black and white photographs of early schooners and fishing boats being chased by swarms of gulls. Brass ship fixtures caught the light of dozens of old-fashioned amber lamps. I was led to a table on the second floor overlooking the wharf, where I ordered a glass of wine and studied the menu.

The evening special was a platter of fresh scallops served with vegetables, a salad and huge bread bar where you could slice off as many different types of home-baked bread as you wanted. Followed by another glass of wine; I was feeling pretty mellow by the time I left. Outside it had started to mist. I hated to leave the cozy restaurant, but knew I couldn't stay in that delicious warmth forever so reluctantly headed out into the darkness.

The meal, drinks and gratuity cost $31 Canadian, the equivalent of around $20 U.S. at the time. A bit pricey, I thought, but after all, think of what I was saving by not splurging on a comfortable, dry, warm hotel room? With a TV and bathroom. And a bed.

Monday, September 16

The thing I hate most of all is striking camp in the rain. I'd had a very shaky night's sleep to begin with — tossing and turning all night and it was still raining steadily when I awoke at 6:30. Unfortunately I discovered the tent had developed a leak since the last time I'd used it.

The temperature had been comfortable the night before, but now I felt chilly, clammy, and wet. I stayed in my sleeping bag for another hour and tried to fall back asleep, but nothing doing. It was time to get up. A nice hot shower. That's what I needed.

During the night I'd managed to keep almost everything dry — clothing, and sleeping bag, most importantly. The last thing I needed was to get them wet, so I rolled everything up in a pile and tossed it on the back seat. I left the wet tent, air mattress and rain fly unfolded and just shoved them in the trunk. I'd have to dry them out later.

Island View Campgrounds featured pay showers. Twenty-five cents Canadian for five minutes. Luckily I had plenty of Canadian quarters with me. I stripped down inside the chilly building, deposited four quarters and turned on the shower. Then I jumped back and waited for the hot water to begin. And waited. Then I waited for *any* water to begin. And waited. Finally I got dressed and stormed up to the office.

The GONE FOR AWHILE sign was still in the window. Poking under the door I could just reach the corner of my payment envelope and worked it back out and returned the $12 to my wallet.

"The heck with you," I shouted at the locked door. I shivered my way back into the car and headed to town. I couldn't get the heater in my Nubira by Daewoo to work.

Geesh! What a way to begin a trip.

St. Andrews or St. Andrews-by-the-Sea, is one of the oldest towns in the province. The original inhabitants were the Passamaquoddies, a native American tribe, a few of which still live in the area. European settlement first began in 1783, years after the American Revolution. Prosperity came slowly — first with shipbuilding and later with tourism, which is now the town's stock in trade.

A pity it was still drizzling; I would have liked to poke around a little. Instead I headed, shivering, to the center of town and the historic Chef's Cafe – Est. 1831, for lots of hot coffee, bacon and english muffins slathered with peanut butter. A pleasant young man was working the counter and we had a nice chat. I asked him if he knew of any internet cafes in the area where I could check my email. He directed me to the local community college where he assured me I could use the computers for free, an excellent recommendation of which I took full advantage.

I left town around 10:00 a.m. and headed north on Highway 1. In an hour I'd reached Saint John (not to be confused with St. John's, New Foundland). It was a rainy, wet drive complicated by the fact the windshield wipers seemed to have a mind of their own, occasionally slipping out of sync and threatening to hit and bend each other into an unusable shape.

The floor heater was still not working properly, but the front heat vent on the passenger side seemed okay if you turned the deflectors just right ...

Saint John was a very interesting stop. It's known as the Loyalist City because of the thousands of late 18th-century refugees who scurried there from the northeastern colonies in order to escape serving in the Revolutionary War. Quitters.

To me, Saint John was famous because it is home to Moosehead Beer, not to mention the Reversing Falls. Moosehead Beer I knew about, but the Reversing Falls were still a mystery.

I soon learned that when the tides are right, the water rushing down Saint John River into the Bay of Fundy gives the impression of reversing itself, as the salt water tide rushes back up the river, causing the water level to rise up very quickly and steeply.

The tides were just reversing when I arrived at the bridge over the falls. I stood and watched the obvious power of the water as it crashed down the steep, narrow gorge toward the ocean only to come rushing back and rising violently.

By this time it was getting close to midday and I was getting hungry, so I hopped back in my less-than-trusty Nubira by Daewoo and headed toward the city center. My destination was the Old City Market.

What a wonderful place it was; all indoors, which was great since it was still raining. I stopped for a bowl of Famous Dave's Chili, a homemade roll and a glass of milk. Comfort food for a dismal day.

162

Afterwards I visited the old courthouse with its three-story spiraling stone staircase, and the Loyalist Burial Ground. If the weather had been more pleasant I would have taken a short detour driving the Fundy Trail Parkway, but decided I would have plenty of time to soak in the shoreline later in the week and kept moving. Saint John was a very nice stop, but a major disappointment was that Moosehead Brewery had closed for the tourist season. Bummer.

By 2:30 p.m. I was northbound once again, cruising along Canada's nifty TransCanada Highway 2, a very pleasant four lane straightaway to the Northumberland Shore!

I soon arrived at Shediac, New Brunswick — Lobster Capital of the World! I was now around 250 miles north of Bangor and standing on the shores of the Northumberland Strait. (A faint memory from Sister Victorine's 8th Grade history class was stirring in my mind that Shediac was a special place, but I couldn't recall what for.) Entering town I was treated to a sight of the world's largest lobster: a monstrous statue some 35' x 15' long, perched on a large rock. It's hard to miss. (Was this the history thingy Sister Victorine was harping about?)

I found the immense Hotel Shediac on the strip, recommended in my *Lonely Planet Guide To The Maritimes*. According to the guide: "This old-fashioned hotel dates from 1853. It's convenient and central, if somewhat overpriced. The locals meet for coffee at the hotel cafe every morning."

Perfect, I thought, a chance to rub elbows with real live Shediacians. I don't care if it's pricey or not. After all, this was my night to sleep indoors. Might as well do it right.

I parked my Nubira by Daewoo, grabbed my bag, and rushed up the wooden steps onto a spacious porch. Entering through a set of huge front doors, I startled a group of businessmen standing in the middle of the lobby. They froze and stared at me as I shook the rain off my jacket and headed for the front desk.

"Can we help you?" said one of the men.

"I need a room for tonight," I replied.

"But ... the hotel's closed. It's up for sale. Has been since June. Now if you'd be interested in buying," he quipped, "you're in the nick of time."

What? I looked around. If you didn't count a worn rug in the middle of the lobby, one card table and three metal chairs in the dining room, it was obviously barren. It turned out the group of men were real estate agents and potential investors who just happened to be there when I arrived, thus the reason the door was open.

Undaunted, I scurried back to my wretched Nubira by Daewoo and continued up the highway. I soon passed a likely-looking place — Seely's Motel. I inquired about lodging. They promised a comfortable room at an excellent price since the season was almost over. I took it. I didn't care as long as they had running water, preferably hot. I was still damp and cold and desperately needed a hot shower. Room and tax cost $49 Canadian, or around $30 U.S. including tax.

I settled in and took a wonderful, long shower before heading out for a lobster dinner. It was time to see what these Shediacian cooks were made of.

Before I go any further, I wonder if you realize there are literally dozens of websites devoted to teaching a person the correct, traditional, New England way to eat lobster? Well, there are, and they all offer a new perspective on the necessity of the lobster bib.

Knowing I would be indulging in several lobster dinners, I had carefully studied these sites before I left home. All were pretty consistent on the procedures to follow and I memorized the critical steps. This Midwesterner wasn't going to show up looking like a rube, no way. At least that was the plan.

My quest for the perfect meal had begun back at the statue of the giant lobster. I'd wanted to take a few pictures before it got too dark and noticed a small "carry out" shop nearby selling live lobsters. I stopped and chatted with the owners and asked where one might go to expect a good lobster meal.

Auberge Gabrielle was the consensus favorite.

Shediac was a small community, and Auberge Gabrielle was easy to find. "Look for the former church, built in 1840 and hauled to

164

town from some distant village over icy rivers pulled by the strength of men and horses," directed my guidebook.

And there it was, a small building on the water's edge. Its weathered dark brown clapboard walls with diamond-patterned muntined windows reflecting a golden glow.

Scattered around inside were seven small wooden tables and a wood-burning fireplace, its flames reflected in the water of a natural stone lobster tank. Fishing nets, harpoons, and old lobster pots adorned the walls.

I know what you're thinking. You're assuming the dinner turned out to be a disaster. Well, you're dead wrong. It was wonderful, it was memorable, it was, how shall I say in the parlance of the locals ... *trés bien*. And I'm quite confident I took the staff's (a cook and a waitress) collective breath away with my unabashed attack on the meal.

The waitress did not speak much English. I think I may have compounded the problem as I thought she was speaking German, which did not go down well. Turned out she was from Quebec and spoke a mixture of French and Acadian dialects. So I did what all tourists did. I spoke louder.

Fortified by a half bottle of local wine, I following her over to the tank and selected a 3/4 kilo lobster, mainly because of its smile. Three quarters of a kilo made it a little over 1 1/2 lbs — a good size, I'd been advised.

A tangy salad and basket of homemade breads and I was ready. First came some cooked vegetables, a bowl of melted butter and a large, cloth bib. Eventually the cooked crustacean appeared, steaming, on an oak plank covered with seaweed and other ocean debris. Head, feelers, claws and little beady eyes intact; one, in fact, seemed to make direct eye contact with me. Did it just twitch or was that my imagination? Perhaps another sip of wine, first. *Bon appétit!*

No pinchers. No pliers. No cutters. No book of instructions. I grabbed and started tearing and twisting and turning and it all came apart just like the internet had said it would. Thirty minutes later this marvelous beast was reduced to a scrap heap of shell and spare parts, several of which ended up on the floor. I polished the meal off with a healthy slice of Acadian chocolate gateaú and a cup of STRONG coffee and was ready to call it a night.

Okay — so the meal cost more than the room, so what? It was truly a meal to remember, and after all, I was in the lobster capital of the world! Sister Victorine would be proud. I left believing Auberge Gabrielle was what she had told us to remember.

Tuesday, September 17

I had planned on checking my email this morning, but the town's library was closed. Bummer. After a quick breakfast, I was on my way to PEI, as it's known to the locals, or Prince Edward Island, as it's called by the unwashed masses.

After a straightforward 100-mile drive east I arrived at the controversial Confederation Bridge, the only land route leading on or off the island. Built in 1997, the $900 million monster is supposedly the longest bridge in the world, at a little over eight miles.

The bridge connects Cape Jourimain, New Brunswick, to Borden-Carlton, PEI, where I visited the Tourist Centre and was able to use their computer to check my email.

This was a night for camping. I'd selected a place on the north side of the island called Marco Polo Campground, which I thought seemed a little odd. Marco Polo? Wasn't he the guy who got lost in China or something? (Where was Sister Victorine when you needed her?)

Later I learned Marco Polo was the name of a sailing ship that went aground on the coastline many years past. I knew that.

As I arrived on the island, almost on cue the sun came out and elevated me to high spirits and jump-started my appetite.

I'd picked an excellent time to visit. The tourist season on PEI is relatively short. Many of the island's facilities shut down after August and stay closed through mid-June. So early in September, the prices drop, the atmosphere is serene and Indian summer is in the air.

I steered my Nubira by DaeWoo, which I must admit, I was becoming slightly attached to despite all its shortcomings, north again and looked for lunch. I soon found the ideal spot; a little seafood restaurant surrounded on three sides by a wide porch and overlooking Summerside's colorful harbor.

I opted to eat outside and ordered a Moosehead beer and a pound of steamed clams served with a bowl of butter and basket of crusty french bread. Excellent! The ambience alone was worth the $6.50 price.

I'd left the rain far behind me by this time, and feeling much better about things I soon neared the town of Cavendish and the Gulf of St. Lawrence.

My guidebook was right. Things were pretty quiet after the 1st of September. I found the Marco Polo campgrounds right on the edge of town and had my pick of grassy sites with wonderful views of the Gulf of St Lawrence off in the near distance. I liked the place right away.

I set up the still damp nylon tent and gave the sun and breeze a chance to blow it dry, after which I stuck my sleeping gear inside and went exploring.

Cavendish was the childhood home of Lucy Maud Montgomery, world famous author of *Anne of Green Gables*. The celebrated home, fictionally set in the town of Avonlea, was just down the road. Off I went.

The home was very interesting. During the middle of the tourist season, I was told, the area was a madhouse, but at this time of year things were very laid back and peaceful.

I was able to stroll though the home, gardens and the woodland paths taking as much time as I wanted. It was great. What I found strange about the location was that it was flanked by Green Gables Golf Course. In fact as I was strolling down one of its garden paths I came upon a brand new golf ball sitting right in front of me. Afraid someone not as keen of eye might step on it and risk twisting an ankle, I picked it up — a Titleist Pro VI by the way — and placed it in my pocket out of harm's way.

Running for miles along the edge of town and the north shore of the island is PEI National Park Beach, where I soon went calling with my metal detector. In a short time I found several dollars in local coins!

One of the most popular Canadian coins is called the Toonie. The Toonie is Canada's $2 coin introduced in 1996 and is not to be confused with the 11-sided, gold-colored $1 coin known as the Loonie, named for the swimming loon featured on it.

Although the weather was bright and sunny, just a handful of people were out enjoying the lovely beach. With coins jingling in my pocket I shook myself free of sand and headed back to town, stopping for a frosted mug of Moosehead beer (paid for with found loot) along the way.

After a hot camp shower and a call home to check in, I headed back out for dinner. By this time it was getting dark and the town had rolled up its sidewalks. Those few tourists that were still about were walking around peering in closed shop windows. It was like ... so dead!

I found a small, friendly diner, had a nice dinner and soon headed back to the campgrounds. By the time I got back, it had turned dark and cool — but remained clear. No rain tonight. I started a fire in the pit, sat and wrote some postcards, did a little reading and turned in.

Wednesday, September 18

I tossed and turned most of the night. It had gotten quite cool and windy. Around 2:00 a.m. I got up, pulled on a sweater and went outside to sit on the picnic table and stare at the stars. The campground was like a graveyard.

Behind me, the Gulf of St. Lawrence shimmered in the bright moonlight. The sky was crystal clear and you could see billions of stars lighting up the hilltop where I sat. Every once in a while a shooting star went streaking across the sky. I love shooting stars. Soon I went back inside and fell asleep.

I got up at 7:30 a.m. and went to take a shower, packed things up and slipped quietly away. Soon I was eating breakfast in a local McDonalds.

It turned into another glorious, sunny day as I headed east and south towards Charlottetown. The road was vacant all the way through North Rustico, South Rustico, Oyster Bed Bridge and Brackley Beach, where I hooked up with the Gulfshore East Parkway, which zipped along within a few yards of the Gulf of St. Lawrence.

Passing by Stanhope Beach I spied a lovely old mansion by the side of the road. It appeared to be a guest house of some type so I turned around and went back to investigate.

Dalvay by the Sea was built in 1896 by Alexander MacDonald, a wealthy businessman and one-time president of Standard Oil Company. This mansion he built looked like something out *The Great Gatsby*. Constructed exclusively with local materials — boulders, island sandstone and lumber — it was a wonderful old place, indeed.

I wandered the grounds and eventually worked my way inside. The going guest rate at this time of year was reduced to $250 ... so look was all I did.

In defense of the price, it did include three gourmet meals and turn-of-the-century guest rooms filled with authentic antiques bought on family trips all over the world. It's on Canada's list of historic places and supposedly the most imposing lodging on the island. That I believe. Maybe some day when I'm rich and famous I'll return and stay for a night or two.

Shortly after noon I arrived in Charlottetown, an old, quiet country town that also happens to be the historic provincial capital. Established in 1763, it's named after Charlotte, Queen of Great Britain and Ireland and wife of King George III.

I entered town near Victoria Park, on the banks of Charlottetown Harbour. It was a nice quiet day so I stopped for awhile and metal detected and found another handful of Toonies and Loonies, and a silver lady's ring. I continued to the city library to use their computers and check my email.

For some reason, all the B&Bs I called were either filled or the owners were gone; perhaps off on vacation now that the season was over. I was planning on staying for the night but now wasn't so sure. Parked outside the library was one of those large, red, double-decker London buses and they were about ready to leave on a tour of the city, so I decided to join them and settle on accommodations when I got back.

The tour was an hour — about 45 minutes too long. It basically drove around three or four downtown city blocks while the guide stopped and pointed out nondescript local buildings. I could have done that myself in half the time, on foot. Oh well, it was a nice chance to ride on one of those neat old buses.

By 3:30 p.m. I still hadn't found a place to stay so I decided to continue on to Wood Islands and stay there for the night instead. I could then catch an early morning ferry to Nova Scotia.

It was a quick drive to Wood Islands which is on Northumberland Strait and the southeast tip of the island. I arrived just as the last ferry for the day was about to leave so I decided to just keep going and spend the evening in Nova Scotia, instead.

I drove up the gangplank with only three minutes to spare, paid my $32 and parked the road-weary, feisty little Nubira by Daewoo. I walked up on deck just as the ferry pulled away from the dock. The sun was still brightly shining as we started on the 10-mile trip across Northumberland Strait.

Early evening the ferry pulled into Pictou, Nova Scotia. Pictou is a colorful harbor town where the Highland Scots first landed from Europe in 1773. Today the place crawls with artists and fishermen. I loved the look of it at first sight; and settled in at The Consulate Inn, an old stone building that dated from 1810 and once housed the American Consulate.

The inn was smack in the middle of the tiny business district on Front Street. I was given a single room with a bath across the hall. A large tawny cat was asleep on the bed when I arrived and was unfazed when I came in and spread my stuff around. That was okay. I like cats.

After a quick shower I headed out for dinner. There was a gourmet dining room right downstairs but I wanted to walk around a little first, so I strolled along the waterfront until I came to the Salt Water Café with a reflection of its shiny red paint shimmering over the bay inviting me in.

A little wine and a huge platter of shrimp, scallops, clams, haddock and french fries made me whole again. After such a wonderful dinner, I walked around window shopping and back to my cat-occupied room, where I soon fell into a sound sleep.

Thursday, September 19

The breakfast room in The Consulate Inn was a large glass-enclosed balcony on the rear, facing the harbor. A basket of homemade breads and pitchers of fresh juice and hot coffee were on the table when I entered. Sausage and eggs on the sideboards. My roommate was already there, hanging around waiting for a handout. I took my time eating and working on my log while watching the lobster boats head out to deep water.

After checking out I drove around town. It was dotted with aged mansions in varying states of disrepair. The whole place reminded me of Galena, IL. A hundred years earlier, it must really have been something.

My goal for today was Cape Breton Island — east and north on Trans Canada Highway 105. My gutsy little Nubira by Daewoo was still running well; perhaps feeling a little loosey-goosey here and there, but all in all, a responsible little auto.

To get on Cape Breton Island, you have to cross over a narrow spit of land called Ganso Causeway leading direct to Port Hastings. Once I arrived I turned northwest toward Inverness, where I planned to stop for lunch.

I reached Inverness around noon. It looked sparse; a declining fishing village on the shores of the Gulf of St. Lawrence. I found a small diner where they served a great bowl of sea chowder with a basket of brown bread. Temporarily sated, I drove down to the town's pier to snoop around. It was deserted except for a woman and her young daughter waiting for her fisherman husband to return.

I spied a large wooden crate with something fish-looking sticking up and over the side. I went over to investigate and was shocked to see it was the head of a very large fish.

"Good heavens," I exclaimed to the woman. "What kind of a fish is that from?"

"Tuna" she laughed. "You're not from around here, are you?"

"No, I'm not," I said, amazed at the size of the thing. "How much would that thing have weighed?" I asked.

"Oh, not too much … around 200 pounds," she said. "If you want to see a big one, stick around for a while. My husband should be here soon. He called me on the ship-to-shore and said me they're bringing in a 400 pounder."

She told me they'd sell it to a middle man who'd ice it down whole and take it to Boston to sell to the Japanese. I waited a bit to see what a 400-pounder looked like, but eventually left before he arrived.

We didn't talk money, but I got the impression that his fish would sell for quite a bit. I later learned a fish that size could easily sell for $5,000! No wonder she was in such a good mood.

By mid-afternoon I reached the village of Cheticamp and the entrance to Cape Bretons Highlands National Park. Tonight was my night to camp and I'd chosen Corney Brook Campgrounds, one of several within the park. The reason I picked this one was it was the only one with a sea view and in fact, was right on the edge of a high cliff overlooking the water. The downside was it was a primitive site with no drinking water and no showers. But I didn't care. I really only need a place to sleep for the night.

The entire campsite was vacant so I had my pick of places to pitch a tent. After setting up camp I drove up to hike Skyline Trail, one of the park's most popular trails. Roughly a four-mile loop over relatively easy terrain which leads out to the edge of a highland cliff right over the water. It was a great hike because of the spectacular scenery, but the most interesting thing I saw along the way were large, illustrated signs educating the hiker on how to understand proper moose behavior.

I copied the instructions verbatim:

1. If the head of the moose is down, it is ready to charge. Be prepared to flee to safety.
2. If the head of the moose is up, it may feel threatened and agitated. Refer to number 1.

Huh? Was this a joke? Apparently not.

As fate would have it and much to my disappointment, I never did see a moose. I was curious to see how they held their heads when they were in a good mood. Maybe tilted sideways or something?

When it started to get dark I headed back to the wee town of Cheticamp for dinner. There wasn't much to choose from so I guess I was lucky to find a cozy little restaurant that specialized in pizza, which turned out to be excellent. I thought it only proper to wash it down with a few bottles of Moosehead Beer.

By 8:30 p.m. it was pitch black and getting chilly. I drove back to my camp site, crept into my tent and spent an hour reading by candlelight.

So goes life in the fast lane.

Friday, September 20

Up at dawn. The ridge where I was camping now had four other tents pitched. No one was stirring as I got up and heated some water for coffee. I'd purchased some ginger cookies and a couple of bananas for breakfast. I hoped I had all the food groups covered.

Sitting on the edge of a picnic table and sipping hot coffee I stared out into the grey water and saw something odd. At first I didn't think much of it but when I looked again, whatever it was had moved. This time I stared hard and was surprised to see it was a couple of whales swimming by. They were bottle-nosed whales, very distinctive looking creatures about twenty feet long with large bulbous snouts sticking out of the water.

I wanted to scream and point them out to my camping companions, but since I was the only one up, I just sat back down and watched them swim past the cliff face until they disappeared from sight. Wow, I thought, no mooses or meece, but whales are way cooler anyway.

I packed up as quietly as I could and continued my trip around the park on the famous Cabot Trail. Soon I came to the intersection of another walk — The Bog Trail. I pulled over, parked and spent an hour on its walk through upland bogs.

The final trail I hiked was the Lone Shieling Trail which led through a dense, 300-year-old stand of maple trees to a replica of a crofter's hut — a reminder of the area's first agrarian settlers.

By late morning I had arrived at the other entrance to the park and stopped at one of its modern campgrounds to take a hot shower and shave.

On to Louisbourg National Historical Site. Time was speeding by.

Louisbourg is located on the southeastern tip of Cape Breton Island. After the Treaty of Utrecht in 1713, the French lost their bases in Newfoundland and Nova Scotia. A fort was built and although it looked daunting, was poorly designed. The British took it in 45 days. It changed hands two more times until The Seven Year's War, when the British took it again and burnt it to the ground.

Today the site depicts, in remarkable detail, what life was like there in the 1700s. All the workers, in period dress, have taken on the lives of typical fort inhabitants and they do it very well.

I arrived at the fortress early in the afternoon and entered — after successfully passing inspection of several wary soldiers. Hungry, I headed for Grandchamps Inn, one of several period eateries within the grounds, where I was served a bowl of pea soup, a large hunk of crusty bread and a mug of warm milk.

The fortress is similar in idea and design to Colonial Williamsburg, Virginia, except these people actually live here and perform their jobs in the way they were originally designed to be done — with no modern conveniences at all. Dozens of buildings were open and work was being conducted as it would have been 250 years earlier; tailors, cooks, guards, blacksmiths, and more.

It was all fascinating and I wandered around and took lots of photos. Incidentally, you cannot drive anywhere near the site. Large parking areas are a few miles away and visitors are shuttled over in special buses. A nice way to protect the integrity of the property.

Continuing west I reached Antigonish and started looking for a place to stay indoors. There was a convention being held in the area and I had some trouble finding lodging but finally located a room at the Oasis Inn. Not very scenic (and no camels), but plenty of hot water and color TV.

Antigonish is a college town with a great Italian restaurant, Frescoes Trattoria, a wonderful little place filled with upscale locals, college professors and the occasional tourist such as myself. The linguine with clams was excellent. It seemed no matter where I went in this part of the world, seafood was a major part of every meal, and I was delighted.

Yet somehow, sleeping in the Oasis Inn with a stomach full of seafood didn't seem quite right.

Saturday, September 21

St. Francis Xavier University sits high on a hill overlooking downtown Antigonish. I'd noticed the 150-year old buildings the evening before and thought it might make a good place to metal detect.

St. Ninian's Cathedral sits in the middle of campus, although for the life of me I'd never heard of him — or her? Later I discovered it was a him and he was a 5th Century Bishop and confessor and the first Apostle of Christianity to the Picts in southern Scotland. Of course.

In a half hour I'd found 10 coins; eight pennies, a dime and a dollar; nothing particularly old or rare, but a good way to start the day. Before leaving town I stopped at the Mariner's Inn for juice, coffee and, considering I was in a British realm, an English muffin. I left feeling right with the world.

South of Antigonish, on Highway 7, was Sherbrooke Village, another highly-recommended historic spot.

I arrived mid-morning and spent a couple of hours strolling around the authentic 1860–1880 town. I found it quite fascinating with its working trade shops ... like a mini-Louisbourg, only a century newer.

The town's photography shop featured a huge, ancient camera that took photos on glass negatives, which then ended up as tintypes. Apparently it was only one of two such studios in the whole of North America. In case you're not familiar with the term, a tintype, or ferrotype, is a photograph made by creating a direct positive on a thin sheet of metal coated with a dark lacquer or enamel, and used as the support for the photographic emulsion. Matthew Brady was a famous Civil War photographer who made tintypes of famous battle scenes during those terrible times.

Before leaving the historic village I stopped at the Temperance Hall, where I received a thorough tongue-lashing from one of the temperate local volunteers. What! How did she know? Must have been the wine stains on my t-shirt.

Soon I was back on the coastal highway, and only three hours north of Halifax. I concentrated on driving the tricky roads with the intention of finding a nice place to camp on the other side of the metropolis.

Although the distance was not much more than 100 miles, I soon understood why the expected driving time was three hours. The highway twisted and turned constantly and passed through dozens of tiny coastal towns: Spanish Ship Bay, East Quoddy, Skip Harbor and Head of Chezzetcook.

By early afternoon I reached the outskirts of Halifax and passed right on by. I really didn't want to fight the traffic and although I hated to skip it, I was running out of time and had a full afternoon's drive still ahead of me.

Peggy's Cove is 25 miles southwest of Halifax and is Canada's best-known and best-loved fishing village. The site, which dates from 1811, has just 60 residents and is picture-postcard perfect. But, to tell you the truth, by this time I was getting a little sated with all the gorgeous villages and just stayed long enough to visit its famous lighthouse, one of the most photographed sites in the Maritime Provinces.

The lighthouse area was, indeed, a picturesque place, artistically placed out on a point of reportedly 415-million-year-old granite boulders. I was very lucky to be there when there were just a trickle of tourists. I was actually able to get several photos of the structure with no one else in the picture. A rarity, I was told.

By late afternoon I arrived in Chester, on lovely Malone Bay, my camping spot for the night. In the middle of the bay was Graves Island Provincial Park — connected to the mainland by a short causeway. Again it was sparsely occupied and I had a pick of several camp sites, so I chose one with a stingy view of the bay but conveniently close to the showers and bathrooms.

I set up camp, took a shower, and went into town for a lasagna dinner in one of the local bars; marginal but filling.

Sunday, September 22

I took my time in the morning — fixed some coffee, ate some fruit and had a long shower. I snuck away before the rest of the campers discovered I'd drained the morning supply of hot water.

By 10:00 a.m. I'd arrived in Lunenburg; not far in terms of distance, but well off the main highway and back on the coast. It turned out that this was the most interesting stop of the entire trip.

Lunenburg was founded in 1753 when the British encouraged German Protestants to emigrate from Europe. It soon became the first German settlement in the country.

It's well known now as being the place where the famous schooner, *Bluenose*, was built in 1921. Today Lunenberg is the only U.N. World Heritage site in North America.

What I loved best about Lunenburg was the Fisheries Museum of the Atlantic, an extremely interesting building and grounds featuring a well-laid-out, hands-on display of the commercial fishing industry. It featured a fascinating aquarium, a room where dories (unique fishing boats) were being built as you watched, and docents who explained the cod-fishing industry from start to finish, including the cleaning thereof.

Speaking of cod, I would like to recommend a book: *COD - A Biography of the Fish That Changed the World,* by Mark Kurlansky. A wonderful read.

The museum featured several actual fishing boats to crawl in and around as well as an eclectic collection of maritime odds and ends. It was a great, and perhaps the best bargain of the entire trip.

I spent a couple of hours looking around and then wandered along the harbor front. There were a variety of activities available and I elected to take a tour of the harbor in a small fishing boat.

Many people went sailing on the original Bluenose but the cost and time exceeded my budget.

High atop Gallows Hill, overlooking town, was the Lunenburg Academy, a huge, wooden, black and white turreted structure that was built in 1895, and the only intact 19th century academy building surviving in Nova Scotia which still functions as a school. Of course, I had to stop and metal detect, and was rewarded with several older silver coins. Lunenburg was definitely a great spot!

Alas, I only had a couple more days before my flight home and there were still several spots I wanted to visit. I was going right through Sherburne on my way and planned on staying there.

I arrived late afternoon and checked into the Loyalist Inn. I was looking forward to rubbing elbows in the hotel bar with some of the surviving Loyalist quitters.

The Inn looked like it might have been built during the Revolutionary War, during which time it had suffered several direct hits! Seedy would be too kind, but the price and location were first rate — right on the middle of town on Water Street.

I hastily settled in and left to explore. The tourist office, placed on the edge of the bay, was ready to close. A college student was running it and cheerily delayed things until I had a chance to look around and pick up a walking tour map.

Sherburne is supposed to be one of the most attractive and interesting towns on the South Shore. The whole town is a sort of museum, and boasts Canada's largest concentration of pre-1800 wooden homes.

Disney Studios filmed *The Scarlet Letter* here in 1995 in one of the few remaining barrel factories in Nova Scotia. But mainly, Sherburne is a shipbuilding town and is known as the birthplace of yachts.

I walked up and down the main part of town admiring the old buildings, most of which were still being lived in as private residences. My mouth watered at the prospect of metal detecting some of those lawns, but I didn't even consider asking for permission.

The John C. William Dory Shop, one of the buildings I most wanted to visit, had already closed and would not open until late the next morning. I had to be content in peering in the windows and seeing the many different boats spread out in various stages of construction. It's actually a working museum and the dories are built there to order.

Eventually, the setting sun and my stomach told me it was time to fill up on fine food.

I chose French Food & Antiques. An unusual spot, and as the name implies, combined a small restaurant with an antique store. It seemed everything in the place was for sale, including my table and chair. I halfway expected someone to come in while I was eating and purchase the plates and silverware I was using. I don't recall what I ordered, but it was definitely French and featured intricate sauces and unknown little squiggly thingies. But everything was quite good. Pricey, but good.

Monday, September 23

Today is my last day in the Maritimes. I catch the "Cat" out of Yarmouth Harbour back to the states at 4:00 p.m. There's only one daily crossing and I'd made a reservation several days earlier. Defending the exorbitant cost, the brochure stated it was well worth the money, saving travelers several hundred miles and a long day's driving time.

I checked, unscathed, out of the Loyalist Inn and stopped at a small pastry shop on Water Street for juice, coffee and muffins. I then wandered around the area to see some of the places I'd missed the night before.

One shop, specializing in commercial fishing supplies, caught my eye. I went in to snoop around and was amazed at the variety of heavy-duty fishing gear they sold. Huge chrome jigs for tuna were displayed on one wall; some weighed as much as ten pounds. The hooks alone were seven inches long.

How in the world someone could stand and jig over the side of a boat all day with something that size was beyond me. I would hope nothing would ever bite on it. I almost purchased one to take back as a souvenir — but common sense prevailed. On the other hand, it might have caused quite a stir passing through customs. (As it turned out, I had enough trouble.)

I left Shelburne late morning and took my time heading down the coast to Yarmouth. Rather than the direct route, I had time to take the more scenic coastal drive and arrived shortly after noon. Although the boat did not leave until 4:00 p.m., I'd read they began loading vehicles around 2:00 and I wanted to make sure I'd get on even though I already had a ticket. It was too late in the game for any screw-ups.

My motto: Hope for the best, expect the worst.

By the time I'd eaten lunch and located the harbor area it was 1:30 p.m. I parked and puttered around looking at all the ocean-going fishing trawlers parked end to end along a huge harbor. I let time get away from me.

In fact, they *did* begin loading at 2:00 p.m., and it was quite a sight. By the time I got there at 2:30 p.m., cars were already queued up in an impossibly long line — with a separate line for motor homes and commercial trucks. I couldn't believe it. The line went back for blocks! There was no way I was going to make it! There was no way they had enough room on the boat for them all ... but they did.

Unlike the Northumberland Ferries, which carted me from Woods Island to Pictou in 75 minutes, the Cat was in a class by itself. It is a huge catamaran type vessel that speeds along at 55 mph, traversing the Gulf of Maine in 2 3/4 hours!

It took an hour to get the car on board and parked. It was quite an operation, and more than a little intimidating maneuvering my nervous little Nubira by Daewoo up and down ramps and around narrow corners. Once parked and locked, I went inside and started snooping around. For a ferry, it was quite amazing, complete with bar and restaurant, duty-free shop, gambling casino and two large lounge areas showing current movies.

I stayed in the lounge until we were well out in the bay when it started to get dark and drizzle. Our arrival time in Maine would be around 7:00 p.m. I realized it would be too late to camp that night so I started looking into hotel possibilities.

Disembarking from the monster ship was the reverse of loading, except this time, everyone had to go through customs. It took forever! Five lanes of vehicles inching their way up to the customs officers, who were taking their jobs very seriously.

Even with five lines, it still took over an hour *just to reach* the customs booths. Once I got there a snippy, 50-something female inspector came over and began asking me questions. Where had I been? Could she see my identification? How long had I been gone? Did I buy anything of value? All the while walking around and peering inside my admittedly extremely messy Nubira by Daewoo. She was not impressed by what she saw.

"Open your trunk, please!" she ordered.

Hmm ... no one else had been asked to do that. I got out, opened the trunk, then stood and waited.

"Get back in your car, please!"

Hmm, again.

Had I mentioned the trunk was kind of messy? I mean really, really messy. I had not yet rolled up and repacked the tent from the last time I had used it. My sleeping bag and air mattress were stuffed back there, too. My cooking gear and lantern were scattered, and my luggage was open, dirty laundry hanging over the edge. And there was the bag of souvenir rocks I'd collected.

She really didn't approve at all. I could hear her muttering and moving things around. She finally called over one of her fellow border officers and they both starting snooping around and talking together in low voices. I was dying to turn around and see what they were doing but decided not to. Instead I positioned myself so I could see them from the rear view mirror. We made eye contact and she frowned.

All this time cars in lanes on both sides of me had been quickly passing through, while I just sat there being stared at by the innocent people. Finally the officer came around to my door and accusingly asked what the suspicious-looking machine in the trunk might be.

"Machine?" I asked, confused.

"The machine with the switches and round wheel sort of thing," she snarled.

"Oh, you mean my metal detector?"

That startled her. "You were detecting for metals and minerals in Canada?" she said in a shocked voice.

"No ... no minerals. Metal ... I mean coins and stuff," I said.

Silence.

"Jewelry and things like that," I added hopefully.

Silence.

"On the beach and parks," I added.

Silence.

"It's a hobby of mine," I whimpered.

"Wait here," she said, her hand hovering near her holster. "Do not advance any further."

No more "pleases" I noticed.

She walked over to a building and went inside. What in the world was going on, I wondered? Surely there's no law about metal detecting in the Maritimes, is there? They must know what metal detectors are, for heaven's sake. Maybe there's a problem with the funky car.

In about ten minutes she came back out and handed me my passport, slammed the trunk closed and waved me on. She was still frowning. I figured she ran some type of license plate check, looked up my passport, and was disappointed I wasn't wanted by the authorities for some misdeed. Whew! Welcome home.

Well, I might have left the Cat around 7:00 p.m., but it was 9:00 p.m. by the time I cleared customs. I was upset, hungry and still needed a place to sleep. I stopped at the first phone booth I came to and started calling. All my first choices were filled by this time, but I was still lucky to find lodging just a few miles away.

The Robbins Motel was one of those old-fashioned, family-owned places that featured knotty pine furniture and low prices. My kind of place. It was around five miles from Bar Harbor, and adjacent to Acadia National Park.

I hurried there, checked in, took a hot shower and dragged in my tent and sleeping bags to dry them before final packing for the trip home in the morning. Then to Bar Harbor for dinner.

Bar Harbor is a beautiful place. I guess I really didn't know what to expect, although I'd heard about it for years. It's one of those famous New England towns steeped in history of the Rich and Famous, and has the old-fashioned mansions lining Main Street to prove it.

By the time I got to town and parked it was almost 10:00 p.m., but the town was hopping! For an off season Monday night, I was really surprised — although to be honest, it had been several days since I had been around any crowds. I think I was just overwhelmed with all the people still out and about.

I walked down the main strip, taking my time, checking menus and prices at all the different restaurants. Every place looked friendly and inviting, and it seemed they all had the same type of food. One thing every place advertised was a steamed lobster dinner, with soup, salad and blueberry cobbler, for $20! Sounded good to me!

Dinner *was* good, although it didn't come up to the standards of Shediac, Lobster Capital of the World! But don't get me wrong, it was wonderful. Afterwards, I strolled around town looking in shop windows and pricing various hotels and inns. By 11:00 p.m. I was bushed and headed back to the motel. It had started misting again and was noticeably cooler.

Tuesday, September 24

I rose early, rolled away the dry tent, sleeping bag, and mattress, and got them repacked. I headed back to town for a little breakfast and a final look around.

First I drove through part of Acadia National Park. I didn't have the time to go too far, just enough to realize it was a very special place, with wonderful vistas overlooking Bar Harbor and hundreds of miles of hiking trails. I'd like to come back some day and spend more time there.

The downtown area was much subdued in the light of day. Just locals and a few tourists stirring about. After stopping for some juice, a few cups of coffee, and an English muffin with peanut butter, I was ready to face the day again.

Just for the heck of it I visited a couple of the more plush hotels to check out the facilities and the prices. Bar Harbor Inn appeared to be the queen of them all. Over 115 years old, it was elegant and inviting, and featured a two-deck veranda facing the rugged beach.

Guest rooms during this time of year ran from $145 to $285, although they had some very attractive all-inclusive vacation packages. All in all I thought that seemed well worth the money for a short splurge.

Perched high on a hill overlooking town was the Bluenose Inn. Equally elegant, it had drop-dead beautiful vistas and rooms that ran $145 to $339. The high season in this part of the world was June 21 through September 1 to coincide with the fall color changes, so these were off-season rates!

I also stopped at several smaller and more intimate inns that looked very interesting. They were in the $75 to $100 a night range including breakfast. I remembered having called several of them the night before, but they had been already filled for the weekend.

By late morning I'd had my fill of sight-seeing, and was ready to head home.

One final time I climbed into my feisty little Nubira by Daewoo, pointed it towards the Bangor airport and left the island.

It started raining lightly again and was getting colder by the minute. The car windows started to fog up. Unfortunately the windshield defroster on my Nubira by Daewoo had left its heart in Nova Scotia. Sigh.

THE VAMPIRE PAPERS

ROMANIA

"Romania?" people exclaimed, raising their eyebrows and the hint of a smirk spreading across their faces. "Why in heaven's name do you want to go to Romania? And where exactly is Romania, anyway?"

Good questions, all — and ones I was not very confident in answering.

Why does one want to go anywhere? What goes into the decision making of a trip location? Doesn't it need to offer a bit of excitement, a taste of the unknown, some type of challenge to make it all worthwhile? And upon returning home, shouldn't one be wiser about the ways of the world?

Yes, indeed. These would all be important elements, for me at least. At any rate, somewhere along the line, the idea of visiting Romania had crept into my subconscious. An article I'd read in some magazine? Perhaps a TV news item I'd seen, or a novel I'd read, or some scene from a movie. I just don't remember. But I do know — we all know — the world is changing before our very eyes.

Borders are shifting. Landscapes are different. Old languages are being lost. Currencies are being consolidated. Soon all the fun will be gone.

But Romania, now they've still got something for us: ancient civilizations just underfoot; the soaring spires of wooden churches; the steamy suspense of spicy, Old–World dishes enjoyed while listening to the tortured violins of gold-toothed gypsies.

And lest we forget, there are the largely uninhabited Carpathian Mountains, rife with wolves and bears and Lord knows what else, including the mysterious fog–shrouded castles of Transylvania, home of You Know Who ...

TUESDAY – SEPTEMBER 7TH

KLM flight 5468 from Amsterdam arrived in Bucharest at 4:00 p.m., an hour behind schedule. I was bushed. Counting the eight–hour time difference between Romania and Iowa, my body assumed it was actually midnight. I was ready to rest somewhere, anywhere. But certainly not in Octopeni Airport, chock full of opportunistic cab drivers, all of whom were apparently assigned to snare me into a "specially priced" cab ride downtown.

Without any Romanian money to work with, I had to exchange $100 to get some working cash now, even though I knew I'd get a much better rate at a bank later. For one thing I had to contact the company who had rented me an apartment and let them know I'd arrived and make arrangements to meet them. And to do that I had to buy a Romanian phone card, which was the only way you could use the phone system. A minimum card cost $3.00 and actually turned out to be a great investment: it was the only card I needed the entire trip, and I made a lot of calls.

I contacted the apartment renters and was relieved to hear everything was all set, and that Laura would meet me at the bus station at Piata Victoriei (Plaza Victoria) in exactly one hour. She advised me she would be carrying a black briefcase and have purple–colored hair. Huh?

I grabbed my luggage and headed out looking for Bus 783, which she said would take me directly to the station. But first I needed to buy an 80¢ ticket, good for two rides and a lot cheaper than a cab which I read could cost up to $20!

But I was tired, weak, and getting confused so when an enterprising cabbie told me he'd take me there for only $7, I caved. I didn't care any longer. I desperately needed to rest!

Laura's hair was actually henna–colored, not purple. But the problem was about half the women in Bucharest dye their hair henna. If she hadn't spotted me, I'd most likely still be looking for her, going from woman to woman: "Laura? Are you Laura?"

My Laura spoke excellent English and seemed very nice and extremely helpful. I started to relax a bit.

"How far away is the apartment?" I said, trying hard not to stare at her hair.

"Oh, just a short walk," she assured me and headed off at a brisk pace. I caught up with her, juggling my small suitcase and backpack.

Well, it might have been a Romanian's idea of a short walk, but it was several busy city blocks before we finally reached the apartment. By this time I was *really* bushed.

It was on the ninth floor of a large unattractive, concrete building on Dr. Felix Street. We crowded into a small elevator that shakily bore us up to a dimly lit corridor of stark cement walls and steel apartment doors. I wasn't impressed. I wondered what I had gotten myself into.

However, once we entered the apartment I was relieved to find it was pleasant enough, quite new, and very clean. It would do just great and I told Laura so. She seemed relieved, I suppose because she wasn't sure what to expect from another "picky American."

After she explained what all the keys were for I paid her $75 in cash for my two-night stay. We also made plans for her to come pick me up in a couple of days and take me back out to the airport where my rental car would be ready and waiting.

By this time it was 6:00 p.m. and I'd already been on the move for two days. It was too late for a nap, so I decided that it'd be best to force myself to stay up until my normal bedtime to speed up jet lag recovery. I quickly showered, changed, and headed out to check out the neighborhood.

As fate would have it, one block from my apartment I spied the Dubliners Irish Pub which drew me like some invisible gaelic magnet across the boulevard and through its welcoming front doors where I quickly ordered a half liter of Irish Harp lager. I realized I would survive.

The pub, as it turned out, was a very popular spot with the locals as well as English–speaking visitors. It was packed with a large crowd watching a rugby match. I settled in at a small table on the screened-in veranda where I sipped my lager and started on my journal. Everyone in sight was smoking. Ugh.

So here are my initial impressions of Romania (mind you, after only four hours in the country): First, everyone I had come into contact with so far had been very friendly and seemed to speak enough English that I had yet to have any problems. Second, and perhaps it was because I was in a large metropolitan community, I found the people to be very attractive, especially the women, who are all dark-haired (or henna-colored), with fair complexions, thin and fit. I'd seen no overweight folks as yet. Finally, there seemed to be a fierce national pride, similar to what I experienced in Turkey.

But physically, the city looked very tired. Worn out. Exhausted. I suppose what you might expect a place to look like after decades of communist rule. I'll revisit these thoughts later to see if my opinions change over the course of my visit.

I finished my lager, left the pub and walked up and down several side streets, unsuccessfully looking for an internet cafe. I did manage to get temporarily lost but eventually spotted my building, and feeling quite exhausted went up and crashed. It was

8:30 p.m. local time, but when you add on an eight-hour time difference and a spotty night's sleep on the plane — well, you get the picture. I was down for the count.

WEDNESDAY – SEPTEMBER 8TH

What a nasty night I had! I was jarred awake at 11:30 p.m., 2:30 and 4:30 a.m., and finally got up at 7:00 a.m. A cacophony of strange sounds disrupted my night: metal doors being continually opened and slammed shut, traffic honking, sirens, and muted conversations. Didn't these people ever sleep?

I looked out the apartment window and down onto a small grassless patch of land. I was surrounded by similar apartment buildings which, in the light of day, looked very bleak. Laundry hanging on balconies, paint peeling off gray drab walls, ripped curtains or sheets covering windows.

I rinsed out a few things in the shower and headed out to see what I could see. Or at least, I started to head out. First I had to remember how to get the apartment doors open. There were two of them.

I should have written down Laura's directions on the complicated key procedure. Each door had two keys, plus a pair of two–stage deadbolts. I don't know how many different combinations that came to, but I'd bet I went through them all at least once before I was free to leave! Not very handy in case of fire.

The major means of mass transportation in Bucharest is the Metro, a spiffy underground urban train system similar to London's. I bought a ticket and headed to Piata Unirii, where I got off and immediately spotted a McDonalds. Yay! I ordered a large orange juice, coffee, and a Sausage Biscuit.

It was a gorgeous sunny day, and I walked down several city blocks to the Palace of Parliament, reportedly one of the MUST SEE sights in Bucharest. Of course, it was closed during the months of September and October. What? How can they close the Palace of Parliament? That would be like closing the White House for a couple of months.

189

Wait, maybe not a bad idea after all.

The Palace of Parliament is the second largest office building in the world — second only to the Pentagon. It was built in the 1980s by the dictator Nicolae Ceausescu when he was at the height of his power. It was supposed to house ministries, Communist Party offices and apartments of high functionaries.

You remember Ceausescu, don't you? He was the Stalin-like cold war ruler who, along with his wife, Elena, was lined up outside the building and shot dead on Christmas Day, 1989.

After his demise, no one really knew what to do with this huge building and it became known as the "Madman's House." The government finally made it the official Senate and Parliament building and a place to host huge conferences.

I was quite disappointed in not being able to tour its 12 stories, four underground levels, 300–foot lobby with 4,500 chandeliers. Maybe next time.

I turned around headed back toward the city center and crossed the River Damobvita to visit the highly acclaimed National History Museum. Of course, it was closed for two *years* for repair. Great — so far I was batting a thousand.

I found a phone and called Nancy and Eugene Georgeisu — friends of my friend-since-grade school, Don Torney, who now lives in San Antonio. Nancy married Eugene, a Romanian architect, when they were in school together in Texas, and they were the only people I knew in the country; well, not actually knew, but who I could talk with. They were expecting my call, and we made plans to meet at a local restaurant for dinner that evening.

I wandered around a little more until I came upon a small church tucked away down a shady side street towered over by gaunt, gray office buildings. It looked so out of place I had to check it out. As I entered, a service was in progress.

Stravropoleos Church is a Romanian Orthodox church built between 1724 and 1730 for the first Phanariot ruler, Nicolae Mavrocordat. It was truly a memorable experience — both the church and the service. Men were standing on one side, women on the other. Deep male voices chanted during the service, which in many ways reminded me of a Catholic High Mass.

Lots of intricately carved walnut furnishings, swirls of smoky incense, wonderful bass–baritone harmony with non-stop icon-kissing. It was obvious I was an "outsider" but after the service, everyone was quite gracious to me, shaking my hand before backing out onto the street and returning to work. It was a marvelous interlude.

I was in a generous, spiritual mood as I walked away and handed a 100,000 Romanian lei note to a beggar lady, thinking it was a 10,000 note. She almost fainted and so did I when I caught my mistake, but if you could have seen the expression on her face it was worth every leu. Of course, that was only $3 U.S. anyway, piker.

Not far from the church was a large urban college campus — the Piata Universitaii. In the area were several local "fast food" places so I stopped and bought a bottle of water and a small, meat-filled pastry called a *pateuri*. Across the street was a book store, where I invested in a map of the country which featured the main roads and all the monasteries.

Afterwards I took the metro back to my apartment for a short siesta to help offset the waning jet lag. I continued to marvel at the attractiveness of the locals, especially the women. But what was the story with this "henna" thing? I couldn't understand why they'd take their naturally glossy, jet black hair and mess it up like that.

After a short nap I got up, showered, changed and headed back out for my early evening rendezvous with the Georgeisus. It was early so I decided to walk. I had a general idea where the restaurant was and figured I could easily find it by 6:00 p.m., our selected meeting time. Wrong. It was time to get lost again.

My goal was the Bistro Atheneu and I eventually stumbled upon it after circling several city blocks at least twice. I was fashionably late when I finally spotted it, sitting midway along a small side street facing the Atheneum Concert Hall. It was a fine little place, full of atmosphere and tempting smells, and very popular with locals and tourists alike.

I found Nancy sitting alone at a table sipping a glass of wine. I introduced myself, and in a moment, Eugene arrived. They were lovely people and we sat and enjoyed ourselves over a wonderful dinner of lamb prepared with rosemary and rice, accompanied by a bottle of excellent Romanian wine.

Eugene was just back from the construction site of a new home they were building. Nancy, I learned, was heavily involved in church volunteer work and had just come from a meeting.

After a wonderful dinner and much interesting conversation, it was time to go. The total bill came to $28 and we agreed to split it. Around 9:00 p.m. we went our separate ways with promises to get back together again on my way back through Bucharest.

Rather than walk back and suffer the indignities of getting lost again, I took the Metro to my area of town and stopped briefly at The Dubliners, which was absolutely packed. I sat and reviewed and recorded the treasured moments of the day over half a—Guinness. So far, so good.

It wasn't until I was back in my room that I discovered I had not paid my full share of the dinner bill after all. My share should have been $14 but all I'd paid was $1.40. Whoops! Those nasty decimal points! They had been too polite to say anything. Obviously I was still having difficulties with the money. To me, the five, fifty, five hundred and five thousand notes all looked alike.

I was leaving in the morning but planned to get together with them before I returned to America. I'd square things then.

THURSDAY – SEPTEMBER 9TH

True to her word, Laura was downstairs in the morning, waiting to take me to the airport. Also waiting were the nervous apartment owners, who collected their keys and immediately rushed upstairs to see what damage the American had done to their new investment venture.

Laura told me she'd arrange for another apartment and a ride to the airport on my way back home. Even though that was still a couple of weeks away, it was a relief to know I had it taken care of.

I paid her $10 for the ride to the airport and gave her a shiny new Sacajawea $1 coin with which he seemed quite tickled.

They were expecting me at the car rental office and had automatically upgraded me from a Romanian Dacia to a Ford Fiesta for the same price. They said I wouldn't have liked the Dacia, and after observing said vehicle during the following two weeks, I agreed. They looked cheap, tinny, and not very dependable.

I was on my way by 9:00 a.m. It was a two-hour drive to the town of Sinaia, the "Pearl of the Carpathians," where I planned to spend the first night.

The road started out just fine, the highway signs clear and easy to follow as I slowly left the flat plains and entered the foothills of the Carpathian Mountain range.

I arrived at Sinaia at 11:00 a.m. and checked out Hotel Palace, a *Rough Guide* recommendation. It looked okay, but nothing to get excited about. I decided I'd look around a little first. In the meantime I decided to visit Peles Castle.

The weather was wonderful and the castle was magnificent. Built between 1875 and 1883 for Romania's Hohenzollern monarch, Carol I, the castle sits on the side of a hill in a park-like setting landscaped in the English fashion of the time. The castle has almost 800 stained glass windows and is stuffed with Persian carpets, Renaissance-era weapons, gorgeous Murano chandeliers, and priceless works of art. I've been in my share of castles and I'd have to say, this one was pretty special.

Adjacent to the castle grounds was an attractive inn and restaurant with the terrible name of Economat. I recalled Nancy telling me this is where they stayed when they came to visit. I wandered in for a bowl of pork soup, hot tea, and tomato salad.

It was still early in the afternoon and time for a decision. Should I stay here in Sinaia, perhaps taking a short mountain hike, or should I go on? It was only 2:00 in the afternoon, the weather was great, and I was in the mood to see some more, so I got back in the car and continued. I was heading towards Transylvania and the village of Bran, the alleged home of Dracula.

Bran is the location of the famous Bran Castle, and is one of the most popular tourist sites in Romania. In 1377 the Saxons built a castle here which the city fathers now advertise as Dracula's Castle.

Although its touted as a major attraction, I found the town small and rather disappointing, more like a country village than a town. Lodging choices were quite limited but I finally settled in at a somewhat downtrodden pension, or country inn, for $18 a night. The room was quite sparse, but for only $18 ...

I parked the car and walked up to the castle for a tour.

Bran Castle was very odd, composed of several floors of small, sparsely-decorated rooms, dimly-lit hallways and unsteady-looking turrets and balconies, all carved into the rock face overlooking town.

The outside walls were covered with thick layers of ivy, the roof matted with heavy, dark green moss. All the doors were huge and strapped with iron. It would have been interesting to see a floor plan of the place, which must have been an architect's nightmare. The views from the upper floors, however, were great, and overlooked the town and surrounding forests. But as far as it being Dracula's castle? I think not.

The character of Dracula, of course, is based on a real person. Vlad Tepes was his name. He was better know as "Vlad the Impaler" because of his nasty habit of impaling his enemies on tall wooden stakes embedded in the ground. The unfortunate victims were left there to suffer a rather gruesome and painful death.

History tells about a "forest" of such victims created by the impaling of 20,000 Turks and Bulgarians along the route of invading armies. Apparently this caused such a panic that they turned and fled back home.

However, his only association with Bran Castle may be that he attacked it in 1460. Of course, if I were a vampire, this might be just the type of castle I'd like; dark and foreboding and definitely creepy enough, if a bit ramshackle.

I suspect that in addition to looking how most movies portray Dracula's castle, this site was chosen because of its location on a road easily accessible to tourists. The *real* Dracula's castle, however, was a day's drive away.

Near the castle were several Dracula souvenir shops, where one could peruse the world's largest collection of vampire–related toys, clothing and food, all made in India. And, of course, walking the cobblestone streets was a local "ghoul" dressed up in a really cheesy vampire costume. For a little money, he would pose with you and slobber at the camera menacingly.

Just to be safe, I bought one of the garlic bulb-chains that were for sale on every corner. You never know.

Although it wasn't very late, the sun set early in the Carpathians and I wanted to eat and get back into my room before it got completely dark. I'm not saying all the vampire stuff was starting to get to me, but one can't be too careful in Transylvania.

I found a funky pizza parlor on the edge of the village and was surprised to find it wasn't all that bad, although a wee bit different from the pizza we're used it. I ordered the special, which came with slices of ham (I hope it was ham), olives, tomatoes, and green peppers. But no sauce. For a small additional sum, you could purchase a small bottle of sauce.

It was dark when I exited the cafe and headed back up the narrow, deserted road toward my pension. The Bran Internet Cafe & Grocery Store (I'm not making this up), which had been open on my way to dinner, was now closed. A bad sign, I thought. In fact, just about every place along the road was now shuttered tightly for the night and completely devoid of warm-blooded humans. Hmm.

I made a dash for my room; no TV but a lukewarm shower and to bed. It was only around 9:00 p.m. but my body's rhythm was still off and I was dead-tired. Sorry. No pun intended.

In the dark of night something woke me. The pension creaked and groaned with the wind. Could that be what woke me or was it something else? Something more sinister?

Let's recap. Here I am all alone, sleeping in a drafty old pension in Bran, Transylvania, somewhere deep in the Carpathian Mountains in Romania. Directly above my head, perched high on a rocky crag, sat Dracula's Castle, a direct line of flight from the turrets right into my cracked room window. WHAT WAS I THINKING?

Of course, I kept telling myself, the *real* Dracula castle was miles away, but this one was creepy enough to be *some* vampire's castle. Quietly I slipped out of bed and retrieved my rosary beads and garlic bulbs ...

FRIDAY – SEPTEMBER 10TH

7:00 a.m. I'm alive. I survived!

I looked out the window and saw others had survived as well. I also noticed everyone was wearing heavy coats and sweaters. A horse-drawn cart clip clopped up the street leaving a pile of steaming manure next to my Ford Fiesta. It gets cold in the Carpathian mountains.

I was looking forward to ordering a bowl of Kellogg's Bran Flakes for breakfast but was unable to find any place open. The town was still shut up tight. Another opportunity lost.

The sun cleared the top of the mountains by the time I got in the car and drove out of town, climbing a winding road toward a distant ridge. My goal was to reach the market town of Curtea De Arges by noon and tour one of the region's famous monasteries.

The scenery was absolutely spectacular, and I stopped several times just to take photos of the hillsides and tiny hamlets that dotted the landscape. The farmers were out cutting hay with long, wicked-looking scythes. Everywhere you looked were huge hay mounds built over large wooden frames.

It was about this time I also noticed that I had yet to see a tractor. Everything seemed to be transported by horse or donkey-pulled carts.

As I crossed over one of the passes, I came upon a local farmer standing at a narrow intersection selling hard rolls, sausages and a honey–flavored drink in recycled bottles. I stopped and purchased some snacks to nibble on as I drove along.

The town of Curtea De Arges is located within the district of Wallachia. And the thing that drew me here was the famous Princely Church.

The church, actually a cathedral, is indeed a magnificent structure. Built by local princes beginning in 1352, the large stone structure is Byzantine in design and quite unlike churches we find in the U.S..

I strolled around the grounds, peeking into buildings and munching on my snacks. It was a brilliant sunny day and the market town was busy with people; too crowded for my tastes, so I decided to forge on into the lake country.

My next stop was the famed Poienari Citadel, site of the *real* Dracula's Castle. After getting temporarily lost and making an disastrous wrong turn up a rocky side road which almost did the car in, I arrived at an obscure junction near a hydroelectric dam in the middle of nowhere. I believed I was close to the citadel but there were no signs or people around to ask.

I got out of the car and looked for some clue. I spotted my goal up the side of a steep mountain, accessible only by a flight of 1,480 narrow stairs. It certainly didn't look very safe but what the heck. I locked the car and headed up.

It became obvious after an hour of climbing why the real Dracula castle was not a popular tourist site. It was not only out of the way, but I doubt there'd be many people willing — or capable — of making the grueling climb.

Once I arrived, panting and wheezing, the castle itself was pretty disappointing. Most of it had collapsed down the steep hillside centuries ago. What remains today is not very interesting and quite unsafe. What *was* interesting, however, and what made the trip worth it to me, was the panoramic 360° view from the top.

It was a scene right out of the forest primeval. All I could think about was how in the world it had ever been built in the first place. It was hard enough to climb there on a concrete stairway. How did anyone manage to get all the building supplies up those rocky, ultra-steep hillsides?

The answer, of course, is slave labor. It was built in 1457 by captured Turkish and Bulgarian invaders. None of whom survived the ordeal.

My second near fatal mishap of the day occurred on the way back down to my car. It was an innocent enough mistake. I thought I could read Romanian.

I'd passed a side path on the climb up and I was curious. The path led though a sturdy iron gate, with a sign attached: ZONA INTERZIS!

Ahh, I thought. A "zone of interest" — apparently what they are trying to say was "something of great interest" must be right down that path. I'd go see. BIG MISTAKE!

With camera in hand I headed down towards the "zone of interest" and after about 100 yards and negotiating a sharp bend in the mountain, I literally ran into an armed soldier who I swear must have jumped five feet in the air. I startled him as much as he startled me.

As he brought his Uzi up into firing position and screamed at me, I did the fastest about-face you can imagine, and without stopping to explain — or argue, or do anything — headed back as fast as I could, hoping and praying he'd figure out I was just another dumb foreigner who didn't know the difference between the words *INTERESTING* and *FORBIDDEN,* which I later found out was the proper translation.

I could almost read the headlines in the Bucharest Daily Bugle:

Crazed American Tourist Shot While Attempting
To Photograph Hydroelectric Dam
and Sell Secrets To The Rotten Russians!

Holding my breath, I hurried as fast as I could down the stairs to my trusty Ford Fiesta and sped away. I never once turned back to see if I was being followed. Whew!

The mountain range in this area of the country is the Fagaras Mountains, and the road I was on is called the Transfagarasan Highway. Normally at this time of year, this is about as far north

198

as one can get but I was told the highway passes were still open and I could probably make it across if I was lucky and it didn't snow. I was at the same latitude of Quebec, Canada at this point. I continued north. What the heck, I thought; it was rental car, after all.

My goal was the town of Sibiu. I knew there was no way I could make it before dark so I just headed north into serious mountains, to a place on my map called Lake Vidaru.

By early evening I arrived at one of the very few places that offered lodging: Cabana Valea cu Pesti, a huge, bizarre hunk of building without a straight line anywhere. Set into the edge of a deep forest, it actually looked like a Disneyland attraction, and turned out to be nearly vacant. In fact, the hotel clerk looked quite surprised when I walked in.

I had my pick of rooms and chose a large double overlooking the lake. The cost including breakfast was $23. I dumped my small bag on the bed and walked down to the sun–drenched terrace to catch up on my log. This was more like it. I ordered a Carlsburg beer and enjoyed the marvelous views.

The inn was reportedly a favorite with fishermen, but the season was pretty much over and I saw very few boats on the lake, which was a couple hundred feet below the inn. The scenery was more than spectacular and I decided to take a walk down to the lake and snoop around.

Afterwards I took a short nap, had a hot shower and went down to the dining room. It was a very formal affair. White table cloths, lit candles and almost empty. Other than a table of three locals who unabashedly stared at me, I was the only other guest staying there. I had my choice of three waiters and twelve tables.

The sun was just sinking below the distant mountains, and the water of Lake Vidaru was changing from deep blue to bluish-black to solid black as I sat mesmerized, staring out the floor–to-ceiling windows. Barak, my own personal waiter, soon arrived to take my order.

The menu had no prices listed. Uh-oh, not a good sign. I ordered a grilled chicken breast, french fries, a salad of sliced tomatoes, a loaf of french bread and butter, and an excellent local wine, Grasa de Cotnari. Although I really only wanted a glass they only had bottles. Uh-oh again.

For dessert I ordered a custard and a cup of coffee served from a large, solid silver urn. At this point it was too late to worry about costs.

Maybe it was the scenery, maybe it was the crystal clean air or maybe it was because I survived the day, but the meal was heavenly.

I sat alone in the dining room when the bill came. Barak, my waiter, discretely placed a piece of paper on the table and quietly withdrew into the shadows. Scrawled neatly across the center was the figure ... ROL 2,275,000. WHAT? How could that be? Two million, two hundred and seventy five thousand! I'm bankrupt! I've been taken advantage of! I should have insisted on asking the prices ... how stupid of me!

Now calm down, Robert, let's figure this out. Just relax. Let's see — there are around 354,000 leu to the dollar. That would make the bill ... $64? No, it couldn't be that much, could it? I wasn't thinking straight. Perhaps I'd had too much wine. Try moving the decimal place over three spots — 64¢? Nah. That can't be right either.

As it turned out, the price of the meal came to $6.43. Perhaps I should have ordered a less expensive bottle of wine.

By 8:30 the sun had disappeared and the hotel was like a tomb. Outside it was black as pitch. There wasn't a street light within 75 miles — actually, there wasn't a *street* within 75 miles. Just a narrow gravel road leading up into the mountains. I started to feel creepy again. I went back to my room, bolted the doors and tightly fastened the wooden window shutters. No TV or radio, of course.

I double-checked the cost of dinner. Still $6.43.

I tried to read, but with a 40–watt bulb hanging from a 20-foot ceiling, I soon gave up and went to sleep.

SATURDAY, SEPTEMBER 11TH

I woke up buried under two heavy wool blankets and was still cold. The windows were coated with a thick slab of hoarfrost and I could see my breath. Forget the shower! I got dressed as fast as I could and went down for some hot breakfast.

A larger group was gathered in the dining room this morning. Everyone was wearing heavy sweaters and jackets and sitting with their hands wrapped around mugs of hot coffee, staring out the window waiting for the sun to peak up over the mountaintop.

I'm was on my way by 9:00 a.m.; away from the lake and up and into the mountains proper. I soon left civilization behind and began climbing — higher and higher — as it got colder and colder. Suddenly I noticed large patches of black ice on the road; I slowed down to negotiate narrow hair pin turns.

About halfway up the mountain I came upon a shepherd in the middle of the road leading a huge flock of sorry-looking sheep down out of the mountain pastures. I had to stop while they swept by me as if I were a rock in the middle of a river.

The shepherd, who looked ... shall I say rather *earthy*, approached the car. He wanted to ask me something. I rolled down the window and he said something. I had no idea what it was. Using sign language he indicated he wanted a cigarette. I shook my head no.

"Matches?" he tried again by pantomiming striking a match on the sole of his shoe.

"No, sorry", I shook my head again. He gave a snarl and turned away.

Now if he'd asked for a bar of soap, I'd gladly have accommodated him.

Other than the shepherd, I met just one other car, driving the opposite direction. I took this as a positive sign that the pass was open and I'd make it to the next highway. I didn't know what I'd do if I had to turn around and head back.

I knew that bears and wolves were quite common in this part of the country, but I never saw any and probably was lucky I didn't, as I was about the only human (as in food) around.

By midmorning, I'd reached the summit; over 7,000 feet and the highest point in Romania. The tree line was far below me and the wind was whistling. I crossed over the saddle and started down the far side, soon passing ski resorts preparing for the season. As I descended the mountain it was amazing how drastically the climate and scenery changed in such a short time. By the time I reached the main highway after a few hours, the temperature had climbed at least 50 degrees.

By 3:30 p.m. I arrived in Sibiu and honed in on my luxury lodgings for the night: Hotel Imparatul Romanilor. I decided I was ready for something nice and this was the most expensive hotel I would stay in the entire trip. $60 for a single room, but hopefully well worth it.

Hotel Imparatul Romanilor is the oldest hotel in Sibiu. Built in 1895, it was a favorite spot of Franz Liszt, Johann Strauss and Eminescu. I was in good company.

Sibiu is a German town. It's also known as Hermannstadt, as it grew to become the chief city of the Transylvanian Saxons. And my hotel was right in the middle of the city center.

I dropped off my bag and strolled down the pedestrian mall, which was lined with beer gardens, all doing a booming business. The day was mild and sunny and, I suppose because it was the weekend, there were lots of families out enjoying themselves. I stopped for a stein of beer and wandered around the town checking out the original old city walls and other ancient landmarks.

The city reminded me of my army days in Germany in the early fifties when I was stationed near the medieval town of Nuremberg; large cobblestone plazas, bronze statues of warriors mounted on war horses, and eight-foot thick city walls.

After a nice nap in a very fancy bed, I showered and walked to Sibiul Vechi, one of the several traditional Romanian restaurants in the area. I ordered a half bottle of local merlot and a mixed grill, which was a delicious combination of veal, sausages and ham, along with a salad and french fries.

The restaurant was known for its folk music but, unfortunately, it was way too early and I finished up and left before it started. Like most of Europe, things really didn't get going until 9:00 p.m.

That's when most of the locals ate their evening meals. Way too late for me.

I found an internet cafe where I was able to catch up on my email messages. I also figured out how to use my phone card to hook into an international AT&T line and called home.

By 10:00 p.m. I was back in my spacious, comfortable room watching some wacky local programs on TV and catching up on my log. Altogether a great day.

SUNDAY, SEPTEMBER 12TH

The breakfast room in the hotel was Old World classy, with a tuxedoed maître d' greeting at the door and waitresses gliding by in ankle-length, fancy dresses. My lodging included breakfast and I took full advantage of the variety of juices, cold and hot cereals, hams and cheeses, brioches, milk, and coffee. I think they were relieved to see me go.

My guidebook recommended a local history museum just a few blocks from the hotel. I planned to spend a hour or so there and then go to Mass at the nearby Holy Trinity Metropolitan Cathedral.

It worked out perfectly, although I could have spent more time at the museum, which was wonderful — full of local and regional artifacts dating back to medieval times. The only bizarre thing about it was that the lights in all the rooms were kept off (to conserve energy, I assume) so I was trailed by a docent who followed me around from room to room, turning off and on lights as we went. Very annoying.

A block away was another outstanding, must-see church — the monstrous Evangelical Cathedral (1320–1520) which houses the crypt of Mihnea The Bad, Dracula's son, who apparently inherited all his father's evil traits and was stabbed to death on the church steps in 1510.

I reached the cathedral just as Mass was starting. The service seemed to go on forever as *all* the readings, as well as the LONG homily were given first in Romanian, then in German.

One last stop before leaving town was the cathedral tower, which provided a great panoramic view of the medieval town, as well as a glimpse of the adjacent new town outside the old walls. I was on my way by noon.

Rough Guide recommended a small village famous for its collection of glass icons that was just slightly off my route to Cluj, my next planned evening stop. I decided to take the detour and check it out.

The tiny village of Sibiel is famous for two things: witchcraft and the Museum of Icons Painted on Glass — a bizarre combination if you ask me.

As far as I know I didn't run into any warlocks or witches, but the museum was eerie enough. Over 700 icons covered the walls of a dilapidated, two-story wooden building. The crone who ran the place insisted I see them all, following me around to be sure I did while talking nonstop. Of course I didn't understand a word she was saying. In my book, a glass icon is a glass icon is a glass icon and if you've see one, you've seen them all. But I was polite and nodded and smiled and couldn't wait to escape.

When I got back to the car I noticed some type of religious service was going on in a cemetery across the street and wandered over to see what was up.

Dozens of people in traditional clothing were standing packed together, passing around large loaves of bread and jugs of what appeared to be homemade wine. A hand would stick out and rip off a hunk of the loaf, and another grab the jug and take a gulp.

In the middle of the crowd was a tall Romanian Orthodox priest, dressed in beautiful, rich, tapestry–like vestments, blessing everyone. I never did figure it all out, but I suspect it was a religious service, perhaps a burial, and I had just witnessed their version of Communion.

The drive to Cluj–Napoca was flat and uneventful with mountain ranges to the south and west while I followed the flatlands north. Early afternoon I stopped at a town for lunch and ended up at some strange fast-food joint that advertised "American–style cheese burgers and fries."

I ordered the special and was handed a sack. In the bottom was a slab of some kind of meat (definitely not hamburger). Fries covered the meat, and over the fries was sprinkled shredded cabbage slathered with some kind of terrible dressing. I ate what I could and hoped I didn't get sick.

I arrived at Cluj-Napoca around 4:00 p.m., and after checking out a couple of hotels settled in the Hotel Melody, where I took a large double room for $30. The hotel sat on the corner across from a park and the huge St. Michael's Church built from 1350 to 1487. I was able to leave my car parked safely in view of the hotel lobby and walk around on my own.

Cluj has a long Hungarian heritage, and is called Kolozsvar by the locals. I took a tour of the local art museum, which was said to offer the best selection of Romanian art in the country. It was housed in the baroque Bánnffy Palace, built in 1774. I enjoyed the building as much as the art and stayed until closing.

For dinner that night I walked several blocks up a hill into the university part of town where there was a great little pizza place. It was a welcome relief. By this time I was getting weary of eating all my meals alone and struggling with the language all the time. I had yet to run into *anyone* who could speak much English.

On the way back to my hotel, which was in the middle of town, I stopped at the famous Continental Hotel, which served as Nazi Germany's military headquarters in Transylvania during World War II. There was a boisterous wedding party going on and I stood and watched the tipsy wedding group stumble through some type of ethnic dance. No one seemed very sure of the correct steps and soon shifted into the Twist ... which was even worse.

I continued on to my hotel and turned in. I had overdone things today and was pretty beat.

MONDAY, SEPTEMBER 13TH

After a solid night's sleep and a decent breakfast I walked across the street to check out St. Michael's church and the adjacent park area.

The "clumsy but imposing equestrian statue" (the guidebook's words, not mine) was of Matyas Corninus, whose Black Army kept the Kingdom of Hungary safe from the lawlessness and foreign invasion of the dreaded Turks for much of his reign (1458–90).

But the most interesting thing to me was found directly in front of the statue: recent excavations had exposed an ancient Roman building. The locals seemed unfazed, but I was fascinated.

I found the post office and bought a dozen stamps to use on the postcards I had written. I was a bit shocked at the price of each stamp — almost $1. (When I got home I discovered not one of the cards was ever delivered!)

I left town around late morning, heading north and west toward the town of Oradea, my destination for the night. Along the way I picked up a hitchhiker along the side of the highway. I say hitchhiker but I'd read, and soon found to be true, that it was common practice for Romanians to pick up people along the road. Public transportation was slow and expensive and it was just considered good manners.

The young man I picked up was heading to the next town where he worked as a waiter. He spoke both passable English and Spanish so we were able to communicate very well. He confided in me he earned about $125 a month, which he considered to be excellent wages. In fact he'd left his home in the eastern part of the country to take this job. He told me he was able to save most of his earnings as he paid only $5 a week for a small room, and his meals were free!

I started a hotel search when I got to Oradea and eventually settled on Hotel Parc, right in the center of things.

Like many buildings in Romania, the outside looked extremely grim, but once you had the nerve to enter, you were usually pleasantly surprised. Hotel Parc was no exception.

Although they had no single rooms available, they gave me a double for the same price of $27. The room was huge! At least 30' x 15' with a separate foyer and adjoining "vintage" bathroom complete with bidet and family-size, enamel claw-foot bathtub. The floors were all inlaid wood and the ceilings had to be at least 20 feet high. Very unique.

I later learned the hotel was built in the early 1800s and had started out as a town casino. In 1833 it was converted into a hotel and, at one time, was one of the most famous hotels in Eastern Europe. I had stumbled onto a legend.

Over the years, some of its celebrated guests had been Prince Carol of Austria, Carol the IV, and the Romanian musician, George Eminescu (Eminescu must be their equivalent of Smith).

After a shower I headed out for an early evening stroll around town; crisscrossing the Crisule Repede river and enjoying the end of the sunny day. I found a lovely little restaurant overlooking the river and ordered a large platter of spaghetti Napolese and a beer, which, along with a basket of crusty bread with butter, cost only $2.75.

It was a lovely night for a stroll. After dinner I followed the river back downtown, admiring many of the elaborate buildings along the way, then on to my lovely Hotel Parc to watch some baffling, local black and white TV programs in my cavernous suite.

TUESDAY, SEPTEMBER 14

I left town after taking breakfast in the parlor and initiating a complicated transaction by asking to buy the fancy ashtray in my room for a souvenir. Before everything was said and done, a cast of no less than six people got involved.

They seemed mystified as to why I wanted to buy the ashtray. "Why didn't I just take it?" they asked. "What kind of cigarettes did I smoke? Would I willing to sell a pack or two?" Many questions needed to be answered.

Phone calls to the hotel owner suggested a price of $4 for the ashtray, to which I readily agreed, but when I tried to pay in dollars, an entire new set of problems were set in motion. They sent off a clerk to the bank with my $20 bill. He returned 15 minutes later with the correct amount of change. Finally the transaction was consummated and amidst smiles and cheers and looks of utter confusion, I worked my way out onto the street with my souvenir Hotel Parc ashtray safely packed away.

I drove north out of town on a back road that paralleled the Hungarian border, until I came to a tiny town a half mile from its frontier crossing.

What the heck, I thought, I might as well mosey on into Hungary and get my passport stamped. I headed down the road toward the border until I reached an armed guard, to whom I tried to explain my great plan. I didn't have much success getting through to him.

I parked the car and walked to the Hungarian border guard, where I was ushered into an office. A guard spoke enough English to understand my mindless request and stamped my passport and passed me through, muttering to himself.

I walked into Hungary a hundred yards or so, at least far enough to determine I was still out in the middle of nowhere. I had hoped I'd find some small shop nearby where I could purchase a Hungarian flag for a souvenir. Nope. On foot now and with no town in sight, I turned around and headed back to Romania ... and into a hornet's nest.

My first mistake was going right up to the barricade, bypassing a long line of cars. This did not please the locals at all. Not so fast, comrade.

The Romanian border guard was not as user friendly as the Hungarian border guard, and did not speak any English at all. Where did I come from all of sudden? Where was my car? What exactly was I up to?

He was not pleased to see this oddball American suddenly appear with no papers, no car, and no purpose for being there in the first place. I stood and waited patiently, bravely smiling all the while.

Eventually the Hungarian border guard noticed what was going on and yelled across to his Romanian comrade for all the world to see and hear. Of course I couldn't understand a word spoken, but from the crowd's reaction I suspect it went something like this ...

Hungarian guard: "What's this American screwball up to?"
Romanian guard: "We don't know. That's why we sent him into Hungary. You guys are all nuts and he'll fit in just fine. Ha ha."

Hungarian guard: "Well we don't want him either, so we're sending him back to Romania. I just called him a schmuck and he's all smiles. Ha ha."

After making me wait a long time, he finally stamped my passport and *presto*! I was free to reenter Romania, more than a little embarrassed. I quickly retrieved my car and left.

I soon entered a region called Maramures, and neared the town of Satu Mare, at which point I was very close to the three borders of Hungary, the Ukraine and Romania. In other words, I was now in the farthest northwest corner of the country. Turning east, I headed towards the village of Sapanta and its Merry Cemetery, mentioned in my guide as another "place of interest."

Maramures, unlike most other regions in Romania, was never conquered by the Romans. It is a hands–down favorite with most tourists because many features of life there appear to have changed little since Dacian times. In other words, it's a time warp.

The fascinating villages are the main reason for visiting the area. The majority of buildings are constructed of wood by skilled craftsmen and the people who live here produce everything they wear, use and eat, or they do without.

The Merry Cemetery is one of the all–time favorite tourist spots and probably one of the least accessible in Eastern Europe; and perhaps the most kinky.

Thanks to the work of one woodcarver, Stan Ion Patras, who lived from 1909 to 1977, the cemetery in the village of Sapanta is one of the most unique in the world. Hundreds of beautifully-worked, colorfully-painted wooden headstones are carved with portraits of the deceased and scenes from their lives, along with witty Romanian limericks. A few translated samples:

Griga, may you pardoned be, even though you did stab me.

Barak, who sought money to amass, could not Death escape, alas!

I strolled though the cemetery and wished I could speak Romanian to fully enjoy the experience. As I left, I passed three local women dressed in traditional garb, talking by the side of the road. It was a photo op too good to pass by. I stopped, got out of the car and pantomimed that I wanted to take their pictures. Friendly nods gave me permission.

It was late afternoon when I arrived in the market town of Sighetu Marmatiei, nestled right up against the Ukrainian border. I was looking for a place called the Hotel Flamingo, about as misnamed a place as you might imagine. I never would have found it without the help of a local student, who jumped in the car and directed me down a warren of side streets.

My room was large and clean, and only cost $20 — so who's complaining? Okay, the shower didn't work, but the large tub had one of those spray-like attachment thingies and I took a long "hosing," changed into some semi–clean clothing and went looking for the Ukraine.

Sighet is not a very attractive town, and if it hadn't been for the balmy, sunny day, would have been downright dismal. My *Rough Guide* says it "has the air of a frontier town." I found this true enough. It also has the distinction of being the birthplace of holocaust surviver and world-famous Nobel Peace Laureate, Elie Wiesel.

The Tisza River separates Romania from the Ukraine. My plan was to drive to the river, park the car, and stroll across the frontier into the Ukraine, get my passbook stamped and return. Sounded simple enough to me.

I started across the bridge. Unbeknownst to me there was an armed Ukrainian guard watching me from behind a tree on the other side. I got about halfway across when he came charging out with his rifle pointed at me. He was shouting at me and holding his hand out in the international "STOP" position.

I stopped and tried to pantomime my intentions while waving my passport like an idiot. He stood and snarled at me, nodding with his head to get out of there. Suddenly I decided it wasn't such a good idea, and turned around and went back. Drat!

Here I was within spitting distance of Old Mother Russia, but it was not to happen. So I went to prison, instead.

The Prison of the Ministers was a true Cold War relic just a couple of blocks off the main "street" of town. A large über ugly, concrete block of a building, it operated from 1898 until 1977, and in that time gained a sinister reputation. Inside were imprisoned former government ministers, high-ranking army officers, academics and religious leaders, or any other "problem people" who needed to be "protected" by the Red Army.

The prison's 72 cells held 180 people, over two-thirds of which were over the age of 60. They were treated appallingly, and not surprising, most died in their dreary cells.

I wandered down among the cell blocks and peered into individual cubicles, many of which had sad little displays about certain famous inmates. It was a very sobering experience and a real downer.

I got in my car and drove around and didn't see any place even remotely resembling a restaurant, so I returned to the Flamingo and went to bed, hungry and depressed.

WEDNESDAY – SEPTEMBER 15

I was glad to leave the bleakness of Sighetu and head south and east toward Vatra Doreni. Almost immediately I entered one of the loveliest valleys of the trip. The landscape was dotted with picturesque villages and the renowned tall wooden churches for which the region is internationally famous.

I stopped several times to take photos and at one place, where a church had just been completed, lucky enough to meet one of the builders.

He came out and waved me in as I pulled up in my car. The church was built by hand, taking over three years. It was huge: two stories tall with a towering steeple. The roof, he explained to me, was covered by 85,000 intricate wooden shingles, all of which were cut individually.

Many of the churches I visited were hard to reach. You could see them from the road, but to actually get to them, you had to park in farm yards and cut across open country.

The valley drive was gorgeous, crossing sparking clear mountain streams and meadows. This is the area where the popular 2003 movie *Cold Mountain,* starring Jude Law, Nicole Kidman and Renee Zellweger, was filmed. With its lack of telephone wires or modern buildings to disrupt the background, it was perfect.

Farmers were out cutting and stacking hay by hand. It was slow driving. The road wasn't that bad, but at this time of year it was filled with hundreds of horse–drawn carts piled so impossibly high with hay they were close to toppling over.

Eventually I came to the Prislop Pass (5,000 ft.) and left the Maramures region and entered Moldavia, not to be confused with the country of Moldova, which was very close.

Of all the regions in Romania, Moldavia has had the roughest go of things. Centuries of invasions, tumult, oppression and corruption have instilled a fatalistic attitude in its peoples. But it is there one finds the Painted Monasteries of Southern Bucovina.

According to my *Rough Guide,* "The Painted Monasteries of Bucovina, in the northwest corner of Moldavia, are rightfully acclaimed as masterpieces of art and architecture, steeped in history and perfectly in harmony with their surroundings."

Keep in mind that Romania, a country only slightly larger than Minnesota, boasts over 260 monasteries! The map I purchased in Bucharest showed the location of them all, and believe me, they were everywhere. However, the *painted* monasteries were something special, and I wanted to see them up close.

Without private transportation, or being a member of a special tour group, it would be a difficult task to visit them. Scattered throughout a fairly widespread area, public transportation would be a long, drawn-out nightmare. I, of course, had a feisty Ford Fiesta.

The market town of Vatra Dornei was my goal for the night. It sounded like an interesting place, and I'd read it had been an old spa town since the days of the Hapsburgs, but now made its living off logging and was in the very heart of the Painted Monasteries territory.

Vatra Dornei, indeed, was an interesting town — not very large, yet with plenty of places to stay and lots of restaurants. I was looking for the Hotel Majestic, a recommendation in my guide, but it was nowhere to be found. I did, however, find the Hotel Maestro, which turned out to be one and the same, the name had been recently changed.

I was given a neat and tidy room with a corner window overlooking the city park and downtown area. It came with cable TV and modern shower, and cost only $24, including breakfast. What a find!

After a quick evaluation of my clean versus dirty clothes, dirty won hands down. I decided to have some things washed (A first for me in all my trips. I must be mellowing.) and dropped them off at the front desk, then went out and searched the town for a phone to call my oldest grandchild, Taylor — it was her 13th birthday. Officially a teenager. YIKES!

After the call and a light lunch, I took a walking tour. As I mentioned earlier, it is quite an attractive place, nestled in the mountains with a river dividing it. There was a lively park adjacent to the hotel and I toyed with the idea of getting my metal detector out, but decided against it because of all the people wandering around.

A large Romanian Orthodox church sat on one corner and I went in to snoop around. Local members were giving tours and gave me permission to take photos. I expected to be refused, but they were most accommodating.

As I exited the church an amazing thing happened. I spied two ladies relaxing on a park bench just outside. They looked to me like they could be Americans. I slowed down as I walked past. Yes, they were indeed Americans — their accents gave them away. Americans! The first I had come across so far on my trip.

I couldn't help it, and went back and introduced myself and asked where they were from. It turned out they were two sisters who were on a tour with an organization called Heifer International. And what was even more interesting was the fact that although they now lived elsewhere, they were both originally from the Midwest.

"Really," I casually said, "Where in the Midwest?"

"Iowa?" they replied as if I may not be familiar with it.

I couldn't believe it. "What part of Iowa?" I probed.

"Well, Boone," they said with a shrug as if I'd probably never heard of Boone, let alone Iowa. "As a matter of fact," they continued, "we were just there last week visiting our mother who lives there in a nursing home."

"Perhaps you know Sherrie Amendola?" I asked, in a moment of wild inspiration.

Their mouths dropped open. They turned to each other, and then turned in unison back to me, staring.

"Why ... why ... yes, we know Sherrie," they said in amazement. "We just saw her last week, as a matter of fact. She's a friend of our mother. But how did you know that? Do you know Sherrie? Where did you say you're from?"

Sherrie is my wife's sister, one of seven, and a manager at a nursing home in Boone. I thought it most likely it had to be her. What a laugh we had about that.

And when you stop and think about it, what are the odds of that happening? Here I was wandering around in the mountain town of Vatra Donei in Moldavia, Romania, when the first Americans I ran into were from Boone, Iowa, and knew my sister-in-law! How bizarre!

It was time to check the progress of my trip, so I stopped at a sun-drenched terrace cafe, ordered a beer and a bratwurst, and dug out my documents. I kind of liked this town and was considering staying over a couple of nights. However after checking the maps and realizing I had just a little over a week to go, I decided I'd better keep moving.

I walked to the market area and found myself in a pastry shop ordering a coffee and a selection of mouth-watering pastries. The display case was filled with hundreds of them, all very ornate, with lots of whipped cream and chocolate. Absolutely sinful.

Back in the room I watched some English language programs on BBC and caught up on my log.

Tomorrow I would visit the Painted Monasteries.

THURSDAY, SEPTEMBER 16TH

Over breakfast I selected two monasteries to visit on my way to my next night's stop at Suceava. According to my guidebook they would be two of the best, and representative of the several in the area.

The village of Voronet was a few miles off the highway, near a nunnery founded in 1488 by St. Stephen the Great. All the interior paintings were done during his time.

But what's unusual about these monasteries is that the *outside* walls are painted as well, and these paintings date from the mid–1500s. Voronet Monastery is known as The Sistine Chapel of the Orient.

It has long been a mystery about painted them and the technique used, since it was all done in seclusion. However, the painters' skills were such that the paintings still look remarkably fresh after 500 years of exposure to the elements!

The nunnery is still being used. Over a stone wall you could see sisters gliding silently down the paths, eyes cast down, dressed head to toe in black Romanian Orthodox habits.

My next stop was the Monastery of Humor, another international favorite, this one because of its tranquil location just north of the wooden village of Humor. Unlike the others, this monastery is protected by a wooden stockade rather than stone walls. Like Vororet, however, it was also built for nuns, but these were cloistered nuns, completely cut off from the outside world.

As in Voronet, the famous mural painted on this monastery is also of the Last Judgment. Here, however, the devil is portrayed as the Scarlet Woman!

There wasn't another soul around as I poked around the various buildings. Adjoining the church was a tall bell tower and I climbed to the top. It was a little scary creeping up an exposed stone stairway and then around the outside of the tower with no protective railing, and once inside snaking my way up an impossibly steep and narrow stone staircase leading to the top floor. Yikes!

But the view from the summit made it worth the climb. I could look over the far stockade wall and see the nuns, dressed in work clothes, silently scratching away in large vegetable and rose gardens. I felt a little like I was spying on them.

Well, these painted monastery sites may be world–famous UNESCO sites, but to be truthful, after several hours I'd seen enough. I couldn't imagine coping with one of the multi-day monastery tours. It might be different if I were an artist, or a church historian, or a monk, but by mid-afternoon this heathen was ready to call it quits. One full day was enough.

I arrived in Suceava around 4:30 p.m. It was still a dreary day. I was searching for Villa Alice, and came very close to getting into an accident after getting lost and checking out street signs instead of the road in front of me. Eventually I found it, and it turned out to be worth the effort.

Villa Alice was a three–star pension. The rooms were spotless and the TV featured several English–speaking channels, a new experience for me; I was delighted. By this time in my trip, I was always glad to hear English spoken.

The people were all quite friendly. The manager spoke passable English and the price, including breakfast, was only $30.

After settling in I headed out on foot to see the sights. I'd read that on Thursdays (today) the market would be going strong and I could expect to see cartloads of peasants wearing their traditional dress: fully–lined waistcoats, white woolen pantaloons, and Cossack caps. Wrong!

I found the market filled with lots of carts all right, but the word must have gone out to not wear anything even remotely traditional today because an American tourist (me) would be there to take pictures. So I walked past tables filled with root vegetables adjacent to tables filled with pirated audio tapes. And the peasants looked pretty much like the same people who show up at the weekly farmer's market at home. Darn! Again I was about five years too late!

The main downtown area very cold and drab, and looked just like you'd expect a communist cold war-era town to look. And the fact that it started raining didn't help.

I visited the Princely Court and the Church of St. Dumitru and that seemed enough. At this point each church had started to blend into the next and my interests had begun to fade.

On my way back to Villa Alice I stumbled onto an internet cafe, where I was able to send and receive some messages from home. And right next door was an art shop selling local crafts. The only things that I found that I even remotely considered buying were the decorated hollow eggs typical of this part of Eastern Europe. I ended up not buying any for fear they would be too fragile to survive the trip.

Suceava was also a university town, and a couple of blocks from Villa Alice I found an outdoor cafe with large umbrellas over tables filled with students talking and laughing. It looked like a nice place to sit and catch up on my log so I stopped and ordered a bottle of Urus, the national beer of Romania at 60¢ for a half liter.

While sitting there I was reminded of several things I'd wanted to record but had not yet had the chance. One was how much Romanian people looked like Americans. They could have been my neighbors back home.

The second thing I noticed, and I guess this axiom fits regardless of which country you visit, is that all towns seem unfriendly when you first arrive. But once you've been there even a short time and start to get your bearings, it's surprising how much your point of view will change, and in a positive way.

And finally I've noticed that when my change was within 5,000 Romanian Leu (about 13¢), it was usually just ignored. I found this a little awkward, and never really knew when to wait for change or how precise I should try to be in settling up.

The innkeeper recommended El Latino, an Italian restaurant, for dinner. It was marvelous. A half-bottle of red wine, fresh tomato, onion and cucumber salad, and some sausage–type dish served over a potato pancake (may sound weird, but tasted fine), hard bread and butter, a cup of hot tea and Amaretto ice cream for dessert. An expensive $12, but delicious.

I walked back to Villa Alice in a light rain and was delighted to find my old friend *Jerry Seinfeld*, on TV.

FRIDAY, SEPTEMBER 17TH

If it hadn't been for someone's automatic car alarm going off about every two hours, I would have had a decent night's sleep. It was early when I got up and left. The dining room wasn't open yet, but I didn't want to wait, and I really wasn't that hungry after the large meal the night before.

I turned in my room key to the clerk at the front desk. She spoke very good English and we chatted a little bit. She told me she was a medical doctor at the local hospital and worked the night shift at the inn to earn a little extra money. I didn't have the nerve to ask what her normal monthly salary was, but it couldn't have been much.

I stopped by (believe it or not) a McDonald's on the way out of town for a cup of coffee, then headed south. I had a long way to drive today — clear to Tulcea, Gateway to the Danube Delta. It would be a full day's drive with few, if any, stops.

It was a good day to spend in the car, anyway. The weather was gray, rainy and cool. The highway I was on went all the way to Bucharest, but I'd be turning east before long.

I passed through market town after market town, a large number of horse-drawn carts in the road making it slow going and more than a little tedious.

Around noon I arrived at the town of Marasesti, site of a savage battle in the summer of 1917.

In World War I, Romania was on the side of the good guys and halted advancing German troops here. On the edge of town stood a giant mausoleum containing the remains of 7,000 Romanian soldiers. I stopped to visit and found it very sobering.

By early afternoon I reached the ancient city of Galati, a town very close to the Romanian, Moldavian and Ukrainian borders. Galati gave new meaning to the word ugly. Virtually destroyed during World War II, it was largely rebuilt with a series of numbingly- identical apartment buildings. It has since swelled to become a sizable city after Romania's largest steelworks was built there.

At this point in my trip it was necessary to cross the Danube River; so I found my way to the waterfront, bought a ferry ticket, and waited. By the time the ferry arrived there was a long line of cars and trucks, and a longer line of people. Everyone wanted on the next ferry.

It was more than a little nerve–racking working my way slowly toward the ferry and, once on, carefully positioning my car into a tiny parking spot. They kept loading cars and people until there wasn't a square foot unoccupied.

The Danube is surprisingly wide at this point, I would guess at least a half-mile. And the landscape had changed dramatically. No more mountains, but gently rolling hills covered with vineyards. I was deep into wine country.

I left the ferry undamaged and headed on. I only stopped once, to take a photo of a family of wine growers heading to market with a couple of grape-laden, donkey-powered carts. The man was so tickled to have his picture taken, he insisted I take a handful of both white and red grapes with me.

I reached land's end, the city of Tulcea, around 3:30 in the afternoon. I say land's end because for all practical purposes, this is where the famous Danube Delta began. I planned to spend the night there.

The Hotel Delta was right on the water's edge, and looked nice, and rooms were only $35. A small tourist concession in the lobby advertised Delta Day Trips leaving at 10:30 a.m. and returning at 5:30 p.m. For the equivalent of $24 it sounded expensive, but interesting. I went for it.

However, rather than do the sensible thing and stay right there in Hotel Delta, in the lap of luxury, I saw notices for houseboats that rented "floating" rooms and thought that would be much cooler.

I checked out the riverfront and soon found what I was looking for. For $12 I got a nifty little cabin with a porthole at water level that looked out over the greasy water of the delta lapping right below my pillow. No TV, of course, and the bathroom (or head, or whatever they're called on a houseboat) facilities featured a combination toilet, sink and shower.

In other words, you could shave, take a shower and use the toilet all at the same time. I'd never seen anything like it before, nor have I since.

Flush with my great success (sorry, bad pun) at not only signing up for a delta tour but latching on to a "floating hotel room" at the same time, I ventured down the gangplank and went searching for a place to eat.

Within a few blocks of walking I found a nice outdoor pizza joint that looked inviting. I opted for a seat on the terrace, ordered a *halba Urus* (1/2 liter of beer) and checked out the complexity of the bar menu. Just in beers, there was a bewildering maze of choices, perhaps thirty or forty different brands.

I won't even get into the dozens of bar whiskeys and mixed drinks listed. A person could work up quite a thirst just trying to decide what to order.

Up the street was an internet cafe. It was jam-packed with kids on their way home from school. The manager, a tattooed, metal-studded teenager who spoke broken English, told me to try back around 7:00 p.m.,when it should be less busy.

I had a couple of hours to kill, so I walked up to the main business area of town to check out some of the three star hotels my rough Guide recommended. Hotels Select and Egleza, both $35, looked very nice. So, I thought to myself, if I stayed here tomorrow night, which I felt pretty sure I would, I'd have a nice selection to choose from.

I worked my way back to the pizza place again and ordered a bottle of the local Merlot and house special pizza. I really didn't want or need a whole bottle of wine, but restaurants that sold half-bottles were few and far between. And places that sold wine by the glass were even rarer. But a whole bottle was so cheap, usually around $3, that I just drank what I wanted and left the rest for the cook.

While chatting with the waitress, I learned she earned *quite a bit* in this touristy area, sometimes as much as $100 to $150 a month if tips were really good. And compared that to the other people I spoke with, that *was* good!

She asked me what food cost in America, and what waitresses earned. I think I really shocked her when I said a pizza the size of the one I had just eaten would cost at least $15, and a decent bottle of wine cost $25. I really floored her when I said a good waitress in a busy restaurant could earn $250 – $300 a WEEK (and I low–balled it, at that).

When I left, I saw several waitresses and waiters in a huddle listening to the amazing story my waitress had to share with them.

I already knew that several international companies had come to Romania to recruit young people as waiters and waitresses in luxury hotels and on cruise ships. Makes sense. They are a very attractive people, speak decent English, and would jump at the chance to earn that kind of money.

True to the manager's word, the internet cafe had emptied out when I returned around 8:00 p.m., and I was able to check my messages and send some off. Around 9:30 p.m. I headed back to my floating hotel to relax and read.

The bed was really just a wooden cot attached to the wall, but the bedding looked clean. The gentle rocking and slapping sound of water against the hull put me to sleep quickly.

SATURDAY, SEPTEMBER 18

I had a wonderful night's sleep and big surprise: my closet–sized bath/shave/potty room had hot water in the morning! I cleaned up and went out and checked on my Ford Fiesta, which I had to leave parked on a side street all night.

Instructions on the rental agreement suggested it was a prudent practice to remove the windshield wipers when parking unattended at night. (Someone would steal windshield wipers?)

Everything was still intact.

A word about the Danube Delta: Every year, the River Danube dumps forty million tons of alluvium (I love that word. Sounds better than sludge.) into the Delta, making it the youngest, least stable landscape in Europe. It's a mecca for bird watchers, as every spring and fall vast migrations pass through on their way home from China, India and Mongolia. It's also home to a wide spectrum of four–footed animals, from wolves to feral pigs, who meander though a seemingly unending maze of confusing side channels and small islands.

Bordered on the north by the Ukraine, the delta is also home to the Lipovani, descendants of the *Old Believers* , who left Russia to escape persecution in the late 1700s. These guys are master fishermen and smugglers, and legendary for their non–stop consumption of vodka.

In 1990 the entire area was declared a Biosphere Reserve, and in 1991 named a World Heritage Site.

At 10:30 a.m., 40 tourists boarded a large, double-decker boat. The day was overcast and cool but we had been warned about that, and everyone had some type of windbreaker with them. The majority of passengers were German, the crew were Romanian and the pilot was a Lipovan!

The tour was very marginal. I don't know what I expected, but I can tell you I see more wildlife along the banks of the Wapsipinicon River back home in Iowa. We motored very slowly up and down a series of canals, passing families out relaxing and fishing, then finally "actual" Lipovan fishing camps.

We stopped at one, and I was shocked to see a man plucking feathers from a handful of ugly black birds. They looked like coots, but I think they were actually black scoters, which I doubted were edible. At least I wouldn't eat one.

We passed several patrol boats, out looking for smugglers. They had very quiet engines and the men manning the boats were heavily armed.

By lunchtime, the sun had come out and it was time to eat. When we had earlier stopped at a fishing camp, the crew bought a basket of some kind of fish from a couple of rugged–looking Lipovans, paying with two bottles of vodka.

I ate with a college professor from Germany who spoke such excellent English I thought she was either American or English. Verena lived in Aachen, Germany. She'd taken a year-long sabbatical to bicycle solo around the world, and was on her way next to Turkey. So far she had come 1,700 miles and was barely getting started. Now that would take guts!

By early afternoon, I think everyone was ready to return, and, finally we did, landing around 5:00 p.m. It was an okay trip. I 'd always liked boat rides, but it got rather monotonous toward the end.

I decided to stay in my floating hotel again. It was just too hard to pass up the bargain price, and after all, I had slept well the night before.

Unfortunately, it turned out to be a near fatal decision.

After a quick shower, I pretty much repeated everything I'd done the first evening. I went back to the same restaurant for a drink, (75¢, gin & tonic), stopped by the internet cafe for messages, and revisited the Hotel Select, where I stayed for a fine dinner of spaghetti Napolese, salad and wine.

Afterwards I walked around the main piazza and visited an interesting version of a Romanian–style department store, kind of like a used clothing store, grocery, and auto supply shop all rolled into one.

I then headed "back to sea" and my cozy quarters.

SUNDAY, SEPTEMBER 19

I made a rookie mistake around 2:00 in the morning: half asleep, I got up to visit the "head" and without thinking, drank a glass of water out of the tap and went back to bed.

Thirty minutes later I suddenly woke up. My stomach was heaving! I immediately rushed to the head, getting there barely in time. Thus began what would be a sleepless night of purging.

What in the world brought this on, I gasped? The spaghetti Napolese? The crafty Lipovani–purchased fish? Or could it possibly have been the tap water I drank? WHAT WAS I THINKING? *Of course* it was the tap water, you dummy!

Drinking tap water can be the kiss of death anywhere in eastern Europe. But to do it on a boat docked 50 yards from an outlet where half the sewers of Europe dump 40 million tons of alluvium annually was plain deadly. The boat drew its water directly out of the river.

Whatever I ingested was after me, fast and furious! In retrospect it was a good thing I had as violent a reaction as I did. Keeping that poison in my system any longer could have caused some serious damage. And it's not like I was safely at home in my cozy bed with my doting wife standing nearby answering my every groan and moan. No, here I was all alone on an old houseboat floating in the Danube River in the region of Dobrogea, Romania. No phone, no television or radio, no more hot water — and I was sick as a dog. Probably as sick as I'd ever been.

The rest of the morning was a hazy, incoherent nightmare. I had chills, of course, and could keep nothing down. I lay buried under covers, sweating and shivering uncontrollably, for several hours before forcing myself to get up and out of the cell of pestilence my floating haven had become.

Slowly and shakily, I got out of my bunk. It took me 30 minutes just to get dressed and ready to go. I was moving in slow motion. My head was spinning.

I walked carefully down the gangplank; the last thing I needed was to fall into the water. It was around 10:00 a.m. but felt like midnight. I stumbled two blocks to the car, got in and left. It was Sunday. Not a soul was around as I lurched south toward Bulgaria, very, very upset with myself.

I had originally planned to attend Mass in the cathedral and later visit the well–regarded Museum of Archeology, but that was out of the question at this point. I knew I needed to get some liquids ingested me so I stopped at a small store and bought a large bottle of water and some saltines. They seemed to help.

I headed south on a fairly major road, as far as roads go in Romania. Several times I was compelled to hurriedly pull over and run behind a large tree, or into a cornfield. I took a series of catnaps in between.

Thus it was that Verena, the German biker I had met the day before, passed me on the road as I was napping. She was headed toward Turkey and needed to go through Bulgaria on the way. When I later caught up to her, I recognized her, pulled over and flagged her down.

I was curious as to how she felt. I was still thinking it might have been the fish and not the water as if somehow that would vindicate my stupidity. But no, she felt grand. We chatted a few minutes, I wished her safe travels, and we parted. I never saw or heard from her again.

I was headed south towards Constanta, a major coastal town and the beginning of a string of resort towns that stretched clear down to the Bulgarian border.

It was along this area I planned to dig out my metal detector and find that elusive diamond ring that would give meaning and purpose to my trip.

Around mid-afternoon I realized that I'd survive. I still felt lousy, of course, but was now able to keep water down, and began to feel a little better. That was good, because I was approaching the turnoff to Istria, a famous Greek settlement dating back to the 7th Century. When I'd told Nancy and Eugene Georgeisu I was coming this way, they told me to be sure and stop. Although I didn't feel much like sightseeing, I knew I'd never come this way again so I turned towards the sea.

The ruins of Istria were five miles down a rough road, and when I arrived I found a wonderful museum plus a large natural outdoor area visitors could explore on their own. The entire site was a maze of ancient Greek building foundations, walls, porticoes and columns sticking out of the sand dunes.

I entered the museum and was surprised to find I was the only one there. On display was an amazing collection of pottery, small bronze idol figures, ancient coins, and spear and arrow points, all just loose in cases where you could pick them up and examine them ... and walk off with them if one was criminally inclined.

After an hour I returned to the car and headed back to the highway. I needed to find a room so I could lie down and rest.

At the turnoff I noticed a large canvas tent had been set up at the edge of a field. I stopped and discovered it was a portable Romanian Orthodox Church. People wearing field clothes were starting to arrive on foot, in old cars, bicycles and horse drawn carts.

And when I thought about it, it made a lot of sense. These people were deeply religious and this was the harvest season.

Rather than expect them to leave the fields and go into town to church, the church was brought to them. I suspected it would remain there until the harvest was complete.

By late afternoon I finally limped into Constanta and checked into one of the first hotels that looked halfway presentable — the Hotel Albatross (at this point my standards had started to slip). I immediately went up to a small room facing the ocean, pulled the blinds tightly shut, and crashed. So much for Sunday.

MONDAY, SEPTEMBER 20TH

I felt much better in the morning, but certainly not ideal. As I look back upon it, I believe I was lucky to get off as easy as I did. Lord only knows what I had ingested that night, but whatever it was, it was nasty. Thank God I was able to get it out of my system as quickly as I did.

I took a good look around the room and decided it was much better than I deserved. I had a private balcony overlooking the beach, cable TV, a writing desk and a wonderful modern shower.

I stayed in bed until 9:00 a.m. before getting dressed and heading down to a meager breakfast of hot tea and toast, my first food in a day and a half. I started to feel a little stronger, so got my metal detector and went out to the beach to find my fortune.

To make a long story short, my fortune eluded me. I found a lot of odds and ends, but nothing of any great value. I did find a fist full of modern Romanian coins; mainly of 500, 1,000 and 5,000 lei denomination, but with 35,000 lei to the dollar, it appeared I wasn't going to get rich very fast.

I also found a bunch of old banat coins, which were Romanian coins discontinued at the end of the Communistic regime, and of some historic interest. However at 100 banat to 1 lei and 35,000 lei to 1 dollar, I'd better keep my day job.

There were two things I found, however, that needed further inspection. One was a piece of brass that had the face of what looked like a ancient Roman figure stamped on it, and another very strange coin or token with no letters or numerals stamped on it, only ancient-looking markings.

I'd spend a couple of hours working the beach, then go up and take a nap, and then go back out to the beach again, and so on.

In the afternoon I drove a short ways up the coast and hunted in front of a lovely resort hotel, Hotel Rex, but only found more of the same. The hotel, however, was worth the visit.

It cost $200 a night, so you can imagine it was pretty glamorous. Sadly, it appeared there were only three or four couples staying there. They outnumbered the dining room staff four to one.

For dinner that night I stopped at an outdoor cafe on the beach and forced down a bowl of cream of chicken soup, a beer, and some hard rolls. It all tasted okay but my appetite was still far away in another galaxy.

As I reflected on it, this stretch of seaside reminded me of New York's Coney Island just before being boarded up tight for the season. With the line of hotels running for miles down the beach, I bet it had been jumping in the summer months.

TUESDAY, SEPTEMBER 21ST

My adventure was quickly drawing to a close. Other than the sickness episode which I seemed to nearly be recovered from, things were pretty much on schedule.

The journey from Constanta to the Bulgarian border was only 50 miles so I slept in, ate a nice breakfast, paid my bill and continued south.

I got on a relatively modern highway and passed through the back–to–back towns of Neptune, Olympus, Jupiter, Aurora, Venus, Saturn, Mangalis, 2 Mai, and finally, Varma Veche, which lay around one mile north of the Bulgarian border and a million light years away from civilization.

Along the way I checked out some of the hotels in the "planet" cities. All of them had ample places to stay, so keeping in mind I could always find a room somewhere, I continued on to the Bulgarian border.

Again I toyed with the idea of parking my car and walking across the border to get my passport stamped. However, a long line of people and cars waiting to cross and some definitely unfriendly– looking armed guards reminded me of the fiasco I'd had at the Hungary and Ukraine borders.

In the end I decided not to risk it. I was heading to Bucharest in the morning and the last thing I needed now was something to go wrong and delay me. I turned around and headed back north to find a room for the night.

Unlike the "planet cities," Varma Veche was the proverbial "end of the road"- type place. Very small, right on the beach, no paved roads. PERFECT, I thought. The lodging choices were limited but I soon found a decent-looking spot.

The owner was surprised someone was interested in a room this late in the season (and an American, to boot). He showed me a selection of second floor, oceanfront rooms. I could take take my pick for $18.

The place was very clean and everything looked fairly new. The price was certainly right, and with less than 200 miles to Bucharest, I figured I could do some metal detecting, enjoy a nice meal, get a good night's sleep, plan a leisurely departure in the morning, and still have time to spend an afternoon in Bucharest checking out some parts of the city I hadn't seen yet.

I spent the bulk of the afternoon on the beach. I was feeling much better, albeit a little unsteady on my feet. By evening I thought I'd be up for a regular meal.

I found a bucket full of coins! It was obvious the beach had never seen a metal detector and I actually got tired from stooping down and uncovering them all. They ended up totaling over $10 US — and at 35,000 leu to the dollar that amounted to a lot of coins. Unfortunately I didn't find anything unusual or of great value. I had a moment, however, when I uncovered a women's Cartier watch, still ticking. Had I hit the big time? No. On closer inspection I discovered it was a knockoff.

I also found a few silver rings, keys, sinkers, and the other normal stuff you always find on beaches, but no diamonds, gold, frankincense or myrrh. Darn!

That night I walked up the rocky road from the beach to a small outdoor restaurant and ordered a grilled chicken breast, french fries, mixed salad and half bottle of wine. This was my first real meal in around three days and it tasted great.

As I sat and pondered my trip, I had to admit that I'd missed English conversation and companionship more than I thought I would. I felt a bit out of my element here, and ready to head home.

The village was incredibly quiet, with no street lights or traffic signs and the rocky path running down to the beach was vacant except for a few kids playing kick the can. In many ways, it reminded me of a small Mexican fishing village. Quiet and peaceful.

I walked slowly back to my room by the light of a bright moon. I set out my last set of clean clothes, disassembled and packed my metal detector, and generally got everything ready to check at the airport when I arrived.

I had one more night to stay in Bucharest, but all I needed was a shaving kit and a book to read. I already had a place to stay and was planning to have dinner with the Georgeisus, so all I needed now was get a good night's sleep and a relaxing drive in the morning. Seemed simple enough, right? HA!

WEDNESDAY, SEPTEMBER 22ND — KNOWN FROM THIS DAY FORWARD AS *THE DAY FROM HELL.*

I'd left the window open during the night and had been lulled asleep by the soothing sound of waves slapping against the beach. With a full stomach, I'd slept like a baby. I woke early feeling energized but slightly groggy.

I didn't want to disturb anyone, so I took a quick shower, dressed, left my key on the bed, slipped out and got in the car. I drove down a side street which ran parallel to the beach to the corner, where normally I would have turned left to the main highway. However, the car was steering funny; it was pulling to the right.

I stopped and got out to inspect things. The rear tire was totally flat. Drat! Of all the times and places. It was not only still dark, but I was wearing my travel clothes.

I looked in the trunk and found a spare ready to go. I had a harder time finding the jack. Then the hard work began.

It took around 45 minutes to change the tire. Jacking a car up in sand is almost impossible. In the process I managed to cut my finger, get mud on my shirt and pants, grease on my hands, and sand in my shoes. But I did get the tire changed. Before tossing the flat in the trunk I looked it over and discovered a wicked-looking gash along one side.

I couldn't return to the room to clean up because I'd left the key there, so I wiped myself off as best I could with some dirty (now even dirtier) clothes from my bag and left.

I'd just have to be careful, I thought. No more spare tire but I only had 200 miles to go and, on the map at least, it appeared to be a pretty good highway. Piece of cake. Right!

Of course I got hopelessly lost looking for the "modern" highway to Bucharest. Somewhere I made a wrong turn and ended up on a truck route featuring deep potholes and sharp rocks. I held my breath the whole way!

I did manage to find a little store open, where I bought a couple of bananas and a honey-filled pastry that weighed about two pounds and dripped all over the car seat and my pants before I could finish it. My travel pants were now covered with mud *and* honey — and a slight smear of black grease. I hoped I could clean them up a bit before boarding the plane.

In about an hour I found the highway I was looking for, only to discover the "modern" highway was only halfway completed; the wrong half, of course. However, if there was any good news, it was that it was still early in the day, and I figured I could still reach Bucharest by early afternoon at the latest.

Don't get discouraged, young man, you're as good as there.

I don't know exactly where I was when I had the blowout. I suppose about halfway to Bucharest. All I know for sure was I had crossed the Danube River again and it had starting raining and turned uncomfortably cool. And I was in the middle of nowhere.

I immediately swerved over to the side of the road, stopped and got out. This time the right front tire was flat. I had no spare. It was raining. I was in a dangerous mood.

What now? I knew I wasn't going anywhere. There were no phones in sight and AAA hadn't been invented yet in Romania.

I got the jack out again and somehow, on the soggy side of the road, got the tire off. It was a dead duck, ripped at least two inches, and the inside of the rim had a huge dent where I suppose I had bottomed out in one of the dreadful potholes. There was no way this tire could be repaired. I took another look at the other tire and thought it might be fixable if I could only get it to a filling station.

Did I mention my clothes were getting, shall we say, a tad messy at this point? Well, you should have seen me by the time I got the second tire off, and the flat out of the trunk. Oh boy.

I carried the tire to the other side of the road and started hitchhiking. I remembered passing what looked like a gas station several miles back. Since I wasn't sure how far it was to the next town I thought my best chance was back-tracking.

I was filthy and soaking wet by this time. I wouldn't have picked me up on a bet ... but perhaps standing with the tire by my side would show my misfortune and elicit sympathy.

I was lucky; in about 20 minutes, a farm truck that looked like it had been pieced together with spare parts from World War I vehicles chugged up the road and stopped. I pointed to the tire and the farmer jerked his thumb toward the back, so I threw it in and climbed in beside him.

We started down the highway, zooming along at at least 15 mph. I don't know how we did it, but we somehow communicated enough that he understood what had happened to me and what I needed. I suspect he figured that out before he even stopped.

After an eternity we finally approached the gas station so I pointed and made signs to stop. He just shook his head no and muttered something I didn't understand, and kept going. I started to panic and tried again. He just nodded no and gave the gas station a look of disgust as we passed it.

Now what? Where was he taking me — surely not back to the town I had passed earlier in the day? That would take forever at this rate. But that's exactly what he had in mind because when we finally arrived, there was a "vulcanizer" shop on the edge of town.

Of course, I thought to myself, vulcanizer. That's what he'd been trying to tell me. I knew what a vulcanizer was from my trips to Mexico, where they're called almost the same thing. They specialize in retreading and repairing tires to keep them usable as long as possible.

I jumped out of the truck, thanked him profusely and lugged the tire into the ancient shop. There were a half dozen workers there, all of whom stopped what they were doing to stare at the unearthly apparition that was me as I walked in.

What? They hadn't seen a flat tire before?

They looked at the tire, showed me the rip on the side, and somehow communicated it could be *temporarily* fixed with a patch on the inside. Great! Thirty minutes later, and only $3 poorer, I was back out on the highway, hitchhiking back.

It was almost a repeat performance. Along came a farm truck that looked like a prop from a *Road Warrior* movie. Nothing matched, things were hooked together with baling wire and duct tape. It was the craziest looking thing you've ever seen, but it was running, and the farmer was grinning as I jumped inside. Again, I somehow communicated what had happened, and we headed back down the highway.

About halfway to my car he indicated that the side road we had just passed was the lane to his farm, but that he would take me all the way. I was very grateful, and when we arrived I insisted he take a $5 bill I kept for emergencies. I'm not sure he knew what it was worth (probably a day's pay), but he knew it was American money, and gave me a firm handshake and toothless grin as we departed.

I eventually got the tire back on the car and was on my way again. Another two hours lost! I was cold, wet and *extremely* messy. My travel pants could have been any color. My socks and shoes were dripping. What else could go wrong now? Just wait.

I finally came to the Super Highway — the new government freeway connecting Bucharest to Constanta which I'd earlier thought had already been completed. Never mind, I was delighted to get on it. It was a smooth road for a change and I was pampering the car like a baby. If I had another flat or blowout now I would be dead out of luck.

By late afternoon I could tell I was getting close to Bucharest by the increasing traffic. I definitely didn't want to go downtown. My muddy map indicated there was a bypass that went completely around the city and exited near the airport. This is what I wanted, and when I came to it I traded the lovely new highway for the world's absolutely — no doubt about it — worst road ever! But it was too late. I couldn't turn around and go back even if I tried.

I was only 20 miles from the airport, but the next two hours found me snarled in heavy truck traffic, in the rain, dodging the deepest potholes and washouts imaginable. At any second I expected one of my fragile tires to blow, and there wasn't a thing I could do about it.

I was in a long line of large, heavy trucks. There was nowhere to turn off or even pull over. If one of the tires went now, a truck would no doubt nudge me into a ditch and keep going. I was a nervous wreck!

But thank the Lord the tires held up, and around 6:00 p.m. I finally came to a turnoff leading to the airport. I breathed a huge sigh of relief; I'd made it.

I returned the car to the rental agency, where they immediately went ballistic.

Actually, I think they were quite fair about the whole thing. In the final accounting, they ended up charging me $175 for two new tires, but overlooked the dented rims and rearview mirror I had broken. It could have been a lot worse; but when they took a look at my disheveled appearance, I think they felt sorry for me.

I called Laura from the airport and explained what had happened and why I was so late. We made arrangements for my room and, then I called the Georgeisus and made plans for dinner. We decided to meet at the same delightful place we'd eaten so many days earlier. I then jumped on a bus and rode downtown. I looked a fright, but so did a lot of other people, and I didn't stick out too much. At this point, I really didn't care.

Laura took me to a different apartment about a half block from the American Embassy. In fact, I could look down on the embassy compound from the apartment balcony and watch the armed guards. It was a much nicer apartment and I later learned it was owned by the rental agency. They gave it to me for the same price since no one else was using it that night.

First thing I did was take a long, soothing shower. Oh, did that feel good. Then I rummaged through my suitcase and dug out some clothes which, although I wouldn't exactly call them *clean*, were at least dry and halfway presentable. I hung up my wet clothes on hangers and left the apartment to meet my friends for dinner.

Nancy was waiting for me and told me Eugene had gotten tied up in a meeting and couldn't make it.

We ordered the same entree: beef Stroganoff, with fresh salads, wine and rolls. It tasted marvelous — probably because it was the first decent meal I'd had in days. We chatted and laughed a long while about my adventures and finally said our goodbyes. I paid for both our meals, remembering how little I'd paid the first time.

I headed back to the apartment, set two alarms and collapsed into bed. I had to get up at 3:00 a.m. Ugh!

THURSDAY – SEPTEMBER 23RD

Homeward bound. Yay!

Donu was waiting for me downstairs at 4:00 a.m. He was Laura's husband and had been commandeered to take me to the airport. He was about as awake as I was but during our ride to the airport became quite animated.

He was very upset with the current government, and told me story after story of the graft and nepotism that were running rampant. Apparently he had been to be a teacher but could not survive on the $100 monthly salary he received so he was now trying his hand at the travel and tourism business.

We arrived at the airport and I gave him my last $10 bill. That was twice what we had agreed upon and he seemed quite pleased.

I didn't mind getting to the airport early since I had a bag full of Romanian coins I was planning to use to buy gifts. However when I got there, none of the gift shops were open and would not open until after the plane left. Just my luck!

KLM runs a pretty tight ship and the security was very strict. All passengers had to go through two face-to-face screenings.

"Where did you travel here from, Mr. Bookly?"

"America," I said.

"And your purpose on visiting Romania was ... ?"

"Oh, just driving around."

"Of course. And this bag of old Romanian coins you are carrying. What is your intent for them?"

"Souvenirs for friends."

"I see. And where did you spend last night?"

"In Bucharest."

"Yes, of course. But *where* did you stay in Bucharest?"

"Well ... ah ... I stayed in an apartment. I can't remember the address."

"Whose apartment was it?"

"Gee, I don't know. I rented it."

"I see. Well, from *whom* did you rent it?"

"Umm ... from Laura?"

"And just who is Laura?"

"Well, she works for this company that rents apartments and ....."

"You may sit down."

I went over and sat; I could feel his eyes following me. Jeez, I thought to myself, that didn't go very well. Why do I feel like I'm a criminal? I mean, my clothes didn't match and may have been a bit wrinkled ... but I hadn't done anything wrong.

We left Bucharest and landed in Amsterdam pretty much on time. But another long, drawn out screening at the airport resulted in a hour delay in reaching Detroit and as a result, I missed my connecting flight to Cedar Rapids. Great!

The next flight wasn't for two hours, which when added to the flight time and hour difference from Bucharest to Amsterdam, when added to the long flight from Amsterdam, when added to an additional seven–hour time difference, when added to the flight from Detroit to Cedar Rapids meant that by the time I reached home, I would have been traveling for what seemed like a week.

Oh well, at least I was heading home. Safe and sound. Full of fascinating stories and experiences. And eight pounds lighter (unless you add in a nine-pound sack of useless Romanian coins).

MIDNIGHT AT THE OASIS

MOROCCO

I was off on my first trip to Africa. Specifically, I was headed to Morocco, a country slightly larger than California, and a place where I was assured, English and Spanish were widely spoken.

At least they were right about the size.

Since Morocco is a Muslim country, I also wanted to visit during the period of Ramadan to see what that was all about. The timing neatly coincided with my preferred fall travel time.

I decided to join up with a group. I'd first done this a few years earlier when traveling in Turkey with Fez Travel, and it had worked out very well. This time, I chose a company called Intrepid Travel, which leads trips almost everywhere on earth. They offered reasonable prices, a 15-day trip, a group no larger than 12, and enough "offbeat" features to weed out the casual tourist. Sounded like my kind of trip.

The tone for the trip was established early, at the Cedar Rapids airport, in fact. I was passing through security when I was asked to unzip my suspicious-looking carry-on bag. A loud alarm immediately went off.

"SECURITY BREACH! SECURITY BREACH!" yelled the Senior Guard. Lights started flashing, machines started "whooping", people started scurrying around and I dropped my shoes in a panic. (It occurred to me then that my metal camera tripod had many of the same characteristics as a rifle!)

Of course it wasn't my tripod after all. It was a surprise security drill that took everyone by surprise and left us all quite shaken. It was several minutes before things got back to normal and I was finally waved through.

Cedar Rapids to Detroit. Detroit to Paris. Paris to Casablanca. Or just plain *Casa* as I soon learned to refer to it. The flight went smoothly enough and I arrived at Mohammed V airport at 3:00 p.m. the following day. I was already confused on the time; my biological clock was shaken!

Nevertheless, I was in Morocco. I looked around me and was pleasantly surprised to hear English still being spoken and people looking pretty much like non-terrorists. I started to relax. This was going to be a piece of cake after all. Then I got off the plane and reality set in.

I'd been warned that the Casablanca airport could be a total nightmare, and that I would be descended upon by cabbies begging to take me into town via a "pretty" route and have a "traditional" Moroccan dinner with their Aunt Jasmine, or somebody equally exotic, along the way.

Not me, thank you. I'd taken the precaution of arranging for an airport shuttle to take me directly to Hotel Guynemer. It was the hotel that Intrepid Travel had selected as the place we would meet and stay the first night.

I'd also decided to arrive a day early so I could rest up and not feel like a zombie the first day or two.

The airport shuttle would cost me 300 dirhams (a dirham, at the time, was about 12¢) so we're talking $36 here, which I felt was exorbitant. I was instructed to look for a man holding up a large white poster with both *my* name and the hotel name written upon it. Seemed easy enough.

It was not easy. It was impossible. There must have been a hundred people running around waving signs in the air, none with anything even remotely looking like my name or Hotel Guynemer. I looked and looked. I started to panic. The freelance cabbies saw me flounder and homed in on me like hounds on a wounded rabbit; they scented blood.

After 20 minutes without locating my man, I gave in and began furious negotiations. They all wanted 500 dirhams. Outrageous! I walked away (as instructed by my guidebook).

"450 dirhams, kind sir," they yelled at my back. I walked further.

"400 dirhams!"

"No!" I said.

"350 dirhams!"

I started to waver. There were only two cabbies left and they both looked insane.

"300!" I said in my bravest voice. They stared in astonishment at my audacity. One whirled and walked away in disgust. The last one started to turn, then stopped and stared at me with his one good eye, shrugged and reached for my bag.

"I won. I won," I said to myself as I followed him to his World War II-vintage Mercedes with white-wall tires and what I believe were bullet holes in the hood. But had I won? Was paying $36 to a half-blind, possibly-insane and oddly-turbaned cabbie a victory? At this point I didn't care. I was exhausted.

I was looking forward to Hotel Guynemer. It had received high marks in my newly purchased edition of *Frommer's Morocco*. Three stars, even: *This Art Deco, family-run hotel is a traveler's favorite and beats all others hands-down for friendly and helpful staff.*

Upon arriving, I was immediately attacked by the "friendly and helpful staff."

"What happened?" shouted the distraught manager. "Where were you? Our driver just called from the airport. He's there waiting for you! Who is going to pay for his time and gas?"

I patiently explained that I had looked for him for 40 minutes. He was not there! We argued for ten minutes and I said I was sorry but there was nothing I could do about it now, whirled away with my key and went to my room. What a way to start! Remind me to write *Frommers*!

The good news was that I felt totally refreshed by 6:00 p.m. when I got up, and against the advice of the hotel staff, walked out into the twilight to find something exotic to eat. Something typically Moroccan to set the correct tone for my arrival. A cold beer would be nice, as well.

As I strolled down the narrow sidewalks of the inner city I could hear the strange discordant sounds of the last of the five calls to prayer being blared from dozens of mosques. The streets were almost vacant. Where was everyone? Maybe I *should* have stayed in my room.

Casablanca has about the same weather we have in the Midwest. Seems strange, doesn't it? You'd think since it is in Africa, it should be hot and muggy. But it's actually about the same latitude as Oklahoma City, and it's right on the Atlantic Ocean. So it was fresh and cool when I started looking for a fancy restaurant to celebrate my arrival. Then a *mediocre* restaurant. Then, *any* restaurant that was open.

Finally it dawned on me: it's Ramadan, stupid. There's not likely to be many places open.

They take Ramadan very seriously in Morocco. Absolutely nothing to eat or drink between dawn and dusk: not a piece of bread, not a sip of cool water. Nothing. And I must say I witnessed this throughout the rest of my trip.

At our first meeting, we Intrepid Travelers were told to be very discreet and respectful about our *own* eating and drinking in public places.

But I was hungry and persistent. I searched and searched until I finally found a little pizza place that was open. Barely. I ordered a Four Cheeses pizza and a bottle of water (no beer, kind sir). 50 dirhams, around $6. Not exactly the exotic meal I had envisioned, but it had to do.

As in Turkey, cats rule in Morocco. Everywhere you go, including restaurants, hotels, museums, wherever, you'll spot cats all over the place. Several followed me back to the hotel. No dogs. Maybe a dozen cats. Rather weird, I thought.

I found my way back unscathed and unscratched and was in my room reading and fighting to keep my eyes open until at least 9:00 p.m. I was dead tired, but knew the longer I could stay awake, the quicker I'd get back on schedule.

I enjoyed a marvelous night's sleep. Eleven hours' worth. Down in the reception area I found pots of hot coffee and warm milk, black tea and hard rolls with four different types of marmalade. This turned out to be pretty standard breakfast fare during the entire trip. Occasionally hard-boiled eggs, sweet rolls and fresh juice would also be available, but that was rare.

My group was not scheduled to gather until 6:00 p.m. so I had the day to myself. My plan was to visit both the famous Hassan II Mosque and Rick's Café. I guess you could consider one as balancing out the other.

I had a local map of Casablanca and thought I could walk without fear of getting lost, so I finished eating and left. To be safe I took my handheld GPS with me to lay down a track. Sounds silly but it saved me on several occasions.

Morocco is a kingdom and King Mohammed VI is the current king. He's married and has two children and a collection of palaces scattered throughout the country. His family claims to be descended through the prophet Mohammed so he walks a tricky line as both the country's spiritual leader as well as ruler. You see his image in every single building in the country.

His father, King Hassan II, commissioned the building of a special mosque and pulled out all the stops when he did. Completed in 1993, it is *huge*; one of the largest in the world. It's built on a rocky outcrop of reclaimed land and can accommodate 25,000 worshipers inside and 80,000 more outside. It cost $750 million to construct, all of it public money.

It's one of the few mosques in the country that allows non-muslims to enter but when I arrived I learned that Friday was not an acceptable day for infidels such as myself to visit. I was able to walk around the perimeter but would have to wait until tomorrow to go inside.

I next headed to Rick's Café which, unlike the skyline-towering mosque, was very hard to find. For those readers who aren't sure what's so special about Rick's Cafe, it was the main location in Michael Curtiz's marvelous 1942 film, *Casablanca*.

Although less than a mile away, it took me over an hour of wandering streets and asking questions before I finally entered the front door and was led to a balcony table. I ordered a bottle of Casablanca beer (anything goes in Rick's) and a tureen of fish soup, hard rolls and butter.

The sea wall was in front of me with the sound of the Atlantic Ocean crashing against it. The Medina, or old city, was behind me, with the tower of the Hassan II Mosque visible off in the distance. Quite enchanting, I thought.

No sightings of Humphrey Bogart, Ingrid Bergman, Peter Lorre, Claude Raines, Paul Henreid, or any of the other "usual suspects", but lots of old movie posters assured me I was in the right place.

The service was impeccable and the meal was delicious, although quite expensive ($18.50 for a beer and soup). But I expected the same and was quite excited to be able to tell folks back home I'd actually eaten at Rick's.

Thanks to my GPS I was able to retrace my steps back to the hotel with only minor mixups. Keep in mind very few streets in Casablanca, or anywhere else in Morocco for that matter, run in a straight line. And the ones that have signs are printed either in French or Arabic.

Casablanca has seven million inhabitants and (I'm guessing here) seven million mopeds. I've never seen so many mopeds anywhere in my life — zipping by at top speed every way you looked. Traffic signs were considered suggestions in Morocco and I came very close to be "moped-ed" down on several occasions.

I got back to the hotel in one piece and after a short nap I went down to meet my travel companions. They were gathering in the dining area when I arrived.

As it turned out, other than myself and a couple from New Orleans, the remaining nine were either from Australia or New Zealand. They comprised two couples and five single women in their thirties who traveled together as a group — mainly school teachers, two of whom were sisters. Our leader, Will, was from Guernsey, England.

So it turned out the best news was I wouldn't have to share a room with anyone for the entire journey, nor did I have to pay a single supplement. This was a welcome relief. Not that I have anything against sharing ... but privacy is always good.

They all turned out to be marvelous companions. Fun, witty and very good sports. Very important in this type of trip when things often don't go according to plan. They were very well-traveled, adaptable and took the good, the bad and the ugly without batting an eye. We became great friends in short order.

After a brief meeting when everyone had a chance to introduce him or herself, Will announced he had made reservations for us to have the evening meal together, and hoped everyone was up to it. We were, and walked together to a restaurant where we shared two large tagines, the traditional Moroccan food I'd read so much about.

It was a fixed price meal consisting of hard rolls, Moroccan salad, chicken tagine, soft drinks and fruit.

A word about tagines, which would became a regular meal for us: Tagine is the name for both the meal and the cooking vessel. Basically it is a type of casserole or stew cooked over a smoldering charcoal fire in a two-piece, cone-shaped earthenware vessel called a tagine.

There are lots of interesting combinations such as beef with prunes, chicken with preserved lemon and lamb with dates (and camel or goat – to be discussed later).

A proper tagine meal takes around three to four hours to prepare, so usually Will would order in advance, as he did this evening.

At one point later in the trip, we had a home demonstration on proper tagine and couscous cooking. We quickly learned there is quite a bit more to preparing tagines than it may appear. For one thing, Moroccans are loopy about spices and tagines have more than their fair share. There is also a prescribed way of preparing the various combinations with the correct placement of the meat and vegetables, and correct timing of adding certain important ingredients. They were always quite delicious and we looked forward to them they were to be served.

A Moroccan dinner salad was always the same: finely-chopped lettuce, diced tomatoes, cucumber and green peppers.

Couscous is really the Moroccan national dish, and would be served after the tagine, but since they require an additional hour to prepare, were rarely served to us. Instant couscous is light years away from the Moroccan kitchen.

Over dinner several of us made plans to visit the Hassan II Mosque the following morning, before our scheduled train departure for the capital city of Rabat.

After dinner I wandered together back towards the hotel with John and Chrissy, the couple from New Orleans, stopping for coffee at a typical sidewalk café along the way.

The last call to prayer had come and gone and the daily fast was over by this time. Sidewalk shops were filled with local men sipping mint tea and talking. And smoking. It seemed all men smoked a great deal in Morocco. Marlboros appeared to be the brand of choice and one was able to buy them, one at a time, from the cigarette runners always found within yelling distance.

John worked with a company called Tidewater and spent most of his career overseas. He was temporarily living in New Orleans where company headquarters were located. He told me that he would be assigned to Dubai within a few months.

Chrissy, his lovely and photogenic companion, worked for a company that staged musical extravaganzas around the world and was as well-traveled as John.

This was John's fifth Intrepid tour and Chrissy's third. They had met on another tour a few years earlier. They were both very nice, and we became good friends in a short time.

Our topic of conversation was Will, our intrepid Intrepid leader. Will was from Guernsey, England, around 25 years old, thin as a rail and very, very droll. He spoke a little French and less Arabic. Honest to a fault, he'd told us that he'd only guided a few trips in Morocco and was a bit nervous.

Over dinner, he'd cautioned us all to pack extra toilet paper because "... very shortly we would all suffer from the *shits*." His words, not mine.

He reminded us of Stanley Laurel of *Laurel & Hardy* fame because of his facial expressions and mannerisms. He was definitely green and made lots of mistakes, but he tried so hard to please everyone that he endeared himself to us all in a very short time.

The Adventure Begins

I enjoyed another great night's sleep, so I began to think my body was already in the correct time zone.The group met for an early breakfast in the lounge area, then piled into taxis for our trip to the mosque.

Our guide was an attractive, very pregnant Muslim woman who spoke excellent English. Although I'd been at the mosque the day before, this was my first opportunity to actually go inside. It was as impressive as I thought it would be.

We entered the mosque proper and learned the roof was retractable and currently open to the heavens. It also had clear-glass flooring enabling worshipers to look down into the ocean 50 or so feet below. A little creepy. A 690-foot tall minaret pointed the way to Mecca each night with an ultra-powerful laser light. The ablutions hall, where visitors ritually purified themselves, had over 40 marble cleansing fountains and two large hammams, or baths.

We were not the only visitors, of course. There were many people from other cities and rural areas, visiting and paying respect. I enjoyed watching them, dressed as they were in their colorful traditional garb, almost as much as I did the mosque itself.

We spent as much time there as we could before rushing back to the hotel, grabbing our bags, and driving to the railroad station for a two-hour train ride to Rabat.

It was hot in the non air-conditioned, crowded train but we made a conscious effort not to drink from our water bottles so as not to offend the other passengers. Remember, for Muslim adults, nothing to eat or drink from sunrise to sunset.

Rabat has been Morocco's capital since 1912 and is considered its most conservative city. The train station was in the city center and after storing our luggage in a hotel room rented for that purpose, we set off on foot to explore. We had most of the afternoon.

Our first stop was a fancy snack shop where we bought food for a picnic lunch. The variety was amazing. We held up fingers and pointed at the various pastries and sandwiches. Somehow it worked out fine.

We continued walking down a gently sloping hill toward the river, Bou Regreg or Father of Reflection, where it empties into the Atlantic Ocean. Our goal was the old kasbah — but first we had to pass through the medina.

The difference between the two is this: a medina means an old walled city; the streets wind every which way and are often very narrow, less than a yard wide. A kasbah is a fortified place, like a citadel, often built on high hills near the entrance to harbors, such as here in Rabat. Many Moroccan cities have both medinas and kasbahs and they are usually in close proximity.

We entered the kasbah gates and climbed to a vantage point overlooking the mouth of the river across from the ancient city of Salé, which dates back to Phoenician times.

We split up at this point and explored on our own. I discreetly finished my picnic lunch and hiked up to the top of the citadel to take photos of the harbor entrance. It was a beautiful day and the views were amazing.

I later worked my way back to the hotel and hooked up with the rest of the group in time to board the next train to Meknes. We would have a late dinner when we arrived.

It was supposed to be a three-hour train trip. However, heavy rains in the mountains the day before had washed out a section of track and we were delayed almost five hours. When the Ramadan fast broke around 7:00 p.m., some young Muslim men sitting in our compartment took pity on John and I and shared their bag of dates with us. It wasn't much, but it was really appreciated. It was a very gracious yet typical thing for them to do.

By late evening we were famished. Our young Muslim friends had long since departed, but the female contingent came to our rescue, laughing at our state of unpreparedness and offering us tins of canned tuna, crackers, muesli bars and raisins. Wow, did that taste great!

We finally arrived in Meknes at 1:00 a.m. By the time we got to Hotel Majestic, we were all exhausted and turned in without bothering with dinner.

Again I enjoyed a marvelous, sound sleep. I should mention that all the beds so far had been to my liking: nice and firm. As in Turkey, they don't use a box spring mattress, just a thin top mattress on a solid wood frame. I found them very comfortable.

Our breakfast ratcheted up a notch the next morning with the addition of croissants, as well as hard rolls with wonderful orange marmalade. Of course, with no dinner the night before, we ate everything in sight.

Meknes is one of Morocco's imperial cities. Usually overlooked by the casual tourist, we were to spend all morning and early afternoon visiting the sights. A lot of walking!

The town itself had been settled in the 10th century by one of the wild Berber tribes, but it wasn't until 1672, when Moulay Ismail came into power, that things really took off. Famous as a prodigious builder of roads, bridges, kasbahs and mosques, he reportedly sired 1,000 children, and was known as a monster of cruelty in his treatment of both slaves and subjects.

On the flip side, he was an extremely able ruler for 55 years, and kept a tight hold on the country, basing his power on a standing army of 150,000 West African slaves called the Black Guard.

We first went to visit the ruins of his Royal Granary. Here, huge amounts of grain were once stored in monstrous rooms with walls over 12-feet thick. Nearby were the Royal Stables built to house his 12,000 horses (How'd you like to be on the clean-up detail for 12,000 horses?), and a four hectare pond built as a water source for his hanging gardens.

Afterwards we walked by one of the present king's many palaces (he has 26 scattered around the country), then on to the tomb of the before mentioned Moulay Ismail. It was quite lovely and featured an abundance of the intricate and beautiful tile work for which Morocco is so well known.

At noon we ended up at the souk (market) and split up for an hour of sightseeing before we were to meet for a lunch of camel burgers. That's right, camel burgers. I could hardly wait.

I found all souks in Morocco to be absolutely fascinating. Usually they consisted of several square blocks, with everything under the sun for sale. I was particularly captivated with all the foodstuffs.

I stopped at one date and fig stand that offered a bewildering assortment to choose from. Dates are sold by the kilo. I love dates and ending up buying a kilo, or 2.2 pounds. I'd forgotten about Ramadan, so I had to sneak them out of the bag one at a time. Do you know how many dates are in a kilo? A lot.

The pastry/sweet stalls were also amazing. I'd never seen so many intricate types of pastries and candies for sale. The whole place was swarming with large honey bees that were flying and crawling over everything. No one seemed to care or notice. I suppose they don't eat that much.

At 1:00 p.m. we met Will at a designated corner of the souk and followed him down very narrow, twisting lanes until we came to a tiny shop. It was time for lunch. Inside we met the owner and his assistant, who were busy preparing our salads and burgers.

We entered with trepidation and were immediately served the requisite cups of hot mint tea in small, heavy glasses, with the mint leaves stuffed in the glass and boiling water poured over. A tray of sugar cubes was nearby.

Soon the burgers were ready, and under the watchful eyes of the grinning, toothless chef we dug in. With all the added spices, it was hard to describe the taste but I think the consensus of our group was ... "not bad." This, of course, can mean anything. Anything but seconds. I'd say it made me think of a blend of zebra and ostrich meat that had been left out in the sun too long.

But we survived and the best part was that the lunch was on Intrepid. Afterwards we walked back to the hotel, put our luggage into a van and left for a brief stop at Volubilis before continuing on to Fes, our evening destination.

Volubilis was the southernmost outpost of the Roman Empire during its heyday. According to our guide, it was a Roman settlement constructed on what was probably a Carthaginian city, dating from the third century B.C.

It was a central administrative city for this part of Roman Africa, responsible for grain production. And since it was a great place to grow olives, it became an important olive oil producer for Rome.

Unlike most other Roman-occupied cities, Volubilis was not abandoned when the Romans lost their foothold there. Even the Latin language survived for centuries, and was not replaced until the Arabs conquered North Africa some 400 years later.

People continued to live in Volubilis more than 1,000 years but it was eventually abandoned in the 18th century, at which time it was demolished in order to provide building materials for the construction of the palaces of our friend Moulay Ismail, in nearby Meknes. If that destruction had not happened, Volubilis would have become one of the best-preserved Roman sites anywhere in the world, and despite this, still is a UNESCO World Heritage Site at this time.

We reached Fes around 7:00 p.m. and proceeded to Hotel Olimpics. The final call to prayer was being sung from a nearby mosque, and the manager was in the lobby kneeling on his prayer rug when we entered. We politely waited before receiving our room assignments.

According to my guidebook, Fes is the spiritual heart of Morocco and is the most ancient and greatest of the country's imperial cities.

Within the walls of its medina lies the world's largest intact medieval city. More than 10,000 narrow streets and dim alleyways wind endlessly up and down, around and about, crammed with people, music, noise, and smells. All this and more were on our guided itinerary for tomorrow. But tonight, I wanted to get away from the group and have a quiet dinner alone. All I had to do was find an restaurant that was open.

The hotel manager steered me to a place called Restaurant Zagora, reportedly very nice and within walking distance.

I arrived shortly after 8:30 p.m. and was surprised to find it was not quite open yet. The waiter, who spoke excellent English (as well as Arabic, French and Spanish), led me to an empty table and took my order.

Up to this point on the trip I'd purchased very few meals so tonight I decided to splurge. I ordered a half bottle of local wine (I was surprised to find it available) and the fixed price meal for $19. A starter of fried cheese wedges was served on shredded lettuce with orange slices and I chose an entrée of veal brochette with french fries, asparagus and carrots. Dessert was a wonderful custard followed by coffee and cream. It was one of the nicest meals I had the whole trip. It was also the second most costly meal I've had. I decided that eating in restaurants was an expensive way to go in Morocco. Street stalls, if you knew what you were doing, were definitely the best option. However I was not overly concerned, as most of the meals on this trip were paid for.

When I tried to pay with my credit card, the waiter said they were sorry but did not accept credit cards. I politely pointed to the decal on the door clearly displaying the international MasterCard and Visa logos.

"But sir," he said carefully as if he were addressing a preschooler, "This is Ramadan. No credit cards are accepted during Ramadan."

Huh? Good thing I had enough cash.

I strolled back toward the hotel, stopping for a chocolate gelato along the way. It was almost 10:00 p.m. by this time and the tea shops were filled to the brim with hundreds of men relaxing, sipping tea, smoking and talking with friends.

I paused at a Kodak photo shop and watched as a long line of mothers and their garishly decked-out daughters had their annual Ramadan photos taken. It was a little strange seeing these preteens dressed up in ultra-fancy satin ball gowns, with their faces heavily smeared with lipstick and rouge. I found it creepy, like watching one of those ridiculous child beauty pageants.

The Medina of Fes

I enjoyed another amazing night's sleep; great bed and zero traffic noise. After breakfast, we boarded our van and left for a city tour with Fesian, our lovely Muslim guide.

First stop was another of the King's palaces, right at the entrance of the medina. We couldn't enter the palace, of course, but spent time admiring its monstrous walls and amazing 30-foot high, ornate bronze and copper doors.

We then entered the ancient medina, where we spent the majority of the day stumbling along gawking at the sights and trying to stay together as a group, which was tough. I can honestly say one could spend a week wandering the twisting paths and alleys and not cover the same route twice.

I've never seen such an eclectic gathering of people, animals and shops crammed within such limited space: heavily-laden donkeys and mules rushing by, numerous open air mosques with men sprawled out, praying, various dripping animal parts impaled on hooks, all for sale, snakes in jars, knife sharpeners working on a piles of wicked-looking blades, the famous dye works, weavers and rug merchants, herbalists hawking mounds of weird medicines, mind readers, and on and on the list could go ... It was truly mind-boggling!

We eventually got sidetracked at the shop of a rug merchant, where something happened that needs to be told.

I'd been at rug merchants before in Turkey, and I think it's safe to say the sales pressure can be intense. This was particularly true at one particular shop in the middle of the medina.

We were escorted in and presented with tea. Then we were given a very brief tour of the large and ancient building before being led into a presentation room. The head merchant began his pitch, going though the three levels of workmanship, and on and on.

He concluded by stressing how fine and strong the materials were, and challenged us to try and break one of the braids of binding used to weave the wool together. He singled out a very expensive rug.

"Just try to break," he yelled, strutting around in front of the twelve of us. "It not possible. Just try."

No one volunteered. I'd seen the exact same challenge thrown down in Turkey. No one could do it, of course. This particular sales tactic must be included in Rug Selling 101.

"C'mon and try," he continued with a smirk of superiority and a smiley-faced glance at his grinning minions standing around the room. "Break and I'll mark 50% off price. Who try?"

Still, no one moved or said a word.

Then he made a fatal error. He paused in front of John, the American from New Orleans and noticeably the burliest of the group.

"How 'bout you?" he taunted. "You strong? Break the cord — I *give* you rug!"

I recalled John's bone-crushing grip when we'd first met in Casablanca. Without a word he took the cord in his hands and without any noticeable strain quickly snapped it in two.

At first no one said anything. There were just gasps of surprise. I looked at the salesman, his eyes now like saucers, his olive complexion visibly pale. For a moment he was speechless, and looked helplessly at his equally-stunned minions.

Suddenly the group broke into a cheer and someone yelled, "Atta way, Yank. You just got a free rug!"

Well, this was interesting, I thought. The salesman's gauntlet had been thrown and overcome. His reputation was now on the line. His honor was at stake. Was he actually going to give John the very expensive rug for free?

After some awkward sputtering about never, ever having had that happen to him before, the sales pitch came to a screeching halt and everyone except John and Chrissy, was politely asked to leave. We waited outside for another forty-five minutes until they finally exited with a rug.

"It wasn't *exactly* free," he told us later. "But it was a *very* good deal." He never told us the details, but I later heard someone say they were given a 90% reduction.

That evening we went to the cliff terrace of the Hotel Sofitel for a drink and a golden sunset panorama looking down on the ancient medina. We all sat mesmerized by the view as over 100 minarets sounded out the final call to prayer. It was quite a magical moment.

A block from the hotel, Will led us to a lovely old riad where there a sumptuous dinner spread was waiting for us. A riad is a traditional Moroccan house with an inner courtyard or garden.

I can't recall how many courses there were — way too many, I know. I'm afraid we didn't do the feast justice and left the hostess feeling a bit bewildered.

By this time in the trip, several of our group were starting to show signs of the dreaded "Moroccan Belly" that Will had warned us about at our first night. A few skipped dinner altogether. Will, himself, reported not feeling that great, and some others only picked at their food. I felt just fine.

We arrived back at the hotel at 10:00 p.m. I rinsed out my nylon travel pants and caught up on my log. At 10:45 p.m. I turned out the lights.

It had been a great day – but maybe a little too great ...

Another exceptional night's sleep; I couldn't believe my luck holding. After a quick shower and breakfast, the group hustled into our van and headed south. Our destination was a quiet rural community called Midelt, located in the foothills of the Middle Atlas mountain range.

We made several stops along the way, the first being a huge cedar forest known for its population of large Barbary apes. We pulled over to the side of the road at a designated rest stop and sure enough, a shrewdness of apes came swinging down out of the trees, scampering out of the dense woods looking for handouts. Yes, a shrewdness! We were told these 20-pound brutes were quite temperamental, and warned not to feed or tease them, so we just took pictures and kept our distance.

Our next stop was an attractive and incongruous community called Iframe. Settled by the French, it is laid out and designed as a Swiss village. We stopped to buy supplies for another picnic lunch.

The most interesting thing to me here was the presence of a very prestigious school called Al Akhawayn University, an English-language, American-curriculum institution. Huh?

Here's how they describe themselves: "Inaugurated in 1995 by His Majesty King Hassan II and Crown Prince Abdallah bin Abdel-Aziz of Saudi Arabia, Al Akhawayn University redefines the classic American liberal arts educational experience on an architecturally stunning modern campus amidst the beauty of Morocco's Middle Atlas Mountains."

What in the world, I thought. How bizarre! Stuck out here in the middle of nowhere? No thanks ... I don't care how prestigious. Might be a good place to come if you wanted to marry a Berber princess but other than that, forget it.

Later in the day we stopped at a co-op also in the middle of nowhere run by Franciscan nuns. What? Another oddity. The nuns worked with local women, helping them achieve financial independence with their intricate needlework. Again a very strange stop in the middle of this Muslim country.

By early afternoon we arrived at a large auberge — a sort of sprawling country estate — in the middle of a stark country setting outside of Midelt. After dropping off our luggage, six of us took off on a two-hour hike to explore the region. Our leader was a 14-year-old boy who lived in a nearby village and worked part time at the auberge.

He led us across a rocky and barren moon-like landscape to a nearby gorge deeply cut by a swift moving river. We trekked along the lip of the gorge until we arrived at a tiny, ancient village that I swear hadn't changed since the time of Christ. We stared at the people. They stared at us. Although our boy guide spoke no English or Spanish, he let us know this was *his* village and he was very proud to take us there.

After a well-deserved 30-minute power nap, I joined the group in the community room for dinner. I only had rolls, soup and salad, which was plenty, and split a bottle of very good wine with my new friends. The wine was a local, Guerrouane Rouge, and was quite nice.

At dinner Will asked the group if we interested in having a local Berber musical group come and perform for us that evening. They had heard we were staying at the auberge and saw an opportunity to make a little money. Since it was only $3 per person, we all agreed. The Berbers are an ethnic tribal group indigenous to North Africa.

After dinner we filed into a small room; a typical Moroccan lounge with raised seating and large pillows around three sides.

The entertainment consisted of four men playing small drums, a strange type of violin and tambourines, and two women who sat and sang Berber folk songs. Soon the music picked up in tempo and the women coaxed (translation: forced) everyone to get up to dance, Berber style, and make fools of themselves.

Well, it was more than a little awkward at first, but eventually everyone got into the spirit of it and started whirling around the room in good-natured fun. It helped that wine had been consumed.

It had been another full day and by 10:00 p.m. I was ready for bed. Reading was impossible with a lone 15-watt bulb dangling from the ceiling so I scribbled in my log as best I could and eventually fell asleep. Outside in the stark landscape, it was as quiet and dark as a tomb.

Sometime during the night, Ramadan ended. I didn't realize it until the smiling face of our Muslim van driver tipped us off that " ... a new day had dawned."

A new day or not, the water was freezing in the auberge. I took a very speedy shower, shoveled down a quick breakfast and tossed my bag in the van. By 9:00 a.m. we were on our way again.

Midelt was halfway between Fes and our Sahara desert camp, our destination that night. We continued traveling southeast toward the Algerian border and the desert of Erg Chebbi.

It was a long day's drive broken up with short stops at small towns and villages until we arrived at a hard gravel-edged road. The topography in this area was referred to as *hammada*: a desolate, windswept, rocky landscape, sort of a no man's land, marked every 50 yards or so with small rock cairns to keep you from meandering off into soft sand where a vehicle would definitely get stuck. No tow trucks in this part of the world.

Far off in the distance you could see mountains of sand, the beginning of the desert.

The Erg Chebbi is one of two huge expanses of sand dunes in Africa — 19 miles long and five miles wide — and part of the Sahara Desert. It took the van around an hour to negotiate the road, until we arrived at a desert auberge where we dropped off our gear, grabbed an overnight bag and prepared to say goodbye to civilization as we knew it.

The auberge was a very strange looking place indeed. The best way to describe it would be to say that it reminded me of French Foreign Legion films I may have seen in my youth; *Beau Geste*, for example.

Here in the middle of nowhere was a huge adobe building, low slung, with massive walls, mostly intact and with very few windows. Add to this a grouping of palm trees, simmering heat waves, and a pervasive odor in the air that recalled ... what? (Deep breath) Ah yes — I remember now. Chicago's Lincoln Park Zoo. In August. On a windless day. By the camel compound.

In fact, to the side of the auberge, which was literally built on the very edge of the dunes, rested an unruly group of camels, awaiting our nervous bodies.

We were led to a pile of dusty, heavy wool rugs and instructed to grab one and slowly approach the camels. The rugs turned out to be both our saddles and our blankets for the evening! Lovely.

There was no rhyme or reason as to who got which camel. I wasn't the first to approach them, but neither was I the last. Yet there was one camel everyone instinctively avoided. Compassionate to a fault, I felt sorry for the poor beast and was drawn to it. It was an error in judgment.

I have a theory as to why things went wicked bad from this point on. If you recall, it was only a few days earlier that I had eaten a camel burger. I later compounded the problem by having my picture taken in the medina of Fes with a dripping camel's head impaled on a hook behind me.

Now we all know that camels have fantastic memories ... or is that giraffes? Never mind. What I think is that they also have an incredible power of smell! I mean, just look at their noses — they're huge! So what was I thinking? I undoubtedly reeked of dead camel. Perhaps dead camel kin, for all I knew.

At any rate this particular beast took a healthy dislike to me right from the get-go, starting with its refusal to stand up. While all the others were upright and ready to go, mine just bellowed and tried to bite my foot with his huge yellow teeth.

The camel driver head honcho guy was not amused and after several minutes of some hardcore ear twisting, he finally got the beast to its feet with me aboard.

We started off to our desert camp site. The other camels plodded along quite politely. Mine kept turning its head to get at my foot, my leg, anything. My perch was precarious at best. These were the Camel cigarette variety of camels, with one huge hump right where we sat. The rug was supposed to smooth things out but with all the lurching, it was all I could do to stay on. So it was a very uncomfortable trek that seemed to last for days but in reality was only a few hours.

There were two Berber herdsmen leading us. One stayed close to me and spoke a little English.

"What is this beast's name?" I asked.

"Fatima," he said.

"Fatima? I thought these were all male camels."

"Fatima is tourist name," he explained. "Easy to say."

"What's its real name?" I persisted.

"Number Seven," he said with a shrug.

It was starting to get dark as we moved along and Number Seven eventually calmed down. The scenery was spectacular as the sun started to sink low on the horizon, turning the dunes all shades of tan and gold. I knew we really weren't going that far but at this point it didn't make any difference. As far as you could see there was nothing but undulating sand dunes broken up with small patches of rough gorse. Other than that, nothing.

I was starting to get a little concerned that we were lost. The two Berber guides were chatting together and really didn't seem to be paying much attention where we were headed.

But just before dark, we crossed over one final tall dune and came upon their encampment — a small oasis. We had arrived.

We stopped in the deep dusk and I quickly slid off Fatima — Number Seven — whatever, and scuttled out of reach of her large, stained teeth. I grabbed my rug and small pack and followed the group to four large Berber tents which were placed in sort of a semicircle. In the middle, several large rugs had been spread out over the sand and a couple of kerosene lanterns were glowing.

In the background, a small grouping of date palms surrounded a shallow pond.

It must have been around 9:00 or 9:30 p.m. by this time and fully dark. The temperature had been steadily sinking with the sun, and everyone pulled on sweaters and sat down and discussed the journey while our two guides prepared hot mint tea. Soon three Berber women appeared out of the darkness and placed a pair of large tagines in front of us. Time to eat.

The food was hot and plentiful. The meat, I think, was camel. It could have been Fatima for all I cared. We were starved and dug in like madmen.

After dinner, a fire was started and we sprawled around and joked. Janet, one of the New Zealand ladies, decided to make a list of all the countries at least one member of the group had visited. The total came to 125! I think the only two unclaimed countries I added were Iceland and Ecuador. This was a well-traveled bunch.

We were all tired and turned in early. I say turned in, but in reality, we spread out our blanket-saddles on the sand and rolled up in them and tried to sleep.

It had started to lightly drizzle during dinner so I partially slipped under one of the tent flaps and lay where I could look up at the sky. As the skimpy rain clouds passed, the stars came out in full force and it was literally bright enough to read a newspaper by. What an amazing sight! I lay back and watched for shooting stars. Soon I fell asleep.

Dawn came early, announced with the sounds of bleating goats and coughing camels. Everyone got up and stretched, and looked around in bewilderment. Where were we? What now? Where's Starbucks?

Stiff as boards, we rolled out of our rugs, climbed a nearby dune and watched the sun slowly rise over the eastern horizon, over Algeria, just a few kilometers distance.

It's hard to describe how the scenery changed as the sun rose. The colors slowly shifted from deep purple to tan to gold. We sat mesmerized, wrapped in our rugs against the morning chill, and just stared.

Around 6:30 a.m. we reassembled by the tents, nibbled a meager breakfast and boarded our "ships of the desert" for the return trip. Fatima lay waiting, her large, ugly teeth itching for a piece of me.

Compared to the trip out, the trip back was a beautiful ride as the sun slowly warmed us. Fatima seemed resigned to her fate by now and gave up her nasty nipping antics. It might have been the sight of a set of bleached camel bones scattered down the side of one dune as we passed. I pointed them out to her … him … whatever.

I learned a camel is able to carry a weight of up to 400 pounds for long distances, and that you could buy a healthy camel for around $2,000. They had a life expectancy of around 50 years. After that, it's all downhill, and into camel burgers and tagines, I imagine.

We arrived back at the auberge around 9:00 a.m., rinsed off our faces, had a cup of tea and loaded back into the van and headed west. Once again it was a long day's drive, punctuated by short rest stops along the way.

By late afternoon we arrived at an inn where we'd spend the next two nights. It was in a beautiful area called the Todra Gorge. We got out of the van and had to negotiate a suspension bridge over a fast-moving river to get to our lodging, but it was worth it. The inn consisted of two large buildings and featured a pool! Of course, it was too chilly to swim, but the idea was nice.

I was assigned to a tiny room in the rear that offered lots of privacy and quiet.

The showers in most places we stayed were iffy at best. It seemed that if you were patient enough and willing to wait for 30 minutes or so, hot water would eventually work its way through ancient pipe systems and find your room. Not so here, where the water only got tepid at best. Balancing out that piece of bad news was the fact they had *free* internet service at the front desk so I was able to receive and send off a flurry of messages.

I decided to have some laundry done, and took a small bag to the desk where I was told I could expect it by the next morning. Twenty-five cents a load. I later learned the local Berber women washed them by hand in the river that flowed by our inn. They not only came back cleaner, but sandier. No extra charge.

I enjoyed another wonderful night's rest, but a not-so-wonderful morning sponge bath in tepid water. I rinsed out my travel pants and shirt and hung them out to dry, then went to breakfast.

It was a cool, clear day until the sun broke into the gorge, at which point the temperature immediately started to rise. Our plans today called for a hike through the palmeries, followed by lunch in a private home in the oldest part of town, topped off with a visit to a rural community hammam in the evening.

Palmeries are lush areas of elongated greenways that straddle streams and rivers. It's here where locals raise their crops, wash their clothes and gather to socialize. The greenways can stretch for miles. I couldn't begin to describe all the different types of fruits and vegetables surrounding us as we hiked down narrow paths on both sides of the shallow river.

Women grouped together to gossip. We were told not to take any photographs. "Don't even think about it," Will warned.

After an hour of hiking, we came to an small village (I never could keep up with all the names) and met a young man who was under some kind of contract with Intrepid to host our group for lunch. I must say that everything Intrepid and our guide, Will, did for us was very well planned out.

We entered an adobe house and went up some stairs to a small room. Before entering we all took off our shoes, then filed in and sat on the floor along the walls. He followed us in and made quite a show of fixing us all a welcoming tea which was standard procedure wherever we went. Then, with the help of one of his female relatives, bowls of hot soup were served, accompanied by large, flat breads.

The soup was some type of lentil soup, which seemed to be a staple, as we'd had it on several earlier occasions. The loaves of bread were hot and crusty, and hunks were broken off and used to sop up the soup. The lunch was very low key and pleasant. We spent about an hour there and left, making sure to thank everyone in the household on the way out.

Afterwards, the group split up and John, Chrissy and I walked back to our inn via another route. I had gotten into the routine of always taking along a supply of Mardi Gras bead necklaces with me and handing them out to children. On the way back, we encountered a young Berber mother with two young daughters and I made a flourish of presenting the girls with the beads. They squealed with delight and my gesture earned us a toothy smile from the mom.

I pantomimed taking a picture. "ABSOLUTELY NOT!" was her nonverbal reply.

Mid-afternoon, Will, Saskia, Anita and I went to a hammam. The others wimped out, perhaps frightened away by Will's colorful description of what would take place. The hammam was in a nearby village. He said all we had to take with a little money, a towel and swimming attire. We could buy everything else we needed once we arrived.

Hammans are similar to Turkish baths, but much more countrified. Locals may take daily sponge baths, but once a week faithfully go to a hammam. The purpose is to get REALLY CLEAN and, of course, to relax.

For women, there is the added benefit of catching up on the local village gossip. It seemed that every single town or village we visited had a public hammam. And as expected, they ranged from semi-fancy to "no-frills."

The van dropped us off at a dusty corner and we walked down a narrow alley until we came to a large, nondescript cinderblock building. There was a man sitting behind a little window selling tickets, reminding me of an old fashioned movie theatre. The price for using the hammam is usually around a dollar or less. But we wanted the 'royal treatment', including a massage & scrub. We also needed to purchase a small bottle of shampoo, a wad of soft, black soap wrapped in gauze, and a small abrasive glove. We also rented a small plastic bucket to use. The whole package cost around $7.50.

Unlike my prior experience in Turkey, at a private bath that was part of a hotel, this was entirely different. This was a public affair. Of course we stuck out like sore thumbs, and even though Will was experienced on what to do, it was still a little unnerving. Men entered on the left, ladies on the right.

Room One was the changing room. Like a high-school locker room with hooks. Here we were to change into our bathing trunks, being very careful when disrobing.

"Whatever you do," Will quietly advised, "never expose your bare butt to anyone. It would be considered a horrific insult."

Huh? What's this, I thought to myself. Don't take pictures of women. Don't eat with your left hand. Don't show your butt in public. They really know how to make things difficult.

Room Two was very steamy and had several hot and cold-water spigots available. We filled our buckets with water as hot as we could stand and proceeded to pour it over ourselves, with the idea of opening our pores. People were seated along the walls sort of lounging around as if they were all in a drug-induced stupor, but constantly sneaking glances at Will and I, uncouth foreign dogs that we were.

After fifteen minutes of soaking with gradually hotter water, we started scrubbing ourselves with the small bars of black soap we'd purchased — then rinsing — then scrubbing — and rinsing and scrubbing until all the soap was gone. Then more hot water to rinse — and rinse again. Then we sat leaning against the tiled walls as if we, too, were in drug-induced stupors.

After another twenty minutes of lounging, a stringy young man came in and motioned for me to follow him.

"What's up?" I asked Will in a panic.

"Go with him," Will said with an evil grin. "He's your scrubber. Good luck."

Room Three was the torture chamber. I was told to lie down on the tile floor while my scrubber climbed on my back, cracking vertebrae as he did and started pulling back my arms and bending my legs and pounding all over as if he wanted to erase centuries of pent-up Muslim hatred against the infidel invaders.

In reality it was a relatively short massage/pounding, maybe twenty minutes, but seemed to go on forever. He seemed to know what he was doing and in the process managed to pop or snap every joint in my body. There were several locals in the room getting the same treatment, and soon Will joined us.

After the pounding was over, the young man took the abrasive mitt and started to rub my arms and shoulders so hard that the top layer of loose skin particles started to scrape off! He made a great theater of this to be sure that I and everyone else in the room saw the visible proof of how unclean the infidels were. Then he started on my back, and legs, and neck, mumbling all the while. This went on for another fifteen or twenty minutes, then abruptly it was over. I was left there on the floor; panting, exhausted, whimpering, too weak to stand.

Soon Will was done and he grinned and motioned for me to follow him. It was time to go back to Room One to get dressed and leave.

"Don't forget. Mind your butt," he whispered.

"Yeah, yeah," I snapped back, " I got it."

Unlike the Turkish bath experience, after which I was wrapped head to toe in warm towels and led to a cot to recover, this was in Morocco. No such niceties here, thank you. We carefully dressed and limped back to the van.

That evening the group had decided on a grilled meat dinner. We gathered on the deck around several small braziers, taking turns pumping air into them, getting the coals good and hot, and then the cooking started. When it was time to eat, we filed into the community dining room and had a wonderful meal of grilled goat, beef and chicken, with maybe a little camel thrown in for good measure. I was so tired and relaxed from the hammam ordeal I almost fell asleep at the table.

Tomorrow we would leave the area; another long day's drive west lay ahead of us.

In the morning I had a bold idea for getting hot water! I turned on the hot water tap immediately upon rising, then packed and read and wrote in my log for around an hour. It worked. After around an hour — presto! — hot water.

We hit the road at 9:00 a.m., heading southwest through a mixture of barren countryside and palmeries. We drove through dozens of small, bustling market villages. I was impressed by how orderly they all seemed to be. The streets were filled with people from local farms, lots of mules, mopeds and an occasional camel. It was quite a change from the isolation and quiet of the last couple of days.

We stopped often for stretching, potty breaks and snacks, and early in the afternoon arrived in the town of Ouarzazate, the film capital of Morocco.

Talk about surreal; this place was nuts!

Once an isolated military outpost, Ouarzazate is now one of the major transport hubs of central Morocco, even though it still exudes a frontier-like atmosphere.

Discovered by Hollywood in the 1960s, dozens of major motion pictures have been filmed there including *Lawrence of Arabia, The Sheltering Sky, Blackhawk Down* and *Jewel of the Nile.*

We stopped at Atlas Studios, one of the largest production facilities in the area, and had lunch around an outdoor pool and signed up for the 2:00 p.m. tour. Although a little suspect at first, I have to say the tour was absolutely fascinating as many important and famous film sets are still standing. We visited several of them and had a great time taking corny pictures.

After the tour we piled in the van again and drove for another hour until we arrived at my favorite spot on the entire trip. And, not surprisingly, a UNESCO World Heritage site: The Grand Kasbah of Ait Benhaddou

The riad we stayed in was like a large B&B. My room was spotless and had three single beds, although I was the only one staying there. The bathroom was also very nice and the shower had ample hot water. The riad had at least a dozen rooms upstairs, plus the family quarters, kitchen, and dining area downstairs. But the magical part was the upper rear terrace that looked out over a shallow river valley and ancient kasbah built up along the opposite hillside. The view was drop dead gorgeous.

We dropped off our bags and gathered on the terrace where our host prepared and poured tea for everyone. I couldn't take my eyes off the scenery however, and it wasn't long before a group of us took off to explore the kasbah — and hike to the summit where there was an ancient, fortified granary! Established in the 11th century, the site was an important stronghold of the clans that controlled the lucrative southern caravan trade.

It was a stiff, rocky climb but worth it. We snooped around until the sun started to set and hurried back before it got dark. There were no towns or street lights for miles.

Later that evening, we gathered in the downstairs dining area and met the rest of the extended family. We were served tagines again, but the owner first wanted to explain the proper way to cook them and invited his sister in to demonstrate. Her name was Erika but he called her *Action Sister,* which we all thought quite comical.

Dinner included glasses of fresh squeezed orange juice, lamb tagine, a variety of cooked vegetables, and platters of fruit for dessert. It was all quite delicious.

Will arranged a scorpion hunt later that evening, but for some reason our "scorpion guide" didn't show up. We waited for an hour on the terrace under a canopy of a billion stars, but finally gave up and went to bed. Darn! I wanted to catch a scorpion.

I awoke early after a restless night: it may have been because of my rather narrow bed. That and the thought of scorpions lurking around.

I got dressed and climbed up to the terrace for breakfast. The sun was rising swiftly as I sat sipping hot coffee, munching on croissants with fresh marmalade and watching the ancient kasbah change colors.

All too soon it was time to leave. We reluctantly climbed into the van and headed up into the High Atlas Mountains, leaving the landscapes of the kasbahs and the Sahara Desert far behind.

Several hours of driving through increasingly winding roads led us over the spectacular Tizi n'Tichka Pass (7,000 ft.) and into the scenic Toubkal National Park. It was slow going but by early afternoon we arrived at the end of the road at the village of Imlil.

Imlil was strange. It reminded me of what I imagine a base camp for climbing the Himalayas must be like. And in a sense that was exactly what it was. A jumping-off spot for treks into the high country; in this case, the High Atlas Mountains.

Mingling around in great confusion were groups of serious trekkers, local guides, and dozens of braying donkeys or mules (I never could keep them straight). Parked helter skelter were rugged-looking Land Rovers and heavily-laden diesel trucks.

We followed a narrow road to a cinder block building where we stored our bags and packed only the essentials for an overnight stay up in the mountains. We had a climb ahead of us.

We were given a choice to rent a donkey or walk. All but three of the women opted to walk. I may have reconsidered if I'd known then what the hike would be like.

We started up a rocky path around 5:00 p.m. The path crossed a creek and got rougher the higher we went. Along the way, Diane, one of the Australian women, had what turned out to be an anxiety attack and was put on a spare donkey. A little scary at the time as no one was sure what was wrong with her. In about an hour we had arrived in the tiny village of Armed. An elevation sign read 6,000 feet, but I think it was much higher.

We were spending the night in what is called a *gite*, or mountain lodge, where sleeping facilities were shared. There were several plain dorm-type rooms, and I managed to stake out a spot in a corner of one. Chrissy and John settled in on the other side of the room. Not too bad, I thought, just for one night. But soon Will came in and politely requested the entire room for Diane and her friend, Tony. She looked very shaken and no one argued.

The rest of the rooms already looked pretty crowded so I decided to go down to the large terrace and spend the night on one of the many couches spread around. It worked out okay.

Before dinner I took a stroll around the village. It was very small and built into the side of the mountain. It was all very strange to these Western eyes, tranquil; but *really* strange.

I passed Berber women climbing up the narrow paths, laden with huge piles of wood from a nearby forest. Off to one side of the path, a man was perched high up in a walnut tree striking branches with a stick, while women in brightly-colored dresses bustled below, gathering up the falling nuts.

Young mothers stood in dark doorways sweeping their earthen floors with homemade brooms. Small groups of children gathered on corners playing some strange game with pebbles — all completely oblivious to me as I quietly passed.

I didn't dare take any photos. We'd been warned.

There were no such things as streets in the village, just narrow, rocky paths following the contour of the mountain. At one point I stopped and carried on a fractured conversation with three men who were sitting outside a small mosque waiting for the final call to prayer.

One of them spoke about as much Spanish as I did and he was translating for the other two. It was quite comical and soon we were all laughing. When the call to prayer began they quickly left. I was kind of hoping they would invite me along with them, but, of course, they didn't. I found my way back to the gite feeling as if I had passed through some kind of time warp.

When I got back I found the rest of the group sprawled out on couches along the terrace playing cards and joking around as they always did. Of course there was nowhere to go. Nothing to do. No TV or radio, of course.

The sun had gone down behind the mountains by this time and darkness was descending as quickly as the temperature was dropping. A few tiny, weak light bulbs hung from the ceiling. We were told this village had received electricity just three years earlier and it was used very sparingly.

Soon Will showed up and asked if we wanted to go and watch the women making bread. Of course we did. What else was there to do? The kitchen was very dark and small and lit by two propane lanterns. A charcoal fire was smoldering, keeping the room warm as we watched the women kneading dough, spreading it out over flat stones in the shape of dinner plates and finally slipping them into a stone oven to bake. The bread was for our dinner that night.

And dinner? What else but lentil soup, hunks of hot fresh bread to dip into it and chicken tagine with lots of vegetables. Hot mint tea and melon for dessert.

We made dinner last as long as we could but by 9:30 p.m. the few lights were turned off, one by one, and everyone headed for a warm corner. It was chilly. And dark. And very, very quiet.

I slept, but not great. I was warm enough under the heavy woolen rug blankets but people kept stumbling by on their way to the toilet during the night and because it was so dark, they kept bumping into things as they tried to navigate down the stairs and across the terrace.

I finally got up around 7:00 a.m. and had a quick breakfast with June and Anita. The shower looked too scary so I elected to pass until the evening, when I knew we'd be back in "civilization."

June (her real name was Mei Jun) was the athletic one in the bunch. Petite and muscular, she was going on a mountain hike with a guide that morning. She lived and worked in New Zealand training computer programmers in India. I remember her for having a head of lustrous black hair and a permanent broad smile.

Anita was Saskia's older sister and I remember and admire her for her common sense outlook on life. Saskia taught in a New Zealand high school and Anita worked as a nurse rehabilitating Australian war veterans. They both had a great sense of humor and were very well-travelled.

After breakfast I took off by myself and went on a hike down through the village, across a river and up a mountain road until it reached a lookout point. There I sat and rested, enjoying the quiet and scenery.

We were scheduled to leave after lunch, but first, Will, who was more familiar with the twists and turns of the narrow streets, gave us a tour of the tiny village. It was all quite primitive by our standards, but all we saw seemed quite happy and content with their station in life. They were still adjusting to the introduction of electricity.

When we got back, a spectacular lunch had been prepared for us on the terrace. Lentil soup and a fascinating selection of salad dishes: artichoke with garlic and lemon, okra with tomato sauce, steamed mallow with lemon sauce, rice with tomatoes and peppers, pureed eggplant with cumin, paprika and garlic, and more. It was one of the best lunches I recall having the whole trip.

Diane and Tony finally showed up. She looked much better and assured everyone she was feeling just fine. We'd see.

Early in the afternoon we headed back down to civilization. It was much easier working our way down than coming up. Of course we knew what to expect this time. We got back to the jumping-off spot, retrieved our bags, stored everything in the van and left.

We were all anxious to reach the coastal town of Essaouira (essa-*wee*-ra) before dark, so we only made one stop at a large — no, make that a *huge* supermarket — on the outskirts of Marrakech. It reminded me of a Mega Super Costco, if there is such a thing. In addition to the usual food products and clothes for sale, this place sold all kinds of oddball things such as cars, motorcycles, live fish, goats and lambs. All I bought were some batteries for my camera, and a few snacks. The women went crazy and stocked up on loads of sweets.

Once past Marrakesh, the drive to the coast took only three hours and we arrived just at sunset. I'm still not clear why we just didn't stop at Marrakesh and then continue on to the coast and end the trip in Essaouira. Everyone knew that in a few days we would have to backtrack and end in Marrakesh anyway. I suppose it was because Marrakesh was more of a major transportation hub. For me, it would have worked out much better the other way around.

Nevertheless, we arrived at the coastal town of Essaouira just at dusk. The van pulled up in front of one of the arched entrances to the medina and we unloaded, said goodbye to our faithful driver and headed in on foot. No motor vehicles allowed. Will assured us it was only a ten-minute walk.

We followed him to a small, dim, narrow side street that led to a wonderful riad. Did I explain earlier that riads were once private residences that had been converted into elaborate bed and breakfasts? You see the term *dar* used as well. They seemed to be used interchangeably but dar really means house, while a riad is a *type* of house, usually an upscale place with several floors and open in the middle.

My room was small but the bath was large, and offered my tired and unwashed body oodles of hot water. It was on the second floor and when I stepped out in the hallway, I could look down onto the dining area, or up towards the third floor. Each floor had around six to eight rooms around the perimeter.

We met on the ground floor (which served as lobby, dining room, reading room and office) and went to a fancy restaurant where we were *supposed* to have reservations. Ooops! A small mix-up. Tomorrow night was the correct night. Will was mortified. No problem, there were lots of restaurants to choose from and we ended up at a pizza joint, where I ordered a tomato salad and a marine pizza featuring unidentifiable sea thingies all over the top. I had no idea what everything was and thought it best not to ask. It tasted fine.

It had been a long day so I left the group and found my way back to my room, read awhile and turned in early. I was bushed!

The next morning I went down to a great breakfast: coffee with hot milk, orange juice, yogurt, small pancake-like breads and lots of marmalade.

I was looking forward to the scheduled city tour, a three-hour outing led by a local college professor.

Everything looked better in the daylight. The evening before I had been a little disturbed that the town seemed to be a haven for the international lost youth one sees bumming around everywhere in Europe and Africa these days. Where are they getting their money? There were still plenty of them around, but not as many during the light of day.

My guidebook talked about Essaouira as being one of the most enchanting spots in Morocco; both a laid-back port town and a chic seaside resort. I guess I would agree. I know I liked it a lot. Settled by the Phoenicians in the seventh century, the town you see today dates from the 18th century onward.

Our tour started on the waterfront and worked its way through key spots in the medina where we visited ancient buildings and wonderful craft shops specializing in wood, silver, pottery and original art. It was truly a great tour and when it ended shortly after noon, we all split up and headed out on our own.

I returned to the waterfront, where I had a lunch of grilled sardines and dorado with a coke, fresh salad and rolls. It took a while to figure out how the system worked, but I watched others and eventually chose a stall, pointed at the fish I wanted, and went from there. Fun.

Essaouira is famous for its fish auctions, so I wandered into the main auction house and gawked at the huge assortment of fish spread out on marble flats, ready to be sold to the highest bidders; shark, octopus, tuna, eels of every size and description, red snapper and dozens of other types of fish I was unfamiliar with. I was so stunned it was several minutes before I remembered to take a picture. Too late. I'd been discovered and was not supposed to be in there, and promptly shooed out. Darn.

I wandered back to the medina again until time to gather for dinner. We were going to return to the fancy restaurant and try again this evening. This time it worked and they were ready for us.

I was surprised to see martinis on the drink menu so I ordered one. Soon a young man came and beckoned me back to the bar area.

"How does one make a martini, kind sir?" asked the embarrassed waiter. Apparently no one had ever ordered one. We muddled our way through in good humor.

I wasn't particularly hungry. I ordered lentil soup and two different kinds of starters; some kind of cheese dish and a fish dish. They turned out to be plenty for me, though. Later that evening I stopped at a street-side pastry shop and ordered a piece of baklava.

Again I slept well but woke feeling a "... little fragile", as the Aussie and Kiwi ladies were fond of saying whenever they weren't feeling in tip-top shape. I hoped I wasn't coming down with something at this late stage in the trip. So far as I could tell, I was the *only* one who hadn't had some stomach problems.

Our departure for Marrakesh, originally scheduled for 3:30 p.m., was set back a couple of hours by group request so more serious shopping could be done. I seemed to be the only one not going nuts buying things. My only purchases so far were three alarm clocks in the shape of Mosques which played the calls to prayer. (Big hits with the boys). Today I planned to buy some silver jewelry I had seen yesterday on our tour.

After breakfast I left by myself to revisit the harbor area, which I just loved. Afterwards I took a long walk along the waterfront. It was a lovely day, sunny and warm.

Lots of families were out strolling and everyone seemed in good spirits and very friendly. I walked a few miles up and down the beachfront and stopped at a sidewalk café for a cappuccino.

Later I ran into Janet, Anita and Saskia in the market and joined them for lunch at an outside stall. Grilled sardines and a salad again.

They were carrying armloads of gifts to take home with them, but were worried they wouldn't have room left in their backpacks. I agreed.

After lunch I went looking for the silversmith area, where I bought silver pendants for my wife and our three daughters-in-law.

We eventually left this lovely sea resort town on a hot, non-air conditioned bus, and after a stuffy ride, arrived in Marrakesh. It was almost dark by that time and Will initiated a crazy taxi negotiation exercise that split us into several small groups for the ride from the main bus station to Hotel Menara — right in the middle of the city. After the off the beaten track places we had been staying in, this was a new experience for us.

Hotel Menara was Old World classy. Oversize rooms, high ceilings, and lots of tile. Everyone was quite pleased. My room had two beds, a large modern bath with instant hot water, and a bidet. Quite civilized.

We quickly freshened up and met in the bar at 8:00 p.m., then walked to the famous Jemaa el Fna — *"the pulsating heart of Marrakesh,"* according to my guidebook. It's described as a place where *"medieval and modern mix — a huge open square that daily plays host to one of the most fascinating spectacles in the world."*

From a historic point of view, its name, which translates "assembly of the dead," refers to the time when the square was a place of public executions, complete with severed heads impaled on tall spikes — a practice that was continued well into the 1800s. Today, Jemaa el Fna is the main social meeting place for locals, visiting Moroccans as well as an ocean of international tourists.

We arrived with eyes agape at the throngs mingling around a open area every bit as large as the zocalo in Mexico City; several square blocks, anyway. We were instantly bewildered. Will kept us all in tow and led us to one side of the square, where dozens of competing open-air restaurants were all hustling for our business. He recognized one of the proprietors, who ran over and welcomed us with open arms.

Dinner was on Intrepid tonight and Will began ordering platters of all manner of things that were quickly rushed to the table by smiling attendants, delighted at their good fate of having such a large group.

I tried to keep track, but am sure I missed most of what was served. I did record helpings of grilled egg plant, calamari, scallops, sausages, potato cakes, chicken and lamb kebabs, spinach fritters, and on and on. It was spectacular. No alcoholic beverages, of course, but just about anything else you could think of. We sampled everything and had a marvelous time, both eating and watching the multitude of jugglers, magicians, snake charmers, henna applicators, story tellers, monkey handlers, letter writers, and I don't know what else pass by in a joyful parade of color and noise.

It was late when we finished dinner, and although we were fascinated, we were all bushed. We agreed to stroll around on our own for an hour and then meet at a large mosque on one side of the square, and walk back to the hotel together. We wanted to see more, but we had tomorrow to do that.

I managed to place a call home and tried to describe everything to my wife. It was impossible, of course, but it was good to talk anyway. I was ready to head home in a few days and mentally winding down.

The next morning I went down to the dining room and joined Olga, Anita and June for breakfast. They invited me to go with them to visit some fancy gardens. I have no idea why they thought I'd be interested in doing that. I suppose they were just being polite. I gracefully declined; I needed to go and buy my bus ticket back to the coast anyway. Our trip with Intrepid officially ended tonight and I wanted to get an early start in the morning.

My plan was to go to a small coastal town called Azemmour and stay my last two nights in a lovely old riad I'd found on the internet. The town was too small for bus service, but the larger nearby town of El Jadida was a popular spot, and from there I figured I could arrange local transportation to Azemmour. I didn't know how at the time, but I'd work it out.

I took a taxi to the bus station and bought a ticket for 40 dirhams, the equivalent of about $5. Afterwards I returned to Jemaa el Fna which had taken on an entirely different look by day. For one thing, the open-air restaurants were gone! In their places were juice and snack stands and in the middle of the square were hundreds of people wandering around watching the henna applicators, snake charmers, storytellers and other oddball characters.

I purchased a glass of juice and strolled around. It was impossible to sneak any photos of the people. They were too clever for that. Once your camera was in hand, they rushed over with *their* hands out. The going rate to take a picture of someone was 10 dirams.

Some of the most fascinating things to me were the African tribesmen sitting around the edges of the square with their wares on display. Spread out on blankets were animal parts, ostrich eggs, vials of who-knew-what magical potions, racks of horns, trays of tiny, live turtles and weird-looking lizards tied to strings and ready to take home. The tribesmen were dressed in bright blue cloaks and looked rather sinister.

By late morning I took a cab back to the hotel area and looked around to find a restaurant. Lo and behold, I found a Pizza Hut within a block. I rushed in and ordered a personal pan and a Coke. It tasted heavenly.

The rest of the afternoon I poked around the hotel getting everything repacked and ready to go. The main challenge was cramming all the souvenirs in my small bag. I had packed pretty sparingly before I left home so it was a little tricky.

My bus left at 10:00 a.m. in the morning, and I was told to be at the station by 9:30 a.m. at the latest. I would be on my own from that point, and didn't want to screw up now.

Tonight would be the group's last meal together. We were going to an Italian restaurant that Will raved about.

We met in the lounge and Will led us on a fifteen-minute walk up the busy streets to a wonderful place that looked and smelled delicious. We were led upstairs to a loft area which we shared with a large, upscale Moroccan family.

I ordered pasta with cream sauce filled with lamb and mushrooms and split a bottle of wine with June and Peter. I splurged for dessert and ordered tiramisu.

It was our last official meal together and gushy toasts were made all around. The girls were getting very weepy-eyed by this time. We had earlier taken up a collection for Will and made an official presentation to him. At this point the girls were *really* getting weepy-eyed. Will made some very nice remarks and presented everyone with a token gift. It was all very touching as everyone had become good friends by this time, and realized it would all end in the morning.

On My Own

I was up by 7:00 a.m. Not a very solid sleep, I'm afraid. Couldn't have been the wine; probably the tiramisu. In reality, I expect it was the uncertainties that lay ahead. This was definitely a trip I would not have tried by myself. The language barrier alone would have made it very difficult. But from this point on, I *would* be on my own.

I had planned to sneak into the breakfast room, grab something quick to eat and slip away quietly. It was not to happen. Most of the group were already up and chatting away. Will was there, looking like death warmed over. At first I suspected it was because of too much wine the night before. But then I remembered he didn't drink.

It turned out he was *really* sick. Unfortunately he was scheduled to travel back to Casablanca later in the day and get ready for a new group making the exact same tour. I really felt sorry for him. (I later learned he got so sick they had to fly in a replacement tour guide.)

Janet, one of my favorites Kiwis, was still, according to her own admission, "... *feeling a little delicate.*" Another euphemism like "*fragile*". I knew she hadn't felt right for several days. A couple of the others had also skipped breakfast so I suspect they were on the "*delicate*" list as well. Things were catching up with them. I still felt fine. Knock on wood.

Between Will's illness and everyone splitting up, it turned into a maudlin breakfast, ending with tears and hugs all around. They were, indeed, a stellar group and I was going to miss them. Everyone realized most of us would never see each other again and it *was* sad.

I left the hotel an hour early for the bus station. Better safe than sorry, I thought — but secretly wished I had spent an extra hour in bed.

At the station I puttered around, bought a bottled water, wrote in my log and finally decided to see if I could board the bus early. I followed people out to the departure gates and showed my ticket to one of a dozen attendants.

"El Jadida?" I said. He waved me onto a waiting bus.

Brilliant, I thought. That was easy enough. I found a seat and sat back and relaxed. The bus wasn't scheduled to leave for 40 minutes but it already seemed unusually crowded. Good thing I did get there early.

You can imagine how startled I was when almost immediately it suddenly pulled out from the station. What's this? I started to panic. A young lady was sitting across the aisle from me so I caught her eye.

"El Jadida?" I said gesturing around at the bus.

"Oui, El Jadida," she said with a smile.

Whew! I was lucky I got on when I did. I could easily have missed it. I've never heard of a bus leaving so early.

The mystery of the early departure was solved miles later while traveling through a very barren patch of landscape.

In addition to bus drivers, and bus driver assistants, and luggage attendants, and turnstile attendants, there are ticket takers on Moroccan buses. I saw him working his way down the aisle and was ready for him when he arrived at my seat.

He took my ticket, stared at it a moment, and then started firing questions at me in Arabic. His body language was not good. I had no idea what he was saying.

Everyone on the bus stopped talking and turned and stared. Soon the young lady across the aisle told me, in halting English, that I was on the wrong bus.

"But you said this bus went to El Jadida," I said.

"Oh, most assuredly, it does," she said. "But your ticket no good on *this* bus. *Your* bus hasn't left yet."

"What?" I said in alarm. "Hasn't left yet?"

Well, you would have thought I had a bomb in my suitcase. The ticket taker whirled around and ran up to the driver, who promptly pulled over to the side of the road and stopped. The door opened. Then they got into a furious discussion on what to do with the dimwit infidel. Soon everyone on the bus was offering his or her own opinions. I became either a source of amusement — or irritation.

In a couple of minutes the ticket taker returned and said in fractured English, "Your ticket very bad. Other company. You must leave." He then stood aside so I could exit the bus.

"What?" I said. "Leave? Here? In the middle of nowhere? Can't I buy another ticket?"

Well, there's a novel thought. And, yes, with a little help from the young lady, it turned out I could buy another ticket for the same price. I'm afraid I caught him off guard. I think he was steadying himself for a furious argument and obviously disappointed when I caved in so quickly. Another sign of my millionaire infidel stupidity. No self-respecting Moroccan would have given up that easily. But I gave him 40 dirhams and everything was cool.

We arrived in El Jadida early in the afternoon. After this last fiasco I asked the young lady, who turned out to be a college student, if she would help me get to Azemmour.

It turned out to be ridiculously easy, although I'd never had figured it out on my own.

We got off the bus and she talked to some locals. They pointed down the street where a line of taxis sat. The routine was this: You could hire a cab to take you to Azemmour. This would cost around $6. But only crazy people would do that. Rather you should tell the cabbies where you wanted to go and they would direct you to a cab that left only after it was filled with the requisite number of passengers, usually four.

The downside to this was you might have to wait a few minutes for enough passengers to show up and pile in. The upside to it was you were acting in a respectable, sane manner and instead of having to pay $6, your portion of the fare was $1.50.

The ride to the bus station in Azemmour took 20 minutes. I had no idea where Riad Azama was and had to take a local cab several blocks before we found it. Well, actually, we found the correct entrance. The riad was inside the walled medina. No vehicles allowed.

It was deep inside the medina — down several blocks of twisting, turning and very narrow alleyways. Everyone was staring at me as I passed by doorways, pulling my small wheeled bag. The entrance to the riad looked stark and severe, but when I pulled a large iron knocker and was let inside, I was stunned.

It was a gorgeous place, right out of the Arabian Nights. My room, on the ground level was huge, featuring a king-size, canopied bed, a sitting area and ultramodern bathroom. Right outside the room was a lush garden area and community reading room. Up a flight of spiral stairs was another rooftop reading lounge that overlooked the entire area. The one drawback was the TV did not work, and I'd been hoping to enjoy a little BBC.

The proprietor/owner invited me to have tea with him in the shaded garden area. He was French but spoke excellent English. He was very cordial, but seemed quite cool toward me. I soon found out why. He had misunderstood my earlier emails saying I would need to hire a car to take me to the airport when I left. He thought I meant I needed to be *picked up* at the airport on my *arrival*! He had sent a driver to get me at 4:30 a.m. that morning and, of course, I'd never arrived. The airport was 50 miles away! Sound familiar?

I said I was very sorry and showed him copies of my earlier emails and pointed out his mistake. He acknowledged same, but was still not happy. Not happy at all. Things got worse when he asked if I was planning to have dinner there that night. No, I told him I would most likely just relax a bit and find a place in town. He didn't like that either! Too bad.

I strolled around the various public rooms of the riad and generally relaxed. It appeared I was the only one staying there and there was no one around to talk with, so I was soon bored. I cleaned up and went out to explore the medina, and then the town. One thing immediately puzzled me. I could find no place to eat, and of course there were no bars or taverns in sight. What was I going to do for two days?

Early evening I hailed a cab and asked him to take me to the ocean, I knew it was only a few miles away. He seemed perplexed as to why I would want to go there, but I had read in my guidebook there was a wonderful seafood restaurant right on the beach and I was getting hungry.

The cab dropped me off at road's end after a bumpy, dusty ride. I got out and looked around. First thing I saw were mounds of accumulated rubbish piled up along the sides of the road.

Yes, there was a restaurant nearby facing the ocean, but it looked like it had been closed for years. Broken windows, sand on the terrace, a sign blowing in the wind and hanging from one corner, squeaking loudly.

The whole area looked deserted and sinister at best. It reminded me of a scene from Stanley Kramer's 1959 film *On The Beach* — when the world was hanging on by its fingernails after a nuclear disaster.

What now? I went down to what was once a boardwalk fronting the ocean and started walking. Many of the boards were missing. After about a half mile, I turned around and returned and spotted a small building down a narrow, sandy, side road with a few mopeds and an *old* crusty pickup truck parked in front.

The building did not have any sign, but looked like it might be a bar. In Morocco? I walked closer and heard the telltale sound of clinking bottles and saw some shadowy activity inside, so I walked up, pushed open a creaky wooden door and entered.

What I had come upon was something as close to an outlaw biker's bar as there is in Morocco. Once inside I could barely make out several tables with shaggy-looking men sitting around drinking beer and smoking. Each table had a stack of at least a dozen empty bottles. Whatever talk had been going on stopped immediately as I entered. Unfriendly eyes locked on me. Great. What had I gotten myself into now?

There may have been a 10-watt bulb, at best, hanging from the ceiling. I stood still for a second, praying for my eyes to quickly adjust, unsure what to do. A dozen frowning men sat staring, waiting for the stranger's first move.

I thought of beating a quick retreat. But where would I go? I couldn't walk back to town as it was almost dark — and not a street lamp within a country mile — or *ten* country miles.

I sighed and walked up to what looked like some type of wooden barricade where an unkept, unshaven barkeep was standing watching me. He was wearing a filthy loose shirt, a turban and baggy pants. I pointed to a bottle of beer on the shelf behind him.

Without a word he placed one on the barricade and picked up the 20 dirham note I lay down. I had no idea what a beer cost but was pretty sure I was safe with 20 dirhams, and I received a wad of change. I was too nervous to count it. I didn't want to offend anyone, let alone Ali Baba, or whatever his name was.

I shoved the money in my pocket, sauntered over to an empty table and sat, smiled bravely at all around. I started to drink the beer and stared into space.

It was the drabbest building I had been in yet. A stiff wind would surely bring it down.

After awhile, the locals just shrugged and began to ignore me. I guess I really didn't pose much of a threat. The beer tasted good but the bottle was small, maybe eight or nine ounces. I quickly finished it off and thought it might seem impolite to leave in such a hurry so I got another and slowly sipped it. Eventually, after an awkward half hour, and as inconspicuously as I could, I stood up and walked out the door.

Of course I still didn't know what to do next. I walked back to the road and looked both ways. I noticed a couple of the men in the bar had come to the door and were watching me. No one else was around. It was quickly getting dark. I started walking.

After a mile or so I saw an old bus coming down a side road so I ran and frantically waved it down before it reached the intersection. Thank heavens it was heading towards town. I got on, bought a ticket and sat down. Whew! That could have been a long walk ... in the dark.

It was still early. Dark, but early; maybe 8:00 p.m. I hadn't eaten anything yet and was famished. Bolstered by the beer and my good fortune with the bus, I decided I would go on in to the larger town of El Jadida and find a place to eat there. When the bus arrived at the depot in Azemmour, I got out and found the cab area and announced "El Jadida" to a group of men standing around talking. That seemed to startle them but they pointed to a nearly full cab. I was number four, so I'd topped it off and was treated to toothless smiles by the other three passengers.

Luckily the cabbie spoke Spanish and gave me the name of a seafood restaurant on the oceanfront. I can't recall the name, but it was very nice.

I arrived early and at first I thought it was closed. But it was just that they were not expecting much activity until after nine. So when a millionaire American appeared, they were pleasantly surprised and I was well attended to.

Then another crisis; I was running low on local money and had hoped to pay for the rest of my expenses with a credit card. Luckily I was astute enough to ask before ordering, and discovered they did not accept credit cards even though the Visa/MasterCard sign was in the window. Uh-oh, I needed to be very careful what I ordered.

Everything turned out fine. They had a wonderful special going; three different types of grilled fish (including eel) with all the trimmings. That together with a small split of local wine and I still had just enough for a gratuity *and* a cab ride back to Azemmour.

All's well that ends well.

Morning. It was my last full day in Morocco. But that was fine with me, I was ready to go home. I slept in until eight, showered, dressed and found breakfast waiting for me on an antique table in the garden outside my room. A bowl, yes, a bowl of coffee, a small pitcher of hot milk, fresh juice, fancy rolls and exotic marmalades.

It was cool, in the low 70s, and lightly drizzling. I had been hoping for a brilliant sunny climax to my trip, but it was not to happen.

The owner came and chatted with me over breakfast. He seemed a bit friendlier than yesterday. How did I like the riad? How did I sleep? Did I like Azemmour? Polite chitchat talk.

He only got excited when he told me about a very famous man from Azemmour who had accompanied the Spanish conquistadors when they landed in Florida and worked their way west — down to Mexico City.

I earned back a little respect when I told him that I did know the person of whom he was speaking. His name was Esteban the Moor, a Muslim slave traveling with Cabeza de Vaca. I think there was even an obscure movie made about his adventures. How I remembered all that nonsense I have no idea. Anyway, he was quite impressed!

If interested, you may enjoy reading *The Moor's Account*, a recent book about Esteban's fascinating adventures.

I wasn't sure what to do with myself for my last day. I left the riad and walked to the cab area. An old hand at mass transit, I jumped in a cab and headed back to El Jadida, where I had eaten the night before.

This cab was jam packed with five people plus the driver but everyone was in a great mood. The driver spoke a little English and good Spanish and soon had everyone in the cab laughing.

He asked me how I was getting along with only English and Spanish. I said I knew some French: *Bon Jour. Merci. Ou son les toilettes?* The Moroccans cracked up at that.

When we arrived at El Jadida I gave the driver a Kennedy half dollar as a present and received my first official Moroccan cheek-to-cheek hug. Quite a milestone, I'd say.

I spent the next several hours strolling along the wharf area watching large ships come in and unload their catches. It was amazing and I saw fish I never knew existed come pouring out of the ship holds. Multiple fish auctions were going on and that was also interesting to watch.

I later stopped at a sidewalk café and ordered a café con leche and sat and worked on my log. Apparently not many Americans visited this part of the world and I was a standout curiosity everywhere I went. But I discovered that when I smiled, I would usually get a big smile in return. I smiled a lot.

By mid-afternoon I decided to skip lunch and head back to Azemmour. I would definitely find a place to eat somewhere tonight and get a good night's rest. I had a 6:50 a.m. departure time from Casablanca — and Casablanca was fifty miles away.

It was turning overcast when I reached Riad Azama. I was slightly chilled and again apprehensive about my early morning departure.

The owner had arranged for a driver to pick me up at 4:30 a.m. The cost was 400 dirhams, or around $50. Expensive, but what could I do?

But what if he didn't show up? Or his car broke down? Or he changed his mind? Still, 400 dirhams was a lot of money for a couple of hours work. Surely he'd come for me.

Late in the afternoon I ventured out from my cozy riad for the last time. I found a small internet café in town and was able to check and send off a batch of messages.

Just as it started to get dark, I got serious about finding a place to eat. I just couldn't understand what I was doing wrong. I walked up and down street after street and couldn't find anything that even remotely looked like a restaurant. Oh sure, there were tea shops every five feet and I suppose I could find some sweets to go with the tea. But I needed something more substantial — something more memorable for my last meal in Morocco.

Suddenly, out of the corner of my eye, I spied a small shop halfway down a dim alley. There were no signs, but I saw some men who appeared to be eating at a small table in front. I slowly headed down the alley until I passed by the shop and casually looked in. I saw a couple more tables inside and a few more people eating. But I still wasn't sure. It really didn't look like any restaurant I'd ever seen. There were no menus on display as at most other restaurants.

Just as I turned around and slowly headed back to the main street, a man inside spotted me and figured out what was going on. He rushed out, grabbed me by the arm and gestured inside. "Tagine? Tagine?" he asked with hope in his heart.

Yes, indeed! I'd surely could go for a tagine all right.

I smiled and followed him in. The aroma was mouth-watering and I saw the others eating with abandon. And sure enough I passed by a small cooking area and saw the telltale signs of tagines steaming away.

He made a flourish of wiping off an ancient, scarred wooden table and asked me something. I didn't have a clue what he was saying.

"I don't understand," I said in a loud voice, reasoning that if I talked loudly enough, maybe he'd understand *me*.

Everyone in the restaurant stopped eating and watched.

"I'm not sure what you're asking," I said. "Could I get something to drink?" I said, pantomiming a drinking motion.

He looking at me quizzically. One of the people at a table across the room said something to him. Then it clicked.

"Coca?" he said hopefully.

"Oui, Coca Cola, merci," I replied in relief.

Well, there's not much to this language barrier thingy after all, I thought.

After several minutes a young boy came rushing in from somewhere with a bottle of Coke. He placed it in front of me and bowed with a wide grin.

"Merci – thank you," I said, saluting him with the bottle.

He whirled around with a huge grin and dashed off.

If someone had filmed the entire transaction, I could have sold it to the Coca Cola company for a million bucks.

First came a typical salad, then, eventually, the tagine. He placed it in front of me with a flourish and murmured, "Bon Appetit." Such service. I could have been at the Waldorf Astoria.

I knew everyone within eyesight was politely watching me out of the corner of their collective eyes. Did the infidel know about tagines ... even how to eat them?

Well this infidel did, and I dug in with relish.

I must say it was marvelous! Spiced layers of freshly steamed vegetables — potatoes, carrots, cabbage and I don't know what else delicately covering the savory, carefully-spiced meat that was simmering in its own juices at the bottom. And the crusty bread was still warm from the oven. Oh my!

I lingered in the warmth of the restaurant as long as I could. While I was eating, it had grown chillier and begun drizzling again. By this time the owner had set out a few antique propane lanterns and was trying to attract new customers. I went to pay the bill. Only fifty dirhams, for everything, including gratuity. A terrific bargain.

I smiled at him and patted my stomach demonstrating how satisfied I was. He seemed very pleased and came over to shake my hand, and turned to report my obvious satisfaction to an older woman (his mother) sitting on the ground in the tiny kitchen area behind him. I hadn't noticed her before. She nodded and gave me a toothless grin and returned to what she was doing — trimming tagine meat from a mound of skinned goats' heads. Oh dear.

The thing is, it really didn't faze me all that much. Definitely another sign I was ready to return home.

EPILOGUE

My return home was, gratefully, uneventful.

Getting up at 3:30 in the morning was a bit painful but I managed. The driver arrived on time and raced me the 50 miles to Casablanca's Mohammed V airport without mishap. It turned out he was the same driver who had gone to pick me up in error. I gave him a healthy tip and the remaining Mardi Gras beads. I do believe the beads were more welcome than the money.

From Morocco I reversed my route home: Casablanca to Paris, Paris to Detroit, Detroit to Cedar Rapids. I arrived home pretty tired. Flying west is always hard for me because of the gain of so many hours. It seems bizarre but I actually arrived home that same evening. Try to explain that to my internal time clock.

In retrospect, I accomplished what I set out to do. I visited a new country — indeed a new continent. I made lots of new friends. I experienced the mysterious period of Ramadan up close. I rode a camel into the desert. I ate a goat's head. What else is there in life?

ON A FREIGHTER LEAVING

MEDITERRANEAN SEA

<u>DAY 1</u>

10 p.m. August 30th, 2012. I am zipping along at 550 mph and 35,000 feet above the Atlantic Ocean on my way to Europe. Milan, Italy, to be more precise.

The trip details were rather iffy just a few days ago. It turns out freighters aren't very punctual. I was originally planning to sail away on Grimaldi's vessel, the Spes, on September 2nd. As it turned out, that was like trying to hit a wild turkey with a frisbee.

Eventually I was switched to another vessel — the Fides — and that's how it stood now. If all works as planned, the Fides will leave Monfalcone, Italy, on September 4th; hopefully with me on board.

But it was too late to worry about it now. Better try to get some sleep.

DAY 2

I landed in Milan at 8:15 a.m. As usual I was traveling with a small pack so I didn't need to claim any baggage, and I quickly left the airport. First stop: an ATM, to get a little local currency. I withdrew €120 at the present exchange rate of $1.25 to the euro.

Standing near the ATM machine was a man selling tickets directly to Milan's central train station. I knew the station was very close to the hotel I'd booked before leaving home. Perfect. I bought a ticket, boarded a swank Mercedes bus and headed to the city center.

As we neared the station I spied the hotel from the bus window; Hotel Monopole, just a couple of blocks away. The room was a little more than I was quoted, but the people were very helpful and the room was perfectly adequate. Besides, I was too tired to go out and shop around.

It was too early to check in so I left my pack and walked back to Milan's monstrous train station to get my bearings. There were dozens of "Fast Ticket" automatic self-service kiosks where one can use a credit card to buy a ticket and thus avoid long lines. I studied how other people did it and figured I could handle it in the morning.

By the time I got back to the hotel, my room was ready. Great! I went up, and lay down for a much needed rest. The bed had a very comfortable firm mattress, and there was plenty of room to spread my things out.

After a short nap I headed for the *Duomo de Milano* (cathedral) via the Metro system (subway), which was very user-friendly. A one-way tickets cost less than a dollar. I exited the Metro, went up a steep escalator, and into a gorgeous sunny day. I was stopped cold by the sight of the cathedral straight in front of me.

Milan Cathedral or *Il Duomo di Milano* is one of the most beautiful cathedrals in the world, and is often compared to the Cathedral of Notre Dame in Paris, St. Peter's Basilica in Rome and the Cathedral of Seville in Spain. It took over five centuries to build and is considered the most important piece of Gothic architecture in all Italy.

I went in and joined a small tour group that was just beginning. We spent an hour and a half going from the basement to the bell tower. It was a great way to begin my stay in Italy.

Nearby is La Scala Plaza where you will find the world-famous La Scala Opera House. I was a bit taken aback; my memory of the building, based on my first visit to Milan as a teenage soldier, was that it was much larger and grander.

I hung around the plaza and did what everyone else was doing: people-watched. It was great. I next visited the world's oldest and most famous shopping center, the Victor Emmanuel Galleria, filled with elegant and extremely pricey shops: Louis Vuitton, Prada and Gucci and the like.

After strolling around the area for a few hours, I headed back to the hotel.

Along the way I stopped for a cappuccino at a quaint little coffee shop. The price in the window read €1.20. While paying, the cashier said something to me I didn't understand. I shrugged and she charged me €2.20. I paid but was confused. "What's with the extra euro charge?" I wondered.

I later discovered that what she had asked me was whether I was planning to drink it at the counter or take it to a table. I was charged an extra euro for the privilege of sitting down.

That evening I went to eat dinner at a interesting-looking place called Swiss Pizzarina, which happened to be run by Asians. My pizza, which was okay, cost $10. I should have asked beforehand what the tiny 10-ounce bottle of Heineken cost. I later discovered they cost $4 each! So with the pizza and a couple of beers, plus another one of those miserable table charges, I ended up paying over $20. Ouch! I needed to watch it.

Back in the room I was fighting to stay awake. The longer I could, the faster I'd acclimate to the six-hour time difference.

The alarm rattled me awake at 7:00 a.m. I felt great after a solid night's sleep. After checking my email I went into the hotel dining room for a great european breakfast: a huge variety of rolls and sweet buns, cereals, cheeses, olives, hard-boiled eggs, fruits, and cafe con leche. Wonderful.

I checked out of the hotel, walked to the station and successfully bought my ticket via Fast Ticket. It was a good thing I knew my MasterCard PIN because it would not have worked without it! (A common requirement these days in Europe to crack down on stolen credit cards is to require a PIN, just like with Debit Cards.) The train ticket to Monfalcone cost around $55.

After a little searching I finally found the correct platform, the right train car, and my assigned seat.

A word about Milan's majestic Central Train Station: It is startling, both in size and architecturally. It was completed in 1931 and has 24 tracks. Every day over 300,000 passengers pass through the station on 500 different trains. I can't imagine how it survived World War II.

It's now 9:41 a.m. and I must say the train left on the dot! Only one more hurdle ahead: I had to switch trains at Mestre (Venice) and get on a different train to Monfalcone. Better not get too cocky at this point.

So far so good. I successfully negotiated the train switch in Venice and boarded a new train heading due east. I got on a First Class car by mistake, but as it was almost empty the conductor just shrugged and let me stay. A little fancier and a little more room.

The arrival time is 1:52 and I'm confident it will be 1:52 the way things are going. I can tell you I'm *very* impressed with Italian mass transit. The trains are comfortable, fast, clean and punctual!

We arrived one minute early. Shame! I exited the station and took a cab to Hotel Excelsior. Francesco, the clerk, a very pleasant young man, was expecting me. I was assigned a lovely, quiet room on the first (our second) floor. I wasn't sure how many nights I'd be there but the room was much more reasonable than Milan — only €50 rather than €70. Remember, a euro was worth about $1.25 at the time.

I checked my email, unpacked, and took a longer nap than planned. The local church bells started ringing around 5:00 p.m. and woke me up. I felt very groggy.

I went out and started exploring Monfalcone, and was very pleased with what I found. No straight streets anywhere, and the central district was just a couple of blocks away. If you look for Monfalcone on a map, you'll find it tucked away in the northeast corner of Italy, right by the border of Slovenia, and on the shore of the Adriatic Sea.

I passed by a Catholic church, Our Lady Marcelliana, and noticed Mass was scheduled to begin in 15 minutes so I went in. It was an old church, very large, with at least 50' ceilings, but I found it rather plain and cold.

After Mass I strolled around town looking for a restaurant and eventually settled on the Rocco. I had a couple glasses of local red wine, a huge mixed salad served in, I kid you not, a mixing bowl, and a plate of ravioli with meat sauce. Excellent. It cost €19, so a bit pricey by our standards, but about average over there, I learned. And yes, there was a €1.50 table fee included in the price. (I was supposed to eat ravioli standing up?)

After dinner I strolled back to hotel, watched a little TV, read for awhile and went to bed.

DAY 4

I woke with a start at 8:00 a.m. Still groggy. I went down to the lobby area for breakfast and was happy to see other people gathered there. These were the first guests I'd seen since checking in. I was starting to think I was the only one.

I decided to go to Trieste today. Trains ran every hour on the hour and cost $7 roundtrip. Just a short 30-minute ride.

Trieste was a lovely place, very scenic and interesting; a harbor town with high hills rising along three sides. Lots of churches, dozens of outdoor cafes, broad inviting plazas and the weather was wonderful; warm and sunny.

I managed to find a couple of geocaches, which was fun; one was hidden in the main plaza and another up on a hill by the wall of an old church. Climbing up almost killed me. I am definitely out of shape. If you're not sure what a geocache is, look it up on www.geocaching.com. It's one of my all- time favorite hobbies.

I spent around five hours strolling around Trieste, taking in the sights and stopping for a Coke break in one of the many colorful sideway cafes to do some more people-watching. I headed back to Monfalcone early evening.

By the time I got back, took a nap and got cleaned up it was time for dinner. The Rocco was closed so I settled on a place called the Local Patriot, an inviting side street cafe. It was filled with locals eating and enjoying an aperitif or wine or latte or whatever.

I ordered a glass of local white wine, a large platter of prosciutto slices and selection of local cheeses served with hard rolls. All very good and very European.

When I got back go my room around 9:30 p.m., I had a real-time, Skype video conversation with Don Torney, a friend of mine in San Antonio. (Isn't it amazing how computers have changed the way we communicate?)

I told him all about my trip and asked him to give my wife, Lois, a call to tell her I was alive and well. I hadn't figured out the phone system yet.

Tomorrow I hoped to hear from the local Grimaldi office on whether the Fides would be leaving port Monday or Tuesday. If not Monday, I'd go to visit Koper, Slovenia.

DAY 5

I called Grimaldi first thing in the morning and was told the Fides was on its way, but because of heavy winds it was doubtful it would enter port until late in the evening. Their advice was to spend the night in the hotel and board the next morning. Darn! I was hoping to save the price of another night's lodging.

Rather than hang around the hotel all day, I did go back to Trieste and on to Koper, Slovenia. Unfortunately my timing was off. I caught the train to Trieste just fine but just missed the connecting bus to Koper.

Koper really wasn't that far from Trieste, maybe an additional half hour, but when I arrived and checked the return schedule I saw I had a problem. There was one bus returning at 3:00 p.m and one at 5:30 p.m. It seems crazy now but I decided to catch the earlier bus back. That left me precious little time to visit Slovenia, but I wanted to be sure I was back in case the Fides arrived and left (without me). I'm not saying I didn't believe Grimaldi, but I didn't want to take any chances. I really didn't get to see much of Koper, but, for what it's worth, I can now add Slovenia to my growing list of countries visited.

So I all-too-soon returned to Trieste, stopped at the same little sidewalk cafe and had my Coke and potato chip fix and caught the 4:30 p.m. train back to Monfalcone.

On the train ride back, I looked out of the window and, lo and behold, there was the Fides almost at the outskirts of Monfalcone. Great! Maybe I could board that evening after all. (As it turned out, I couldn't.)

I took a short rest and headed back to the Rocco, the great little restaurant where I ate my first night. It was after 7:00 p.m. By our standards it seemed like a reasonable hour, but as it turned out, I arrived before the cook!

I didn't care. It was a lovely, balmy evening so I sat outside on the veranda at a wine keg table, sipping a glass of chilled wine. I felt very cool sitting there among several small tables of people speaking a variety of languages. I looked out on the plaza and couldn't help but notice that everyone seemed to be Indian or Pakistani sitting around on various benches, just chatting away and having a nice time.

The hotel clerk later told me there was a rapidly growing number of Muslims in Monfalcone and one of the largest groups was from Bangladesh.

One more observation: I have yet to see an overweight Italian. Literally everyone seems to be in wonderful physical shape. What a difference from what we see now in America. On the flip side, most everyone here smokes! It would be interesting to compare lung cancer rates.

For dinner that night I had a tuna salad and a plate of ravioli with lamb. With the wine, table charge and gratuity, my bill came to $30, the most I had spent yet. But keep in mind, it was the only meal I was paying for each day. Breakfast was included with my room and I usually skipped lunch. And from the next day on, all my meals will be on board the ship.

Back in the hotel I got busy making final plans and fine-tuning my packing. I turned out the light at 10:00 p.m. I wanted a good night's sleep. Tomorrow we set sail!

DAY 6

I awoke at 8:00 a.m., and still felt very groggy. My body was very slow in adjusting to the time change this trip.

After breakfast I checked out of the hotel and called a cab to take me to the dock area. We pulled up right beside the Fides, which was busy loading and securing cars. The ship was huge!

I paid the cabbie, got out and stood by the gangplank. No one paid any attention to me so I just headed up the ramp until a Filipino crew member finally stopped me. He checked my ticket and passport and passed me off to another crew member who took me up in a tiny elevator to the 9th level before passing me on to another crew member whose name was Fitz. I'm guessing Fitz was in his twenties and very smiling and polite. He took me to my cabin and told me I had the run of the 9th level. There were 10 levels in all.

My cabin was more than adequate, perhaps 12' x 12'. The upholstery on the couch was a little frayed but other than that I was pleasantly surprised. A tidy little bathroom and shower. A small closet. Two bunk beds. A couple of chairs and writing table, two reading lamps and a functioning porthole that looked out over rows of new cars.

The freighter was chock-full of cars. I later took a brief snoop around and discovered hundreds of a compact four-door model called the Suzuki Splash. Interesting: here we had a boatload of Japanese cars manufactured in Hungary on an Italian freighter heading to Israel.

Fitz told me breakfast was at 7:30 a.m., lunch at noon and dinner at 6:00 p.m. There were a total of three passengers besides myself and I would be meeting them shortly.

This was going to be fun!

1:15 p.m. I'd just experienced my first meal on board and met my fellow passengers; an Italian couple (the man speaks excellent English and will be my info source), his name is Mauro and his wife's name is Maria. They are both consultants. He for Cinzano, she for some financial institutions.

The other passenger is Winfried, a tall, dignified German fellow from Stuttgart who also spoke very good English. He retired from IBM after 35 years, so I guessed he is around 65 years old. He rode his bike from Stuttgart, Germany, to Monfalcone! When we arrive in Israel he planned to ride it from the port city of Ashdod to Jerusalem and later arrange a flight home.

We ate in the officer's mess. All four of us sat at one table, with large bottles of water for each person. Shortly after we sat, three Italian officers came in and sat at an adjacent table and paid us no mind, almost as if we were invisible.

According to Mauro, all the ship's officers were Italian and all the crew members were Filipino.

First course: Pasta Alla Norma, a pasta dish with squash and tomatoes. Gag! Second course: Merluzzo Lesso, pouched cod. Double gag! Third course: Costoletta Di Maiale In Padella, a piece of grilled pork steak with garlic. Very good.

A fresh lettuce salad was served with bottles of extra virgin olive oil and red wine vinegar. There was also a basket of hard rolls on the table. For dessert, a bowl of plums. All in all, very European and very Italian.

The Fides did not leave port until 4:30 p.m., a slight discrepancy from the scheduled 2:00 p.m. departure. I was lying in my bunk reading when I sensed a slight shift in motor noise and, looking out the window, saw land passing by ... always a good clue one is moving! I rushed out on deck and stared in fascination as we slowly pulled away from the pier and headed south. I fired up my handheld GPS and saw we were already moving at 14 mph. Not bad for a ship this size.

Forty-five minutes later we were passing by the Bay of Trieste and heading out to deep waters. Like the other passengers, I was rushing from one side of the ship to the other, taking photographs. It was all very exciting.

Before I knew it, it was time for dinner. Fitz, as it turned out, was not only our cabin steward, he was also our waiter and "go to" guy. He knew everything.

Our first evening's menu was extensive: First Course: Risi E Bisi, a rice dish with lots of vegetables. Good. Second Course: Caponata Alla Siciliana, a cooked vegetable salad made with chopped fried eggplant and celery. Gag! Third Course: Fettine Ai Ferri, a thin slice of grilled beef, served with fresh quartered tomatoes and cucumbers. Very good. A fresh peach for dessert. Winfried and I each ordered small airport-size bottles of red wine.

So far I was impressed with the food! As long as the *Goods* outweighed the *Gags*, I'd be fine.

By 7:30 p.m. the sun was low on the horizon. My new friends and I were out on the deck admiring the sunset and quietly chatting. I was really enjoying myself so far. Everything was so new and exciting. I only hoped it stayed that way. We'll know in a few days.

Later I returned to my cabin and continued to edit my second novel, *Ophelia's Brooch*. I'd already finished the first three chapters!

DAY 7

I slept very well despite heavy rain, thunder and lightning during most of the night. The bunk was just fine for someone my size but had to be a bit cramped for anyone much taller, such as Winfried, who is well over six feet.

I entered the dining room early and tried a cup of their horribly strong coffee.

All our breakfasts were fairly standard: Cold cereals, boiled eggs and rolls with marmalade. And ultra-strong coffee, which I never did get used to. Our small group was loosening up a little more with one another.

Master Gilligan came in the dining room this morning and sat at the officer's table. Gilligan was my name for the Captain.

He'd been the only one so far dressed in white. The rest of the officers wore tan outfits. He seemed pleasant enough and practiced his English on us, apologizing for the fact the TV in the lounge was not working. (According to Mauro, the TV never works on these ships. Neither does the VCR player.) I had a hard time understanding his English, so Mauro was very helpful.

I later found out his real name was Falanga, which is Sicilian for *gangplank*. Well, that didn't sound very promising considering we are on a ship.

I looked at the GPS and it showed we were opposite Bosnia at the moment, heading southeast at 16 mph — 582 miles to Piraeus, Greece, our first stop.

This morning we participated in a safety drill: what to do in case of a fire, what to do with a man falls overboard, and so forth. The drill was conducted in "English" of which I understood about half.

We then took a tour of the entire 9th level of the ship which was very interesting. The 9th level was the "main" level where the bridge (control center of the ship) was located. We were told we could visit there whenever we wanted as long as we stayed out of the way. I was looking forward to this as there were lots of very cool electronics there.

We were also told the best time to look for dolphins and whales was at sunrise and sunset, and that at night there were loads of shooting stars to be seen out here in the pollution-free air. All true.

On our tour we passed a smaller group of cars under tarps: Luxury BMWs and a pair of gorgeous Porsche roadsters. Besides the Suzuki Splashes, I still don't know what other kinds of vehicles were on the lower eight decks, but I do know that all total there were 2,500 automobiles of one type or another.

By mid-morning the sun came out and the clouds turned from grey to white to fluffy and white.

Lunch consisted of some kind of tube pasta in tomato sauce, followed by a filet of salmon, followed by a slice of grilled beef with a lettuce salad. All very tasty. Dessert was a large slice of some wonderful kind of locally-grown melon.

There were several new officers in the dining room with us today, sitting at their own table, of course.

With the exception of the Master Gilligan, the officers looked like the cast of *The Godfather*, or my senior class at Dowling High in Des Moines, where half were first generation Italians.

During the meal, Master Gilligan, in a power move of some type, found fault with something served. The chef was summoned out of the kitchen and in front of everyone received a barrage of uncomplimentary comments from Gilligan. From all the pointing and gesturing, I think it had something to do with the cheese.

That afternoon, we passed by the Yugoslavian coast and came up even with the Bosnian border. The radar units on the bridge pin-pointed our position exactly; we were probably less than five miles from the coast as we continued south. The sea was a sparkling, deep blue and the air cool and fresh.

Dinner tonight was another wonderful experience. Potato soup with pasta, zucchini with crusted cheese, a slice of grilled veal and lettuce salad, and a slice of watermelon for dessert. All this was washed down with a bottle of local white wine. I could get used to this.

During dinner, a passenger ferry passed in front of us going from Dubrovnik, Yugoslavia, to Pescara, Italy. I was reminded it was the same trip I had taken years earlier with a dear friend of mine, Fr. Frank O'Meara. When was it? 1976 or 1977? Good Lord, where has the time gone ... it seems like only yesterday ...

I asked my Italian friend Mauro about the incident between Master Gilligan and the chef. I was right: it was an argument about cheese. Gilligan was chastising the chef for leaving the cheese unrefrigerated. The chef's position was that to refrigerate it would be a sacrilege and ruin the flavor. It would be perfectly fine for several days.

Mauro said the chef was correct, but he was just a chef and not a Master, so you know how that turned out.

I sensed the weather getting warmer as we headed further south. We were now around 400 miles from Greece and almost at the tip of Italy, closing in on the bottom of the heel.

By morning we would be in Albanian waters. The sea was much calmer today and I could see two other freighters in the distance. All quite lovely.

Bringing my laptop along with me turned out to be a smart decision. I almost left it at home. Although I can't hook into the internet I spend a few hours every day editing my book. In the evening I use it to watch DVDs. Tonight I will finish watching *The Assassins* with Sylvester Stallone and Antonio Banderas.

My social calendar is very flexible at this point.

DAY 8

Up early to wander outside before breakfast and up to the bridge to check out the radar screens. They're fascinating and filled with detail. I should point out that when I was in the army, I worked with large radar devices, tracking down mortar locations. Radar holds a special attraction for me.

The screens showed we were just passing by the edge of southern Italy and getting close to Greek waters. We were also passing out of the Adriatic Sea and moving into the Ionian Sea. The weather was still quite lovely.

I spend my daily hours working on my trip log and the edit of my new book, *Ophelia's Brooch*. I am already past page 200. When not doing that I go for a stroll around the perimeter of the ship and end up at the bridge, where I go in and check their fancy electronics. Since the vessel is so large, all the walking is pretty good exercise.

Later in the day: All right, I'll admit it. I'm borderline bored. Thank goodness I brought along my computer. The problem is I am the only native English speaker on the vessel and while almost everyone can communicate in English, I think it is very tiring for them. So we interact in spurts. That's fine with me at this point.

I continue to be impressed with the meals. Breakfast is fairly standard with an occasional surprise. This morning's surprise were slices of grilled ham as well as yogurt and coconut cookies?

Pranzo (lunch) started with slices of more cold cuts and something like potato salad for appetizers. Then a pasta with meat sauce followed by a slice of pork in Ragu sauce. A wedge of lettuce and a banana.

This afternoon the Fides crew conducted an impromptu fire drill. If I'd been prepared I would have filmed it and posted it on YouTube. It would have instantly gone spiral, or viral, or whatever. It was hilarious!

It all began with a very loud alarm bell, followed by garbled yelling coming over public address speakers alive with static. After what seemed like an inordinate amount of time out came the twenty-five chuckling crew members, running helter-skelter on deck with high pressure hoses, life jackets worn every which way, running and colliding with each other, while whistles were being blown and with absolutely no organization that I could see. Think *Keystone Kops*.

Suddenly, to everyone's surprise, one water hose actually did come on. Unfortunately it was aimed directly at two crew members and almost blew one of them over the side of the ship.

It soon turned into a scene out of a Rocky Balboa film, with the crew sparring in pairs, punching each other in their life vests like a crowd of goofy high school boys. Just when I thought it couldn't get any worse, there was a rush for the life boat. Several members charged up the narrow steps and into the boat itself. Oh no, I thought, they're not actually going to try lowering it into the water. Thank goodness they didn't, but they did start the diesel engine and let it run for a while. Thirty minutes later, following a loud pep talk by the Chief Petty Thingy, the fire drill was over to loud cheering and high fives all around.

Apparently it went very well. Master Gilligan was nowhere to be seen during the exercise.

Please God, don't let there be a real fire until after I disembark.

Cena (dinner) tonight was quite delicious: a healthy bowl of rice soup with beans, a quarter baked chicken in some type of red sauce, and a plate of cheeses, apple slices and lettuce. For dessert, a bowl of chocolate chip gelato.

I don't know where I'm putting all this food. And I'm not sure why I'm writing about it so much. I guess because everything is so different and I still find it intriguing. That, plus mealtimes are the only scheduled social events that take place. Remember, this is a freighter, not a cruise ship.

We were told to set our watches ahead one hour tonight which will make an eight-hour difference from home. We also learned we would arrive at Piraeus, Greece, tomorrow evening, later than planned. Not sure if we'll have much time to visit Athens.

We are definitely in a warmer clime now. Tomorrow I planned to switch into shorts.

DAY 9

We were getting close to Piraeus, the port city of Athens, and the ship traffic was getting heavier and heavier. Very soon we'd be weaving in and out of islands on the way to port. After a few days at sea we are finally making our first stop. Should be interesting, and definitely scenic.

Last evening I finished making my initial changes to *Ophelia's Brooch*. When I get home I'll order a few copies and get the proofreaders busy.

I'd been thinking of a devilish practical joke. I'd noticed all 2,000+ Suzuki Splashes were unlocked and each car had its own ignition key sitting on the passenger seat. Now, what would happen if someone were to switch the keys around? Especially on those vehicles at the head of the line leading off the ship? Now, that would be something to see.

I obviously have too much time on my hands.

We were now passing very close to the Greek Islands and had come around the southernmost tip of Greece and made a very slow turn north toward Athens. I went up to the bridge and found Gilligan doing something at the electronic controls. I think he was programming in new coordinates, while a group of his minions crowded around him trying to look impressed.

I was eager to see how the docking procedure takes place. Stopping one of these big freighters must be a little dicey. If I remember correctly, the Fides is over two football fields long. I'd think it would be easier to stop a runaway freight train.

I hoped Gilligan was up to the task.

One thing I've learned is the Filipino crew speak Tagalog and do not speak Italian. The Italian officers do not speak Tagalog, so they communicate with each other in English. I can barely understand them as they shout nautical commands back and forth in fractured English. It was a little scary.

It's interesting to note the people on board are comprised of Filipinos, Italians, one German and one American. But, as it turns out, the official language is English. America rules!

Apparently passengers are expected to exhibit common sense on freighters. We basically have the run of the 9th deck, including the bridge. But one must watch where one is going. The deck is crowded with cars, cables, tie-downs, lifeboats, buckets of paint, welding equipment, and who knows what else.

The Fides, as was made clear to us on numerous occasions, is a working freighter, not a cruise ship.

The waters we were in at any one moment seem to shift from name to name. We started off on the Adriatic Sea and headed south. In a couple of days we entered the Ionian Sea. Then as we headed around Greece we were in the Mediterranean Sea for a short time until we headed north into the Aegean Sea.

Okay, another interesting, yet unappetizing meal today: a pasta with meat sauce, a couple of grilled, skinny, long fish and a slice of very lemony tasting meat. Lettuce, rolls and watermelon.

We were just 50 miles from port and expected to dock around 6:00 p.m. None of the passengers were sure what that meant as far as sightseeing was concerned. I didn't think we'd have much time. We would have to be satisfied with a tour of Piraeus and forget Athens.

The ship really slowed down as we neared the busy port. Soon a boat headed out to us from shore, coming to drop off the Port Pilot, the Big Cheese. When he walked into the bridge, you could see how important he was. All the officers seemed to drop in rank at least one notch as he started shouting out nautical commands, which were repeated starting with Gilligan, and on down the chain of command.

It was fascinating to watch as the pilot babied our freighter into the harbor and softly against the dock. There was no superfluous talk going on, I can assure you of that. Strict silence except for his lordship's commands. No room for error here.

We passengers were excited and anxious to go sightseeing. We had a quick dinner (hamburgers, Italian style), headed down the ramp and left the dock area in a cab. Winfried decided he only wanted to go the local docks in Piraeus and send some emails. Mauro, Maria and I dropped him off and continued to Athens to an area close to the Acropolis, where we got out and split up.

I wandered through the twisting side streets filled with families and couples strolling and eating at small sidewalk cafés. Believe it or not, I could hardly find the famous Acropolis and walked for quite a while until I suddenly came upon it. By that time, it was getting pretty dark.

The Acropolis with its amazing Parthenon were built over 2,500 years ago and reportedly the most-visited archeological site in the world. I learned the word acropolis is the combination of two Greek words: *akro,* meaning high, and *polis,* meaning city.

After walking around the area for a few hours it was time to leave. I took the Metro back to Piraeus (around seven miles distance), found an internet cafe, and sent off a hurried message to let everyone at home know where I was. I then jumped in a cab and returned to the ship.

I was a little nervous in the strange city, and about navigating myself back to safety. The last thing I wanted was to be left behind. I must admit I was disappointed we didn't have more time to visit more museums, but that's freighter life for you. It was still a fascinating day!

I found my way back to the Fides early and without mishap and watched the end of *Capote*, another one of the DVDs I'd brought along with me.

I should slip in a word here about Grimaldi, the company that owns the Fides. The Grimaldi Group is a family-owned enterprise and is part of the House of Grimaldi, the 700-year-old rulers of Monaco, and of Grace Kelley and Prince Ranier fame. It is one of Italy's largest shipping companies and is a huge operation, with business ties all over the world.

When I was stationed as a young soldier in Europe, I remembered going to Monaco and visiting the Ranier castle, which overlooks a yacht basin crowded with mega-million-dollar boats. Grace and the prince had just recently married. It was shortly after the release of her wonderful Hitchcock-directed film with Cary Grant, *To Catch A Thief*.

<u>DAY 10</u>

I woke at 5:30 a.m. and couldn't get back to sleep. I stumbled into the bathroom, or head, or whatever its called on a freighter, and brushed my teeth. Unfortunately, since I was half awake, I grabbed the wrong tube and brushed with Triple Antibiotic Ointment. Unflavored!

Winfried and I ate breakfast alone this morning. No sign of Mauro or Maria. We assumed they'd slept in. It would be easy to do. The gentle motion of the ship and the subtle drone of the engines was quite soothing. Did they make it back last night? We talked about what would happen if, for whatever reason, one missed the departure time. Simple answer. You would be left behind in a heartbeat.

That could prove very troublesome, as we were required to leave our passports on the ship.
This morning I decided to do some laundry. There was a wash room just up the corridor from our cabins. Fitz left me some laundry soap and I went up and figured out the machines. He

offered to do it for me, but I don't like the idea of some stranger washing my delicates for me. I must admit: I didn't separate the darks from the lights.

Our next port of call was originally scheduled to be Alexandria, Egypt. But that was not in the plans now. We were bypassing Egypt altogether and heading directly to Israel. No reasons given. The crew seemed quite tense, however. What a disappointment! I had been studying up on Alexandria and had several "must see" places lined up to visit.

We had just passed Libya. I just checked my GPS (another piece of equipment I'm glad I brought along). We were 700 miles (as the crow flies) from Ashdod, Israel. We should arrive early on Monday, September 10th. That would be great, as it would give us the whole day to explore the old city of Jerusalem. The first mate told us they had 1,000 cars to unload there, and it would take at least 10 hours.

I was in my cabin working on the computer, not really paying much attention to anything when I took a break and looked out the window. There were no cars in sight. Huh?

I ran out on deck and discovered that *all* the cars on the 10th *and* 9th levels had been moved to lower levels. I got out in time to see the last one driven down the ramp. Wow! What a difference that made. Now there were no cars anywhere in sight. The ship looked kinda naked.

It was very windy today and you could detect much more side-to-side movement of the ship. The twirly thingy on the bridge showed the wind at 19 knots which translates to around 22 miles per hour ... I think. On deck, you had to hold on to your cap, or off it went.

Lunch today was a little different. First course was a type of pasta and vegetable dish, second course was a slice of grouper in tomato sauce, and the third course was tripe and boiled potatoes. Ugh! I took a very small portion, just to say I ate tripe. (If you're not familiar with it, tripe is the stomach lining of a cow or other ruminant and the principle ingredient in *menudo,* a popular Mexican soup, especially if you're suffering from a hangover.)

Life on board had fallen into a predictable pattern. Up in the morning, a walk around the ship, a visit to the bridge to make sure all the officers were awake, then breakfast followed by ... a walk around the ship, a visit to the bridge to check our positions on the radar scopes, back to my cabin to work on my computer followed by ... a walk around the ship, a visit to the bridge to make sure we're still heading the right direction, followed by lunch followed by ... a walk around the ship, a visit to the bridge to check out the changing of the guard, back to work on my computer, read a little, a short nap followed by ... a walk around the ship, a visit to the bridge to see if El Capitan has shown up yet, followed by dinner, followed by ... a walk around the ship, a visit to the bridge, which was all lit up by then, back to work on my computer and watch part of a movie, then read and sleep.

And so forth and so on. Life in the fast lane.

I know that all must sound terribly boring but I should point out there were always unexpected and exciting happenings to look forward to. A good example would be the drastic change in scenery as suddenly (as in this morning), hundreds of cars were moved to another part of the ship.

Or the sighting of dolphins and flying fish off the front of the ship. Or the appearance of a cruise ship off the starboard. Or the proximity of some large island. And, of course, every evening the drop dead gorgeous sunsets and the star-filled skies to gaze at. I hope you get the idea.

My fellow passengers and I were getting very comfortable with each other. Mauro and Maria could always be found together, relaxing and reading. Mauro took a lot of photos and had some excellent camera equipment compared to my basic point and shoot.

Winfried and I spent time talking and he shared a lot with me. He told me his wife was home taking care of her 88-year-old mother and that's the reason he was able to get away for the three weeks he'd be gone. One daughter is a consultant, one son works for a large, international corporation. I can't remember what the other daughter does. He has six grandchildren and one more to be born any day. His parents were married on D-Day and very few people attended the wedding. (Remember, he's German).

He has a double major in mechanical engineering and business. As a Catholic, this trip to Jerusalem was very important to him. He had been to Rome to visit the Vatican, and he'd walked the famous 500-mile trail, *El Camino de Santiago*, or St. James Way. The last commitment he has made to himself is a trip to Jerusalem. An interesting chap!

I successfully finished my laundry. It looked like everything got mostly clean, but the dryer was not working properly. As a result I had various pieces of underwear, socks and shirts hanging around the room on hangers, backs of chairs, and shower curtain hooks. I hoped to have no unexpected guests tonight.

Dinner this evening was wonderful. Spaghetti served with butter, garlic and hot peppers. Spicy! Second course was pizza, not like we're used to but very tasty. Third course was a slice of some type of grilled mystery meat — lamb or beef I hope. Wine, salad, rolls and a banana.

I plan to finish watching *Capote* tonight, saving *Bucket List* for the long voyage home.

DAY 11

I enjoyed another solid night's rest in my cozy little cabin.

I folded and put away my laundry and walked up to the bridge. The sea appeared to be a little calmer today, although a slight side wind gently rocked the ship.

One of the Filipino crew members excitedly pointed down to the water where I spotted dolphins zipping back and forth in front of the ship. They're much smaller than porpoise and very swift. I tried to take a picture but they were too fast for me.

I finally managed to finish an entire cup of Italian coffee this morning, but I still had to cut it with lots of milk. I do like their yogurt, however, and I eat Frosted Flakes almost every morning. Tony the Tiger would be very pleased. For some reason, hard boiled eggs have disappeared from the menu.

As I wrote earlier, other than the officers, the crew is made up of Filipinos. Fitz told me they sign up for a nine-month tour of duty and earn about the same as they would during four years at home. Wow!

They apply through an agency in Manila and have to exhibit a high level of general knowledge (including fluency in English) before they are hired. Most of them are married and save all their money and wire it home. Fitz is married and has a six-year-old son. Although he looks around 20 years old, he's obviously older.

It was noticeably warmer this morning and I have permanently switched to wearing shorts. I lounged around a lot on the deck today using the canvas lawn chairs provided for us.

Lunch consisted of a selection of sliced meats, green olives, hunks of tomato, and large slices of grilled eggplant with garlic sauce. Hmm. That was the first course. Next we had some type of pasta with tuna-fish gravy. Yikes! Next, small roll-ups of beef and vegetables. Water, hard rolls and peaches. I know that must sound like a lot, but the helpings are as large or small as you want so we all take just a little of each. Fitz, the steward, served everybody, always with a smile on his face.

Today I was pleased with myself because I finished the meal with no silverware left in front of me. Usually I have a few unused pieces, while no one else does.

When we are first seated, each place setting consists of a stack of large bowl-shaped plates, plus a side plate. There is a liter and a half bottle of water for each person plus three forks, three knives and a large and tiny spoon.

There is a wide selection of olive oils, vinegars, and spices from which to choose, plus the standard salt and pepper shakers, plus metal containers of sugar and grated cheese and a large basket of hard rolls. No butter. Butter only in the morning with jars of marmalade.

I glanced ahead at the menu for this evening and it showed we'd be having Spinach Ice Cream for dessert. I could hardly wait.

7:00 p.m. (not sure where the day went) and we've just finished dinner. It was quite good. First course was a bowl of rice soup with spinach, second course was a quarter roast chicken with side serving of spinach — very healthy, I think — and third course was a selection of several cheeses and watermelon. Dessert was a dish of some strange kind of berry ice cream with cookies. Water, wine and crusty bread. Ho hum, another day on its merry way. (Apparently spinach ice cream was a misprint, thank goodness.)

I received a piece of sobering news after dinner. One of the young officers (we were alone on the bridge) told me, in confidence, that there was no chance I'd make it back to Monfalcone until the 21st or 22nd! What? (My flight was scheduled to leave early on the 18th, and out of Milan).

One of the reasons, he said, was the Fides had been running on only one engine to conserve fuel (a savings of 200 gallons of diesel per hour). But the major reason was because of unscheduled stops along the way. I think bypassing Alexandria, Egypt, meant Grimaldi had to hustle to find new places to unload the extra cars on board.

Unless things drastically changed, he said I would definitely need to change my flight schedule. Great!

As soon as I get to a computer I could cancel my room in Milan but I couldn't change my airline ticket until I had a definite arrival date back in Italy. I suspected the airlines would make me pay a fine and doubted my travel insurance policy will cover it.

Freighter travel rules, passengers don't.

I walked around the ship before calling it a night. I'd finished watching *Capote* last night, and tonight planned to watch the special movie extras.

Although the acting was excellent, I felt the story was kind of a bummer. When I returned home I plan to reread *In Cold Blood*. Was it really that great?

It was now almost 10 p.m. and I was back in the cabin. I'd just returned from the darkened bridge, where there were several new and unfamiliar crew members looking around. I got the impression that was a rare place for them to be. It was a bit spooky walking back to my cabin in the dark.

Another gorgeous, clear day. A brisk couple of turns around the deck (a half mile each way) followed by a stop at the bridge before breakfast. The crew pointed out an Israeli war ship following us off in the distance. Hmm.

Frosted flakes, a cup of their terribly strong coffee, a hard-boiled egg (yay!) and bowl of yogurt, and I'm ready for the day.

We're roughly 50 miles from Israel. A large United Nations ship passed us this morning. Something's going on but the crew's not saying anything. Wonder what's up?

There are two small wren-like birds that I see every day that must live on the ship. I'm sure they have a nest tucked away somewhere. I also saw a dove perched on the railing. Where did it come from? And down in the water, I spied what I thought was another small bird skimming along just above the waves, when all of a sudden it dove into the sea. What was that? A single flying fish? It was too large for a flying fish and you usually see several flying fish if you see any. Mysteries of the sea.

Things were suddenly getting a bit frantic. The Fides had just entered what is called the "chute" leading directly to Ashdod on the Israel coast; a relatively narrow lane we must use. We were just passing by the Gaza Strip. Soon there would be lots of action to observe. Off in the distance, another Israeli navy ship kept an eye on us.

It's almost 9:00 a.m. We're told we had three or four more hours before we reached port.

Big excitement a few minutes ago was when one of the small, wren-like birds flew into one of the bridge windows and dropped to the deck. We all gathered around. Maria was quite upset and lightly stroked it and coaxed it in bird talk back to life. Soon it wobbled to its feet and before long flew off.

Strangely enough, in just a few moments it returned and landed at Maria's feet and walked around as if wanting more attention. Very bizarre.

1:30 p.m. We finally docked at Ashdod but no one seems to know the procedure for getting our permission slips to leave the ship. Winfried, in particular, is very anxious because his plans are to *bike* to Jerusalem, a distance of around 40 miles. The rest of us plan to share a taxi.

We wait by the bridge patiently. Eventually we learn we'll be able to leave the ship around 4:30 p.m. — maybe.

But, this is a freighter, we are reminded, not a cruise ship. Yeah, yeah, yeah. Got it already.

Around 4:00 p.m. all the crew and passengers were summoned to the purser's cabin. Inside were three, tough-looking Israeli security people. One by one we were summoned inside and asked questions: Who are you traveling with? Why are you on a freighter? Where are you going? Why? Where have you been? Who are you meeting in Jerusalem? Do you carry firearms? Where did you get on this boat? Why? And on and on. Goodness gracious.

Finally the four of us were all allowed to leave the ship and I said goodbye to Winfried. We exchanged contact information and he pedaled away.

We learn the ship would be leaving port at 5:00 a.m. the next morning, so Mauro suggested we stay in Jerusalem until midnight or so. Well, I didn't know about that. I doubted I'd last that long.

As it turned out, that wasn't an option. After a lot of arguing, the cab driver agreed to a fare of $175 round trip, but he would only wait for us two hours. Later the bill jumped to $210 so we could stay an hour longer. What could we do? We were taken advantage of, and we had no choice if we wanted to see Jerusalem.

We arrived at Jaffa Gate at 5:30 p.m. and decided to split up and meet back there at 9:30 p.m. Keep in mind we had been on the ship for three days. Nothing at all to see except 360 degrees of water, with a rare ship in the distance. And lots of water. Making the giant leap from such a quiet and peaceful setting into the sensory-loaded atmosphere of Old Jerusalem was a bit disorienting.

The old city was amazing. By this time we only had a few hours of good light, but I made the most of it. I first headed down through the Jewish Quarter and made a beeline for the Western Wall, also referred to as the Wailing Wall, the most cherished place on earth to the Jewish people. It has been the center of Jewish yearning and memory for more than 2,000 years.

Hundreds of Jewish men and women were standing at or near the wall and praying and rocking and chanting. The vast majority were dressed in black with wide brim hats, rather different hair styles and mostly bearded. It was bizarre and humbling at the same time. I accidentally headed down the woman's side before I was stopped and sent back. Oops! Later I was chided for not having my head covered. Oops again!

I stuck a prayer request for an ailing friend between the ancient rocks of the wall where there were hundreds of thousands already placed. And I sat and contemplated things awhile. I was very moved by the whole experience.

Next I started off to find the *Via Dolorosa*, the route believed to have been taken by Jesus through the ancient city on His way to Calvary. It was fascinating and I stopped and studied several active excavated areas. Honestly, I could have spent hours just wandering around, but time was flying by so I kept moving. I really needed to send an email home and asked if there was an internet cafe in the area. There was, but it was like looking for a needle in a haystack. Oddly enough it was right off the famous Via Dolorosa! I sent off a flurry of quick messages alerting friends where I was and that the next time they'd hear from me would be from Izmir, Turkey. I also managed to cancel my hotel reservation at the Hotel Linate in Milan.

By this time it was too late to visit the Church of the Holy Sepulcher, the only other place I'd really hoped to see, but I was terrified of getting lost in the bewildering maze of ancient cobblestone streets and missing the cab, so I had to pass it up.

After receiving a couple of misguided pieces of direction, I stumbled out of the maze and found the Jaffa Gate. I spied a restaurant right across the street from where we had planned to meet so I entered and ordered a beer. Mauro and Maria soon joined me. Perfect timing.

Our driver showed up right on time and we got back to the ship around 10:30 p.m. We had to go through the same security searches as before. I must say, they really take terrorism very seriously in this part of the world. Can't say I blame them.

Lights out at 11:00 p.m. ... late for me. The Fides would be well on its way by the time I awoke.

DAY 13 - The Day of the Benghazi Attack

I overslept. It was already 7:30 a.m. and we were moving. Lying in bed you could feel the gentle vibrations and hear the low throb of the engines, very much like being in an airplane cruising at 40,000 feet. I splashed some water on my face, ran a comb through my hair and headed to the dining room.

We'd had a 25% increase in the number of passengers since yesterday, we were now five instead of four. The scary news was I was now surrounded by Axis forces; two Italians and two Germans. I must be on my toes. I hadn't met the new arrivals yet.

On the bridge I noted our estimated arrival time in Izmir, Turkey, was 2:00 p.m. on Thursday, September 13th, two and a half days from now. I checked our the vessel's speed on my GPS this morning and recorded 18 mph. Four miles faster than before. Either Master Gilligan was speeding up on purpose or with so much less weight it was a natural reaction. After all, we did unload 1,000 cars in Ashdod. Estimating each car weighed one ton, we were now at least 1,000 tons lighter.

Speaking of Master Gilligan, I think he has a very easy life. I very seldom saw him on the bridge. There were always two or more other officers who seemed to do all the work. He made an appearance when we neared ports, walking from radar screen to radar screen, perhaps making a modest adjustment in direction from time to time. When we got close to the port, a local pilot came on board and took over ... so I'm trying to figure out what Gilligan did the other 90% of the time. I'd seen him in the dining room more often than on the bridge. He enters walking fast, never smiling, and sits at the head of the table. The only time I'd seen him really doing anything was the evening he barked at the cook about the cheese.

Well, I suppose that's important to Italians, so who am I to criticize?

1:00 p.m. and lunch was over. A pasta and meat dish, grilled cod and garlic, hamburger patties, watermelon, rolls.

I have met my new shipmates: Karin and Niels, a young couple from Berlin. They have been on a sabbatical since July, living in Haifa studying Hebrew. Their English is very good.

They left Monfalcone heading to Haifa, Israel, and are on their way back to Germany. Niels, 30, works for Germany's National Sports Organization (not clear what that is or what he does). Karin, 28, had been working with mall associations but was in the process of changing jobs. She is a movie buff and we talked about the DVDs we brought with us. We planned to do some swapping.

I finished watching all there was to watch on the *Capote* DVD; all the special features and all the previews of upcoming movies. There were several titles that looked interesting and I planned to check them out when I got home: *Thumbsucker, Memory of a Killer, Friends with Money, Breakfast on Pluto,* and *Cache.* I hadn't heard of any of them.

One last visit to the bridge to check our position. We were just coming up to Crete, directly north of the Libyan-Egyptian border. I head back to the cabin and am in bed by 10:30 p.m.

Of course, I had no idea, at the time, that our embassy in Benghazi was currently under attack.

DAY 14

The wind came up during the night. Yesterday's calm sea was now covered with whitecaps. When I took my early morning stroll up to the bridge, the little wind speed measuring thingy (nautical term) was spinning so fast it was just a blur.

314

There is more ship traffic as we approach the maze of Greek Islands. It feels cooler and I keep my light sweater handy. At breakfast, Karin (a vegetarian), spends her time filling a small dish with dislodged pomegranate seeds. She say she will snack on them during the day. The process looks more complicated and time consuming than getting the nut meat out of black walnuts.

It's really too windy to stay out on deck for long. I struggle back and forth from the bridge to my cabin taking in my special stops along the way. Finally I settle down and finish watching *Whatever Works*, the DVD Karin has loaned me. It was enjoyable and funny in true Woody Allen fashion. Hard to forget what a bum he is, however.

Lunch was pasta with tomato sauce followed by a dish of raw octopus with potatoes and pickles (Gag!) followed by a slice of wiener schnitzel, which Neil, our new German passenger, really got excited over. Fresh peaches, rolls and water.

We were told during lunch that we'd arrive at Izmir the next morning. The ship would be in port all day as they were scheduled to unload 600 cars. I was looking forward to visiting Turkey again.

Izmir has bittersweet memories for me. I happened to be there when the World Trade Center was destroyed almost eleven years ago to the day. I witnessed it live on a tiny black and white TV set in a gas station. The local announcer reported the Japanese Red Army had just bombed the White House! It was days before I learned differently. Very scary times.

After Izmir there were *unscheduled* stops at Izmit, Turkey, and Gemlik, Turkey, and then on to Ravenna, Italy, where I would most likely disembark. I was now convinced I would not get back in time to make my flight no matter what. Time to work on a back-up plan.

The officers say there are lots of uncertainties ahead; a possible strike in the Turkish dock area, very heavy fog, and more important ships (such as warships) taking precedence over us.

It was a shock to everyone this morning when a Russian nuclear submarine surfaced to take a closer look at us. We were cautioned to take no pictures but c'mon, how often do you get to see a Russian submarine? I'm afraid I sneaked a quick photo.

Yikes! Was that a sun flash on the sub from some Russian's binoculars? I held my breath. We passed unscathed.

I was becoming a fixture on the bridge. I made routine trips up there at least five times a day and the crew had come to expect me. Yesterday when I overslept and didn't show up, one of the officers told me he was afraid I hadn't made it back to the vessel on time.

This evening before dinner one of the Italian officers on the bridge wanted to know if I'd like some tea. (By this time they all know I don't like their horrid coffee). I really didn't want any tea either but I said yes as it gave him something to do. They are all non-stop coffee drinkers, constantly sipping their muddy little cups of espresso. I don't see how they do it.

It must get mind-numbing up there on their individual watches — and I suppose I gave them some kind of comic relief. They all make a point of practicing English on me. Ironically it was the Filipinos who spoke the clearest English and were easiest to understand. The Italians were much worse although they have no idea. They think they are quite fluent. It was actually a little scary as the Italians and Filipinos communicated on the bridge in English; shouting commands and changing directions of our huge ship in a language that sounded like gibberish to me.

I found their radar scopes fascinating. All the information shown was in English (although full of acronyms and initials). I figured out how to use them and I think I could lay out a course to get us into, or at least close to, a port. The stopping part still escapes me. I suspected that within a few days however, Master Gilligan would be willing to turn over the bridge to me.

The wind today was still fierce and no one was spending much time on deck. Dinner tonight was rather bizarre: a thick soup of rice and potatoes, a soft boiled egg served over a bed of peas and sliced onion, a slice of grilled beef, lettuce, wine, and a pear. My stomach was very accommodating.

The passengers (me included) were slightly hyped about tomorrow. It sounded like we'd have most of the day to snoop around Izmir and do plenty of shopping, sight seeing, sea side relaxing, and internet messaging. Although we were close to Ephesus, Turkey, no one was planning to visit because there was really not enough time, plus the added confusion of transportation. I had been there before.

Karin offered me a DVD of *Goodfellas* but I declined, having seen it earlier and finding it ultra-violent. She instead gave me Monty Python's *The Meaning of Life*. I hoped this young German couple was not forming opinions of American culture from these two films!

Niels found my proofing copy of *Ophelia's Brooch,* my book in process, which I'd left in the lounge, and was reading it. His comments and questions should prove interesting.

DAY 15

I woke at 6:30 a.m. and looked out the window. We were already docked and had begun unloading cars. We had arrived at Izmir, known in ancient times as Smryna, a city inhabited since the forth century B.C.

I quickly picked up my "shore pass" (no security screenings here) and was told to be back on board by noon as the ship was scheduled to leave around 1:00 p.m. Mauro, Maria and I left the ship around 8:00 a.m. and caught a cab to the *Agora*, the ancient market place dating back to Roman-Greek times.

We arrived at the ruins early. The entrance gate was locked and wouldn't open until 9:00 a.m., but the fence was low and you could see all you needed from the road.

We split up and I wandered back towards town, stopping at an ATM to withdraw 20 Turkish Lira (I was confused and should have withdrawn more). The Turkish lira was only worth around 40¢ those days; what was I going to do with $8? The last time I was in Turkey you received over 3,000 lira for a dollar. Quite a difference.

I stopped at one of the many street stalls and bought a large glass of fresh-squeezed orange juice and a roll and sat to watch the world go by. I had earlier written down a few recommended places I wanted to visit, two of which were the Alsancak Railway Station and the Asansoer (elevator).

I really didn't care which one, and when I showed the list to a cab driver he just nodded and took off.

He apparently knew where the Asansoer was and it turned out to be several miles in the opposite direction. This amazing building is 200 feet high, sitting on a bluff overlooking the bay and town. People living up on the bluff take the free elevator down to the lower level to go to work. It reminded me of the Fenelon Street Elevator in Dubuque; not only providing a wonderful vista of the city, but a short cut for people to get down to street level. The view was stunning.

There was a small snack shop overlooking the bay. I ordered a cappuccino and some sweet rolls and sat and enjoyed the view. Since I was short on local money I asked to pay in dollars, which created quite a commotion. Eventually it all worked out and I was able to pay my modest bill in dollar bills and conserve my meagre amount of Turkish Lira for a cab ride back.

I believe the novelty of receiving American money was a blast for the shop owner and he waved my money to everyone who walked by.

I still wasn't sure if I had enough lira for a cab, so I took the elevator down and decided to walk along the oceanfront promenade back to town and look for an internet cafe and post office. Having successfully negotiated all that, I headed back to the dock area. It was a little after 11:00 a.m. I had an hour to get back to the ship.

Then commenced a comedy of misdirections and errors which almost ruined everything. In short, I dallied too long, forgetting where I was and what I was doing.

The next thing I knew it was 12:15 p.m.! Yikes! I was supposed to have been on board by noon as the ship was leaving at 1:00 p.m.

I still had a long way to go so I flagged down a cab. I didn't know the name of the dock area, so I just shouted "Grimaldi! Fides! Boat!" The cab driver nodded and we took off.

The next thing I knew he was stopping in front of a Costa Cruise ship. He pulled over and smiled. A long line of tourists were walking up the gangplank.

"No. No," I yelled. "The *freighter* area. The *cargo* ships! Grimaldi. Grimaldi," I repeated over and over.

"Yes. Yes, of course (you stupid tourist). Boat. Ship. Straight ahead. Right there ..."

I started to panic. I had less than half an hour before the ship left and I had no idea where we were. Seeing I was getting nowhere with the cabbie, I dropped my lira on the seat and jumped out.

I ran up to the first official-looking person I saw and started in again, "Grimaldi ... Grimaldi ... freighter ... Fides ... I'm late!" I pointed frantically at my watch.

"Oh, yes, my kind sir. Absolutely no problem. You board here," he said, smiling and pointing to the end of the tourist line.

Twenty minutes to go. I'm not going to make it, I thought. In a panic I turned away and headed toward the only commercial-looking dock area in sight, ducked under a "No Trespassing" sign and began running.

"Wait! Stop, sir!" shouted a number of uniformed people. "No, no. Wrong way you are going! Come back, please. Cruise ship right here."

I didn't dare stop, I just ran as fast as I could. The crowd turned to watch what the idiot American was up to. I rushed down one lane of ship-going containers stacked nine high, probably 100 feet. It was like running down into a narrow canyon. I kept going, turning and going down another.

With less than 15 minutes to go I saw a dock worker driving a huge forklift. I waved frantically at him and he stopped and stared at me in shock.

"Grimaldi. Grimaldi," I shouted. He looked at me for a moment, sizing up my terrorist possibilities, and finally pointed in an entirely different direction. Ten minutes to go. I ran like crazy and eventually found myself surrounded by more boxcar containers. I couldn't see anything.

"Oh, Lord," I gasped. "Is he sending me back to the Costa Cruise Ship?" I kept running.

Suddenly, like a heavenly vision, through a gap in the piled containers, I spotted the smoke stack of the Fides two blocks away. Hallelujah! I was saved.

I was a mess. I raced by the startled workers and up the gangplank just as they were getting ready to raise it. I rushed into the tiny elevator, went up nine floors and into the dining room. Everyone was there calmly eating their lunch of Frutti di Mare (pasta with octopus and squid.) I was too embarrassed to share my close call. The ship was already moving.

So I'd learned an important lesson. The dock areas in these larger ports were huge, sometimes stretching around the bay for miles. From now on, I told myself, always keep the name and number of the specific dock written down and tucked away.

Soon we were steaming away from the Bay of Izmir. It was lovely out; sunny but cool. Lots of ships all around us, and hills on all three sides. Far off in the distance, I could see the Asansoer. I have to say, Izmir is a very attractive city. I still can't believe I made it back in one piece.

I took a well-deserved nap and puttered around the rest of the afternoon, standing on deck and watching the islands pass by, and chatting with the boys on the bridge until supper.

Soup of pasta and peas, quarter baked chicken with weird vegetables, a platter of four different cheeses and a fresh peach. Dessert was beloved strawberry gelato and cookies. Wine, rolls. Very nice.

Table talk centered on what was going to happen from here on. According to Mauro, tonight we were moving north into the Dardenelles Strait and into the Sea of Mamara to our next port: Derince, Turkey.

Actually Derince is the *port* city, the city is Izmit (not to be confused with Izmir). We'd be there for a full day and then continue on to Gemlik, our last stop before heading back to Italy, stopping first at Ravenna before continuing to Malfacone. At this point, no one was willing to say for sure when we'll arrive.

My plans, at this stage, were to disembark at Ravenna, stow my luggage at the train station and go and see the sights. Then, in the afternoon, take the train to Bologna and stay there the night. Then, depending what change in my ticket was required, I'd continue by train to Milan, board a plane and fly to London.

Granted, a little daunting but I was not going to worry about it since I couldn't do anything about it anyway.

It was now a quarter to eight in the evening and I had just come back from the bridge. I learned that a heavy-duty — special pilot would board the Fides sometime during the night and lead us through the entire length of the Dardenelles. There we'd proceed to the far northeast corner of the the Sea of Mamara to Derince, passing by Istanbul on the way.

Tonight I would finish watching the strange Monty Python movie, *The Meaning of Life*. It had been an interesting, albeit stressful day. Somehow I survived. I refused to ponder what would have happened if I'd missed the ship.

DAY 16

A riot of slamming doors woke me in the wee hours of the morning. The crew was up and about, rushing down the narrow hallways. I remembered that we were scheduled to enter and pass through the Dardanelles during the night. Tense times.

The Dardanelles is a 38-mile, narrow waterway leading from the Aegean Sea to the Sea of Mamara. The crew was nervous, therefore I was nervous. I got up and went out on deck. What a sight! The stars were brilliant. On both sides of the ship we were close to shore, and even at this hour you could plainly see the lights of tiny villages dotted along the banks. Although the Dardanelles is 38 miles long, it's less than a mile wide in many spots and the water flows in both directions.

There were numerous other ships jockeying for the middle of the channel. It's a particularly dicey bit of water and thus the need for a special pilot to take us through this dangerous stretch.

I stayed on deck for over an hour, mesmerized by the sight of it all. With the special pilot on board, no passengers were allowed on the bridge, but there was plenty to see anyway.

Eventually I went back to bed. Sometime during the night we passed the Island of Patmos, where the Apostle John lived in exile around 95 A.D. I had hoped there would be an opportunity to visit later — but there wasn't.

The breakfast room was empty so I sat and ate my bowl of Frosted Flakes and slice of focaccia, or flat bread, and drank a little of the dreaded coffee. Just as I was finishing, Master Gilligan entered and sat at the officers' table. Just the two of us in the room by ourselves.

It was a little awkward in the complete silence. After finishing, I stood up and, trying to be polite, asked him what time we would arrive in port today. He muttered something about this afternoon. I thanked him and tried to sneak away when *he* asked *me* something. I couldn't understand him at first so he repeated something about about my intentions for debarkation.

I told him I was not sure. It depended on when we arrived back in Italy. He nodded sagely and said he thought we would be in Ravenna, the first Italian port of call, late in the evening of the 18th. But that could change, of course. Of course.

So I still didn't know much more than before, other than it was now absolutely certain I would miss my flight out of Milan. I'd attempt to contact American Airlines as soon as possible and inform them of my dilemma.

The weather remained balmy. There were quite a few ships all around us now. We had navigated through the Dardanelles without mishap and were now in the Sea of Mamara steaming northeast toward Derince, Turkey. We'd be passing by Istanbul early in the afternoon, as well as the entrance to the bay to Gemlik, to which we'd be returning later.

Monty Python's *The Meaning Of Life* was utterly stupid, disjointed, irreverent and interrupted by occasional funny stuff. As I watched the Special Features section I could understand why. The wacky cast of actors/writers had no idea what they were doing and admitted as much. It certainly showed. Tonight I planned to begin watching *Bucket List*, which I'd downloaded to my laptop before leaving home.

It was approaching 10 a.m. and my disjointed night's rest had left me feeling tired. I lay down to read and prepare myself for lunch. A tough life.

Back on my feet after a short rest, and things on the bridge were very busy. We were surrounded by all kinds of ships.

Standing on deck I could count a dozen various size ships flying flags of several different countries. Looking at the radar screen there were dozens more in the immediate area and the chatter on the bridge radio was nonstop. The officers on deck appeared tense. Master Gilligan, himself, absent. Perhaps he was resting before a new pilot arrived to take over.

I mentioned this in a light-hearted manner to Mauro, and he began lecturing me about how much responsibility the commander has: the lives of all the people on board, the vessel and all its contents, all other ships in the area, yada, yada. (He forgot to mention the important role Gilligan played in the selection and proper preservation of cheese.)

I'd heard we'd already unloaded approximately 2,000 of the 2,500 cars we started with. I assumed we would drop off the rest at the remaining ports in Turkey.

As opposed to container ships, The Fides is considered a car-delivering ro/ro freighter (roll on/roll off). There were also several large containers in the hold, each the size of a semi truck. It was quite a sight in the large port cities, such as Izmir, to see thousands of them stacked three or four high, row after row, several city blocks long.

A new concern: Since the decks were now empty of cars I had been noticing oddball pieces of things lying around. For example, this morning I'd found a silver dollar-size washer. Later I found a piece of some type of important looking plastic thingy, various sized slivers of painted deck metal, an odd screw or bolt here and there, a piece of rubber tubing, a woman's brown plastic barrette ... Where were they coming from? Was the Fides coming apart on us? I wondered if Master Gilligan was aware of all this.

We hurriedly finished lunch to be ready for shore leave and were now patiently waiting for the pilot. He was already an hour late.

Lunch consisted of pasta with garlic and tomatoes followed by a slab of dentex with tomato. Dentex is a predator fish common to the Mediterranean, very well-regarded for its taste. All this was followed by a grilled pork cutlet. Water, hard rolls and plums.

Izmit has 300,000 inhabitants and is a fairly important city. Originally named Nicomedia, it was the eastern and most senior capital of the Roman empire between A.D. 286 and A.D. 324. When Constantine came along, it became his capital city and remained so until A.D. 330, when the honor was moved to Byzantium, aka Nova Roma, aka Constantinople, aka Istanbul which is 62 miles west.

Where was the crazy pilot? It was now 2:15 p.m. and we'd just been informed he may, or may not, show up in an hour or so. There were rumors of a long soak in a hammam somewhere. Perhaps there were more important ships ahead of us. Perhaps the pilot and Master Gilligan were at odds with each other. Or perhaps there was a legitimate problem with a ship in our assigned berth (which is what it turned out to be). Whatever, here we sat on this lovely day, twiddling our thumbs just ten miles from shore.

Again we were reminded this is a working freighter, not a passenger ship. Yeah, yeah, got it already!

I passed the hours the best I could. I worked on my rewrites, I tried to take a nap, and walked the bridge a few times. An early dinner came and went: Lentil soup, Venezian style corned beef, cheeseburgers, hard rolls, coffee, pears.

The wretched pilot finally turned up around 5:30 p.m. and we finally, slowly moved toward port. Because of the delay we again would have limited shore time. The ship would be leaving before dawn and arrive at Gemlik at a decent time tomorrow. I hoped if I didn't get to an internet cafe and purchase some gifts this evening, I might have the chance in Gemlik, our last stop before the long haul to Ravenna.

9:00 p.m. and we're still on the ship, can you believe it? We just learned we pick up our shore passes in 15 minutes. Everything takes so long. Here we originally thought we would have the whole afternoon to explore, but now would have to be content with two or three hours at most.

However, the docking procedure is always interesting to watch, pushing and pulling this monstrous vessel with the help of a couple of tug boats into a single, empty space along the pier with barely 20 feet to spare on each end. Amazing, really. I can't imagine how they manage in a heavy wind.

There was a ship from Beirut tied up in front of us, off loading cattle onto trucks as fast as possible. Cattle from Beirut to Turkey? That's just strange.

Well, as opposed to the near disaster in Izmir, things started out badly but ended up splendidly.

Our shore passes were finally ready by 9:30 p.m. and we left the ship and walked a few blocks to the main entrance of the port where I approached two young men who were filling up their car at a Shell station.

I tried to explain to them that we wanted to go to the city center (Cetrum) but they didn't understand. Finally I said "ATM" and "EFES" and they knew exactly what I was getting at. Efes is the local beer and ATM is a universal term.

They offered us a ride, and drove us a few miles to the main business district where they dropped us off at a modern-looking bank. We offered to pay them for their trouble, but they refused to accept anything. I withdrew 100 Turkish Lira and the three of us split up, deciding to meet back at the same place at midnight.

I went to look for an internet cafe, quickly found one, and sent off a batch of messages warning the folks back home that my schedule was messed up and I'd be delayed returning. More to follow.

Across the street I spied a tiny side street café and ordered an Efes. Things were looking up.

There was a baklava shop nearby and I went and gobbled down four small pieces with a coffee. My, they were wonderful. I was so impressed I ended up buying a large box of assorted pieces with the idea of treating the crew tomorrow night. It cost about $10 but weighed around ten pounds.

We arrived back at the Fides around 1:00 a.m. and found the crew loading new cars. They were replacing the Suzuki Splash models with Fiat Doblos, a great looking little van that looked very similar to a large Fiat 500.

All in all a pretty good day. Tomorrow: Gemlik.

DAY 17

I slept in. It was now 9:00 a.m. and we were already approaching Gemlik, Turkey. The day was clear and the temperature was very comfortable, perhaps in the low 70's.

I'd heard the pilot would be boarding soon. I guessed we'd be in port by 10:00 a.m. and allowed to leave the ship around 11:00 a.m., but the way things normally work, maybe noon or 1:00 p.m. would be a safer bet. Either way we should have plenty of time.

It *was* close to noon before Mauro, Maria and I left in a cab and landed in the city center, split up and went our seperate ways. We needed to be back on board by 5:30 that evening. Five hours to explore. Yay!

The German couple seldom left the ship but stayed on board, read and lay around on deck chairs. Karin was not feeling well.

Gemlik is kind of a funky town spread out along the waterfront at the end of a deep bay facing the ocean. It gives off a very small town feeling, with none of the hustle and bustle of the other places we visited. There were dozens of outdoor cafes where mainly men gathered and talked over a cup of their beloved chai. Very casual and informal.

Again, there was virtually no English spoken, nor Italian, Spanish or German. But I still managed to find an internet café and send off my usual messages.

Afterwards I stopped at an attractive bayside restaurant for a bottle of Pepsi where I sat, rested and soaked in the ambience of the town. I looked and looked for a suitable gift for my wife but could find nothing at all. Most of the shops featured inexpensive, every day clothes, shoes, and furniture. A tourist stop this was not.

It was Saturday and the streets were loaded with people. I passed several mosques, maybe one every three or four blocks, with services going on non-stop.

Since it was a coastal town, all along the colorful waterfront fishermen and their families tended small stands selling their morning catches.

Mid-afternoon I stopped at another small seaside café and ordered a bottle of Efes. A smiling shoeshine boy stopped by looking for business and I was happy to help him out. He attacked my dusty shoes with gusto and chatted away a mile a minute. The fact that neither one of us could understand one another didn't slow him down a bit. What a great little kid!

Before heading back to the ship, I found yet another friendly open air restaurant and ordered a wonderful, spicy baguette of grilled chicken and another Pepsi. Although I was a figure of interest (I suspect very few tourists, if any, find their way here) everyone was quite polite and smiled at my awkwardness.

Around 5:00 p.m. I caught a cab back to the Fides and took my box of baklava to the dining room and instructed Fitz to ensure all the crew got a piece with their coffee that night. It turned out to be a big hit.

Karin, who had not been feeling very well was feeling better tonight and offered me a DVD of *Edward Scissorhands*. I'd seen it before, but it was fun to watch again.

The Chief Petty Officer told us we should be getting underway around 8:00 or 9:00 p.m. Probably closer to 10:00 or 11:00. At any rate, once we left Gemlik there'd be no more stops until Ravenna. With all the snacking I'd done during the day, I skipped dinner and began watching *Edward Scissorhands*.

DAY 18

I woke at dawn and looked out the porthole. We were just reentering the Dardanelles and passing by the famous World War I battlefield site of Gallipoli. I rushed out on deck and took several photos just as the sun was coming up behind me. Magical.

327

I had toured the battlefield years earlier when I visited Turkey with a tour group from Australia and New Zealand. The place has great historical significance to them because of the horrible losses to their troops during that war. Many thousands of Australian and New Zealand troops are buried there.

It was the battle that propelled a brilliant, young Turkish officer, Mustafa Kemal — better known as *Ataturk* — into the world's limelight, and was his stepping stone to becoming one of the most beloved rulers of Turkey in the years that followed. His image is still seen on every piece of Turkish money, and in every nook and cranny of the entire country: storefronts, schools, and public buildings. His tomb, in Ankara, is the size of a city block.

I visited the bridge before breakfast and found Master Gilligan nervously pacing back and forth. Of course, the Turkish pilot was already calling the shots. Pilots have immense power in these circumstances and his word was law.

I was approached by one of the officers who wanted to know if it was still my intention to get off at Ravenna. I said it was and he said he would pass that information along to the Master, who would decide. Decide? Decide what? I was getting off!

I looked at the radar scopes for the estimated time of arrival at Ravenna and it showed late on the 18th. It would be my hope to spend the night on the ship and disembark the following morning. I suspected that would work, but it may be I'd have to get off at some other inconvenient time. I would await Master Gilligan's ruling.

It was close to 10 a.m. and the sky was clearing after a stubborn rain cloud slowly passed. The sea was a little choppier once we had exited the Dardanelles and entered the Aegean Sea.

I could still see dozens of large ships around us, but I knew this would change in a day or so as we entered the vast expanse of the Mediterranean.

I was still finding odd bits and pieces on the deck. This morning I picked up a hunk of frayed cable, a square piece of steel plate, and pieces of tan canvas strap. Where were they coming from? Surely no birds were dropping them.

I consulted my handy little Garmin GPS and learned we were, as the bird flies, 762 miles from Ravenna. Unfortunately, as we're not flying, we had the country of Greece in our way so we were heading the opposite direction at the moment in an attempt to avoid running into it. I assumed Master Gilligan is up to the task.

I looked out my porthole and saw another Russian submarine close by! Wow. I went to the bridge and learned we were in some kind of sensitive naval exercise area. The radio was alive with orders from various warships ordering merchant ships, such as ours, to alter their courses.

I didn't know if this would affect us or not. Just in case, PFC Robert E. Buckley — RA18519383 — stood ready to flex a little American muscle, if necessary.

On a serious note, it was at this point in the trip we heard sketchy details about the Libyan terrorist attack in Benghazi a few days earlier. Although no one was talking much about it I suspect it had something to do with not stopping in Alexandria, Egypt.

That night we were treated to a delightful dinner. Wine, pasta soup, lasagna, gelato. Poor Karin sat outside on deck, still very ill and worsening according to Niels. He called and left several messages for his German doctor but had heard nothing.

Today I agreed to an international trade deal with Francis, one of the night-shift Filipinos and a favorite of mine. The deal: My extra pair of Levis for a Grimaldi cap and wool sweater. We'd see if it would happen.

I finished watching *Edward Scissorhands* tonight. Kind of fun, but I think I would have come up with a different ending if I were Tim Burton.

DAY 19

We passed the southern tip of Greece sometime during the night and this morning were well on our way back north. It was a gorgeous, clear day, around 75 degrees. The sea was a little choppy but blue and clear. A handful of ships were in view.

We'd be heading north the rest of the voyage, passing by Albania today and Herzegovina the next. I chatted with my favorite Italian officer at breakfast this morning. He told me he lives on Istria, one of the large islands off Naples. He's nearing the end of his four-month enlistment and is not sure if he is going to sign up again or not. He confided to me that he earns good money but doesn't like to be away from his family that long.

He confirmed we'd arrive at Ravenna very late the evening of the 18th. So, it appeared I'd be able to stay on board that night and visit Ravenna the next day which would be great. From Ravenna, it's a short hour and a half train ride to Bologna.

I'll admit I was growing more and more concerned about my return flight plans. It all boiled down to whether I could successfully contact American Airlines from Ravenna. Up to this point nothing had worked. I guessed my odds were 50/50 at being able to exchange my expired ticket. My next step would be to make a new reservation. I thought I had enough Frequent Flyer miles left.

My last resort would be to buy a new ticket at the counter. That would be very painful.

I noticed the deck was relatively free of unidentifiable debris this morning, with perhaps just an odd piece of metal or two. Nothing to be alarmed about.

I spent a lot of time pondering the crystal clear horizon, no fog or sea haze, just a straight line in every direction. Some lovely puffy clouds, that's all. I thought back to Father Swartie's geography class at Dowling High and vaguely recalled his argument that the earth is round, not flat. However, all empirical data I have amassed so far shows that it is indeed flat. Would a Catholic priest lie to his students? I'm keeping an open mind on the matter.

Francis, the Filipino worker I mentioned earlier, walked up and tapped on my window while I was sitting, writing. (Scared me to death). The swap was on! So now I had a brand new Grimaldi sweater and cap. And he had my used, slightly soiled Levis. We were both extremely pleased. (My graduate studies at the American Institute of Foreign Trade, circa 1962, now known as the Thunderbird School of Global Management, Glendale, AZ, were finally paying off.)

The big news at lunch today (pasta with egg plant, grouper with tomatoes, a slice of some odd piece of beef, water and plums) was that Karin learned she is pregnant. She was not seasick after all, but with child. She finally talked to her doctor in Germany, who told her to eat everything she wanted, and I think the news mentally set her straight. She looked and acted 100% better.

She and Niels asked Master Gilligan if they might also disembark in Ravenna instead of waiting until Monfalcone, and it looks like this would also happen. They now wanted to get home as quickly as possible.

The crew would have to do some juggling when we got in port to uncover the couple's stored BMW, but apparently this would not be a big deal. Their doctor had prescribed some type of medication which they would pick up in Ravenna, and then they'd drive straight back to Berlin (10 hours drive).

Niels, in the meantime, had finished reading *Ophelia's Brooch* and told me he really enjoyed it. I'm very impressed he was able to work around the slang and oddball terms. He seemed to understand almost everything, judging by the comments he made.

DAY 20

I rose early and went out on deck. We were opposite of Albania's coast line now and would soon be level with the very bottom of Italy, where the "heel" sticks out. This time tomorrow we'd be closing in on Ravenna.

Master Gilligan was alone in the dining room when I entered for breakfast, perhaps drinking his twelfth cup of coffee. After a few moments of awkward silence, I offered a levity.

"My plane leaves from Milan in twenty minutes," I said with a smile. "Any chance we can make it?"

"Milano?" he said. "Yes ... very nice, Milano. Yes, very nice. We no stop Milano."

This is the guy who gives orders to the crew in English?

I found the face of some kind of enamel-coated dial laying on the deck this morning. It was white with official-looking numbers, about five inches in diameter. I looked up and around to see where it might have come from. I couldn't see anything. It looked rather important. Some kind of thermostat cover? Heat gauge? Diesel fuel level? Blood pressure gauge? Expresso machine part?

We had just passed by Montenegro and Bosnia-Herzegovina on the east and were about ready to come even with the Dalmatian Coast. On the left or port side, we were passing by Pescara, Italy. There was a lot of ship traffic.

A slightly hazy day, cool with a slight breeze. I certainly hoped we'd go rain-free the next day or two. I hadn't brought any rain gear with me.

10:30 a.m. I'd just finished reading *Galore*, by Michael Crummey. It was one of the strangest novels I've ever read. Beautifully written, but profane. Yet I had to admit, a bit of genius. When I got home and settled, I would look into his earlier works: *River Thieves, The Wreckage,* and *Flesh and Blood.*

1:30 p.m. I'd just returned from the bridge where I was tactfully informed that in the future, passengers were to keep any visits brief and take no photos at all. Apparently Grimaldi has issued a new set of policies because of current problems in this part of the world. Something about a recently released "low budget film"portraying the Muslim world in a poor light.

We were also *officially* informed that the American embassy in Libya had been attacked and our ambassador killed. What? And it had happened on the 11th, when we were originally scheduled to be in Alexandria, Egypt.

What a tragic mess!

I was frantically packing everything away in anticipation of leaving the ship early in the morning. Since Niels and Karin were also leaving at the same time, there would only be Mauro and Maria left to keep Master Gilligan on his toes.

It would soon be time for my last dinner on board. I know I've kidded a lot about things but I've come to appreciate the Fides, and would miss my daily interactions with the crew, including Master Gilligan.

I was now packed and ready to leave, and very apprehensive about getting transportation home.

I talked to the Chief and asked how difficult it would be to send an email message from his office. I was told it would be simple and no charge so I sent a message home telling my wife not to go to the airport to pick me up as per my original schedule. I told her I'd contact her when I knew more.

Dinner was very glum as everyone realized this was our last evening together. We chatted about our departure plans and afterwards went out and took some final pictures of the sunset, which was quite lovely.

Fitz says there was no charge for the wine consumed during my meals. That was unexpected. I left him $20 American, 10 Euros, 20 Turkish Lira, a handful of Greek, Israeli, Turkish and Italian coins and two DVDs. I don't know if that's enough, but that's all I had to spare and he appeared quite pleased.

8:30 p.m. Time to shut the computer off, charge up the batteries and read. Tomorrow will be filled with uncertainties. I'd better get a good night's sleep.

DAY 21

Ravenna, Italy. It was almost noon and my day had been filled with ups and downs. Let me start at the beginning: I woke around 2:00 a.m.. The ship had docked some time earlier and the lack of movement and silence of the engines woke me. I tried to get back to sleep with no success. Finally I got up at 6:00 a.m., showered and got ready to depart.

At 7:15 a.m. Niels, Karin and I walked down the ramp one last time. Soon their car arrived and it was packed to the gills. No room for me in there. I had been hoping for a lift to town. But the dock attendant offered to drive me in his own car and took me directly to the train station.

I checked my luggage at the station, bought a street map and headed out for the world-famous, 1,400-year-old Basilica di San Vitale with its amazing mosaics.

Ravenna is a lovely coastal town with dozens of sidewalk cafes strung along the cobblestoned streets. I selected a popular-looking one and stopped for a café con leche and sweet roll.

Feeling refreshed I set out again and soon found the Basilica, where one was required to purchase a €10 entrance ticket. Hmm ... a bit expensive I thought.

The price was worth it however. The Basilica dates from the sixth century and contains what are probably the finest mosaics in the western world, making the church one of the most important examples of early Christian Byzantine art and architecture in Europe.

The mosaics around the altar were truly marvelous. I walked around in awe and took loads of pictures. It was hard to believe the intricate murals, which covered all the walls and ceilings, are actually comprised of a bazillion pieces of tiny colored tiles. I almost had the place to myself, which I found strange.

I spent an hour wandering around before heading out to find the local Tourist Office. I desperately needed assistance in reaching American Airlines.

Of course, when I found the right building, they were not able to help me at all, but suggested I visit Dante's Tomb which was just a block or two away. Hmm. That seemed odd. Not exactly the kind of help I needed, but I went anyway.

The only thing I knew about Dante was he was an ancient poet, or mystic or something, who wrote *Divine Comedy*, which I had never read but was considered a big deal by my priest teachers at Dowling High. Sorry, ancient texts are not my strong point, but I went and snooped around. I found the tomb quite funky.

While pondering Dante's Tomb I ran into a couple of Australian backpackers, who told me to go to a place called the International Computer and Call Center (ICCC) ... again just a few blocks away. Now that sounded more promising, and off I went. I thought with a name like that I could be confident my problems would soon be over. Think again.

The International Computer and Call Center was about the size of my bathroom at home and, no surprise here, they weren't able to help me either. Three of their four clerks were engrossed in some violent computer war game and really didn't want to be disturbed. The one remaining clerk could hardly speak English and steered me out to the street and told me to use local phones.

Well, that didn't work either so I returned to the office and after sufficient whining, one of the war game players took pity on me, painfully paused in his game and somehow got American Airlines on the line ... an office somewhere in the Philippines.

After 45 frustrating minutes on the phone with some guy called Rommel (The Desert Fox?) and accruing $20 in long distance charges, I did manage to change my ticket without a fine. Yay! Same route, but completely different times, which meant I not only had to stay overnight in London, I also had to stay overnight in Dallas. OUCH!

They promised an email confirmation within a day.

So anyway, here I was sitting at *Binaria* 6 (Platform 6) in Ravenna, Italy, late in the afternoon hour, waiting for the next train to Bologna (I just missed the last one by five minutes). I would spend the evening in Bologna before going on to Linate Airport in Milan the following morning to catch a 1:50 p.m. flight to London. Whew! Hope it all worked out.

We arrived in Bologna at 5:30 p.m. and I headed out to find a hotel. Unfortunately there was a large *Congress* (We call them conventions) in town and all the hotels on my list were filled. But kind fate was with me once again as the manager of the Millenn Hotel broke his rule and offered me his *emergency single room* for one night only. I grabbed it.

The room was tiny, but spotless. A single bed with hardly any room to move around, but a dazzling bathroom with one of those great little his and hers toilets. Indeed, I was back in Italy.

I immediately took a shower in a real shower stall with controllable hand spray. And unlike the wretched bathroom on the Fides, here the water drained immediately, not five hours later.

I lay down for an hour but could not sleep. Up and out I went, heading to Plaza Maggiore via a broad and colorful avenue. The Plaza Maggiore is home to the world-famous Fountain of Neptune, a rather risqué piece of sculpture and one that is beloved by the locals. It's been on the Catholic Church's hit list for centuries but so far has managed to survive.

Once there, I settled immediately at an outdoor cafe and enjoyed an glass of local wine while watching people stroll by. The late afternoon sun finally broke through the clouds and flooded the people-filled plaza with a golden hue. It was wonderful.

The library adjacent to the plaza offered free wi-fi so I went and checked for messages and had another live video chat with my friend Don Torney in San Antonio. I described, in detail, my transportation problems, and asked him to call my wife and explain.

Seeing as this would be my last night in Italy (I hoped) I planned to splurge at a nice restaurant. But at 8:00 p.m. all the restaurants were still empty or not yet open. The Bolognesi don't go out to eat until very late.

I walked the streets checking menus and prices and in the end decided to forget it. I was not in a mood to spend $50 or $60 for a meal, especially when I was eating by myself. So I found a cozy little pizza parlor and had a couple of slices of sausage pizza and a glass of beer for $6, followed by a wonderful pistachio gelato for $2. A much wiser decision, I think.

It was now 9:30 p.m. and I was swiftly winding down while the city appeared to be swiftly waking up. Dozens of families with young children appeared and were out strolling the wide avenues. Hundreds of bicycle riders filled the streets. Again I was struck by the overall attractiveness of everyone. Very, very few overweight folk around.

Although I was only in the city for a short time, my impression of Bologna was that it's like Ravenna on a larger scale. A very handsome place indeed.

I was slowly closing in on Milan, now some 150 miles away. I checked the train schedule and found there was quite a selection. The 8:35 a.m. Express (Bullet) Train makes the trip in one hour and five minutes at a cost of $50. The other trains make the trip in a little over two hours and cost $40. I decided on the faster option.

I was now more than a little concerned, having not received the promised email confirmation from American Airlines about my tickets. I was assured this would be done right away when I talked to them in Ravenna. Of course, it was their office in the Philippines who were the ones who told me.

If it was not here in the morning, I would act on faith alone.

10 p.m. and I was back in my delightful little room at the Millenn Hotel after my wonderful stroll up to the Plaza Maggiore, with photo stops at the wicked but wonderful Statue of Neptune. Tomorrow was going to be a challenging day. Better get a good night's rest.

DAY 22

I arose at 6:00 a.m. feeling a little disoriented. Everything was so quiet and still — my room wasn't moving. But the bad news was I still had no email confirmation from American Airlines.

After breakfast and a short walk to the train station, I bought my ticket and boarded the Express Train to Milan. The train is gorgeous and sleek, inside and out, and zipping along at 200 mph!

In theory, my plane to London was not scheduled to leave until 1:50 p.m. If things went as planned I would arrive at the airport in plenty of time. In theory.

The old adage "plan for the best, expect the worse." paid off in spades this morning. My "bullet" train arrived in Milan right on time, 9:30 a.m., and I quickly managed to find where to buy bus tickets for Linate Airport. The bus left in less than half an hour.

Okay, so far so good.

The bus arrived at Linate around 10:45. I found my way to British Airways and finally learned I was scheduled *but not ticketed*. (Huh?)

It turned out I had to go to another part of the airport to get my actual ticket. That took more time, and when I got there they would only ticket me to London but no further. They told me I would have to work that out with American Airlines once I arrived in London. Okay. Okay. Don't panic. One step at a time.

11:45 a.m. and I was safely within sight of Gate B28, but no boarding until 1:00 p.m. So whereas I started out this morning thinking I would have *hours* to kill, it turned out I'd be cutting it very close.

I used the rest of my Euros to purchase a glass of beer and a ham sandwich served on a long, thin and crispy bun. I finished just in time to board the plane.

2:30 p.m. We have just passed over the snow-covered Alps, heading to Heathrow. Too bad I wasn't sitting by the window or I would have taken some great pictures. I was just glad to be on the plane.

We would land in 30 minutes and I pray I would have a ticket waiting for me. That would be the first order of business to attend to. My *tentative* schedule with American Airlines called for a 10:30 a.m. departure which would put me into Dallas at 3:30 in the afternoon.

Next thing I would need to do is find a reasonably-priced London hotel near the airport; a place close to some local pubs where I could get a pint of beer and some inexpensive food.

The wheels came off my careful planning as soon as we arrived in London. I was confronted with long, long, long lines through security and customs. It was terrible! They tore my bag apart — as they did everyone else's — and tempers flared, I actually thought there was going to be a fight at one point.

Then I had to go and talk to American Airlines about my next ticket. That took more time. The good news was I *was* scheduled and ticketed. The bad news was I would have to spend the night in Dallas. More meals and another hotel expense. Darn!

But don't panic. One step at a time. I was getting closer.

Although I was now in London, naively expecting to deal with English speaking Londoners, everyone I had dealt with so far was from India, or Pakistan, or Nigeria, or God knows where else and

I was having problems understanding them. So, yes, it was still hectic.

By this time I was bushed, and in a futile attempt to find a low cost room I ended up falling victim to a hotel placement scam in the terminal that booked me in the Sheraton Skyline near the airport to the tune of hundreds of dollars (I'm not even sure how much at that point). They insisted I was lucky to get a room any place at such short notice, which turned out to be a big lie.

The Sheraton Skyline was out of my league: a typical business hotel where they added something to your bill every time you took a deep breath.

Exhausted, I eventually stumbled into my room and took a nice hot shower to relax. By this time it was after 7:00 p.m.

I was shocked to hear they charged $25 to use the internet — but upon further probing learned they begrudgingly offered an hour's free use in the lobby area. So, feeling clean and semi-relaxed again, I took my computer with me and went down stairs.

I ended up skipping dinner (I refused to pay $18 for a cheeseburger) but I did sit in the bar area and had a $6 pint of Guinness, ate a bowl of *free* peanuts and watched a soccer game on a really big TV. Then I went and did my email thing, watched a little TV in my room, and called it a day.

It was somewhere in the middle of the night when I woke with the sudden realization I was now paying in British Pounds instead of Euros. The financial damage would be much more than I had earlier imagined. I only got back to sleep after telling myself I might be able to make some kind of claim on my TravelEx insurance policy. I doubted it, but it gave me temporary relief.

DAY 23

I woke at 6:00 a.m., cleaned up and began packing things away. I wanted to get to the airport in plenty of time, knowing the bedlam I'd be headed for. I noticed a piece of paper on the floor by the door. It was a bill for the Guinness and gratuity, which I expected. What I didn't expect was the $25 charge for internet and the $5 charge for my automatic contribution to UNICEF. Huh?

I went downstairs prepared for battle but they quickly backed off and removed both charges.

I caught the shuttle to the airport and got in long lines again. Finally I worked my way to the American Airlines window and was relieved to find I had a seat as promised. Whew! This time I decided to check my luggage. I didn't think I could survive another search like the one I had the day before. Each time I repacked I was having more trouble getting the zipper closed.

It was almost two hours before my flight left for Dallas. I could now see the light at the end of the tunnel and I'm starting to feel better about things.

I was confident I'd have no problems with my Cedar Rapids flight tomorrow morning, and I'd show more diligence in selecting a hotel tonight.

Finally! A piece of good news. We landed in Dallas early and I quickly retrieved my bag and checked in with American Airlines. It seemed I would *not* have to stay overnight after all. After some pitiful whining on my part, they were able to get me the last seat on a plane leaving in *one hour*. But I would have to really rush to make the gate, which was in a distant part of the airport.

They'd finished boarding by the time I rushed up to the gate, out of breath and ready to pass out. Bless American Airlines, they had waited for me. Just before entering the plane I slipped one of the gate attendants my home phone number and asked her to call and alert my wife of my itinerary change: I would be arriving tonight at 6:00 p.m. instead of tomorrow. I got on the plane not knowing if this would happen or not.

Iowa looked especially welcoming as the plane approached the Cedar Rapids airport. It was a calm evening, with the sun low on the horizon casting a warm, golden glow over the freshly harvested fields.

Apparently the attendant in Dallas came through and did call Lois, because when I arrived she was there waiting.

Yes, indeed. Iowa looked pretty good to me right about then. I was glad to be home.

ABOUT THE AUTHOR

Robert Buckley was born and raised in New York. A graduate of Iowa State University with majors in Psychology and American Literature he spent his career as copywriter and creative director in the advertising agency business.

I'm Lost Again, as well as his four earlier works - *The Slave Tag, Ophelia's Brooch, Two Miles An Hour* and *The Denarius* are all available in eBook as well as printed format on Amazon.com.

Buckley lives with his wife in Marion, Iowa. They are the parents of three grown sons and seven grandchildren. Autographed copies are available. Contact the author at repb35@gmail.com.

44384366R00195

Made in the USA
Middletown, DE
05 June 2017